INTERNATIONAL

BOOKS BY *Vladimir Nabokov*

NOVELS
Mary
King, Queen, Knave
The Defense
The Eye
Glory
Laughter in the Dark
Despair
Invitation to a Beheading
The Gift
The Real Life of Sebastian Knight
Bend Sinister
Lolita
Pnin
Pale Fire
Ada or Ardor: A Family Chronicle
Transparent Things
Look at the Harlequins!

SHORT FICTION
Nabokov's Dozen
A Russian Beauty and Other Stories
Tyrants Destroyed and Other Stories
Details of a Sunset and Other Stories
The Enchanter

DRAMA
The Waltz Invention
Lolita: A Screenplay
The Man from the USSR and Other Plays

AUTOBIOGRAPHY AND INTERVIEWS
Speak, Memory: An Autobiography Revisited
Strong Opinions

BIOGRAPHY AND CRITICISM
Nikolai Gogol
Lectures on Literature
Lectures on Russian Literature
Lectures on Don Quixote

TRANSLATIONS
Three Russian Poets: Translations of Pushkin,
Lermontov, and Tiutchev
A Hero of Our Time (Mikhail Lermontov)
The Song of Igor's Campaign (Anon.)
Eugene Onegin (Alexander Pushkin)

LETTERS
Dear Bunny, Dear Volodya:
The Nabokov–Wilson Letters, 1940–1971
Vladimir Nabokov: Selected Letters, 1940–1977

MISCELLANEOUS
Poems and Problems
The Annotated Lolita

Speak, Memory

Speak, Memory

An Autobiography Revisited

Vladimir Nabokov

Vintage International

VINTAGE BOOKS
A DIVISION OF RANDOM HOUSE, INC.
NEW YORK

First Vintage International Edition, August 1989

Copyright 1947, 1948, 1949, 1950, 1951, © 1967
by Vladimir Nabokov

Library of Congress Cataloging-in-Publication Data
Nabokov, Vladimir Vladimirovich, 1899–1977.
  Speak, memory: an autobiography revisited / by
    Vladimir Nabokov.
    p.   cm.—(Vintage international)
  Rev. ed. of: Conclusive evidence. 1951.
  Includes index.
  ISBN 0-679-72339-0
  1. Nabokov, Vladimir Vladimirovich, 1899–1977—Biography.
2. Authors, Russian—20th century—Biography.   3. Authors,
American—20th century—Biography.   I. Nabokov, Vladimir
Vladimirovich, 1899–1977. Conclusive evidence.   II. Title.
PG3476.N3Z477   1989
813'.54—dc 19
[B]   88-40528
                                                            CIP

Manufactured in the United States of America
579C86

To Véra

Speak, Memory

Foreword

THE present work is a systematically correlated assemblage of personal recollections ranging geographically from St. Petersburg to St. Nazaire, and covering thirty-seven years, from August 1903 to May 1940, with only a few sallies into later space-time. The essay that initiated the series corresponds to what is now Chapter Five. I wrote it in French, under the title of "Mademoiselle O," thirty years ago in Paris, where Jean Paulhan published it in the second issue of *Mesures*, 1936. A photograph (published recently in Gisèle Freund's *James Joyce in Paris*) commemorates this event, except that I am wrongly identified (in the *Mesures* group relaxing around a garden table of stone) as "Audiberti."

In America, whither I migrated on May 28, 1940, "Mademoiselle O" was translated by the late Hilda Ward into English, revised by me, and published by Edward Weeks in the January, 1943, issue of *The Atlantic Monthly* (which was also the first magazine to print my stories written in America). My association with *The New Yorker* had begun (through Edmund Wilson) with a short poem in April 1942, followed by other fugitive pieces; but my first prose composition appeared there only on January 3, 1948: this was "Portrait of

My Uncle" (Chapter Three of the complete work), written
in June 1947 at Columbine Lodge, Estes Park, Colo., where
my wife, child, and I could not have stayed much longer had
not Harold Ross hit it off so well with the ghost of my past.
The same magazine also published Chapter Four ("My English Education," March 27, 1948), Chapter Six ("Butterflies,"
June 12, 1948), Chapter Seven ("Colette," July 31, 1948) and
Chapter Nine ("My Russian Education," September 18,
1948), all written in Cambridge, Mass., at a time of great
mental and physical stress, as well as Chapter Ten ("Curtain-
Raiser," January 1, 1949), Chapter Two ("Portrait of My
Mother," April 9, 1949), Chapter Twelve ("Tamara," December 10, 1949), Chapter Eight ("Lantern Slides," February 11,
1950; H. R.'s query: "Were the Nabokovs a *one*-nutcracker
family?"), Chapter One ("Perfect Past," April 15, 1950), and
Chapter Fifteen ("Gardens and Parks," June 17, 1950), all
written in Ithaca, N.Y.

Of the remaining three chapters, Chapters Eleven and
Fourteen appeared in the *Partisan Review* ("First Poem,"
September, 1949, and "Exile," January–February, 1951),
while Chapter Thirteen went to *Harper's Magazine* ("Lodgings in Trinity Lane," January, 1951).

The English version of "Mademoiselle O" has been republished in *Nine Stories* (New Directions, 1947), and *Nabokov's
Dozen* (Doubleday, 1958; Heinemann, 1959; Popular Library,
1959; and Penguin Books, 1960); in the latter collection, I
also included "First Love," which became the darling of
anthologists.

Although I had been composing these chapters in the
erratic sequence reflected by the dates of first publication
given above, they had been neatly filling numbered gaps in
my mind which followed the present order of chapters. That
order had been established in 1936, at the placing of the

cornerstone which already held in its hidden hollow various maps, timetables, a collection of matchboxes, a chip of ruby glass, and even—as I now realize—the view from my balcony of Geneva lake, of its ripples and glades of light, black-dotted today, at teatime, with coots and tufted ducks. I had no trouble therefore in assembling a volume which Harper & Bros. of New York brought out in 1951, under the title *Conclusive Evidence;* conclusive evidence of my having existed. Unfortunately, the phrase suggested a mystery story, and I planned to entitle the British edition *Speak, Mnemosyne* but was told that "little old ladies would not want to ask for a book whose title they could not pronounce." I also toyed with *The Anthemion* which is the name of a honeysuckle ornament, consisting of elaborate interlacements and expanding clusters, but nobody liked it; so we finally settled for *Speak, Memory* (Gollancz, 1951, and The Universal Library, N.Y., 1960). Its translations are: Russian, by the author (*Drugie Berega,* The Chekhov Publishing House, N.Y., 1954), French, by Yvonne Davet (*Autres Rivages,* Gallimard, 1961), Italian, by Bruno Oddera (*Parla, Ricordo,* Mondadori, 1962), Spanish, by Jaime Piñeiro Gonzáles (*¡Habla, memoria!,* 1963) and German, by Dieter E. Zimmer (Rowohlt, 1964). This exhausts the necessary amount of bibliographic information, which jittery critics who were annoyed by the note at the end of *Nabokov's Dozen* will be, I hope, hypnotized into accepting at the beginning of the present work.

While writing the first version in America I was handicapped by an almost complete lack of data in regard to family history, and, consequently, by the impossibility of checking my memory when I felt it might be at fault. My father's biography has been amplified now, and revised. Numerous other revisions and additions have been made, especially in the earlier chapters. Certain tight parentheses have been opened and allowed to spill their still active contents. Or else an object, which had been a mere dummy chosen at random and of no factual significance in the account of an important event, kept bothering me every time I reread that passage in the course of correcting the proofs of various editions, until finally I made a great effort, and the arbitrary spectacles (which Mnemosyne must have needed more than anybody else) were metamorphosed into a clearly recalled oystershell-shaped cigarette case, gleaming in the wet grass at the foot of an aspen on the Chemin du Pendu, where I found on that June day in 1907 a hawkmoth rarely met with so far west, and where a quarter of a century earlier, my father had netted a Peacock butterfly very scarce in our northern woodlands.

In the summer of 1953, at a ranch near Portal, Arizona, at a rented house in Ashland, Oregon, and at various motels in the West and Midwest, I managed, between butterfly-hunting and writing *Lolita* and *Pnin*, to translate *Speak, Memory*, with the help of my wife, into Russian. Because of the psychological difficulty of replaying a theme elaborated in my *Dar (The Gift)*, I omitted one entire chapter (Eleven). On the other hand, I revised many passages and tried to do something about the amnesic defects of the original—blank spots, blurry areas, domains of dimness. I discovered that sometimes, by means of intense concentration, the neutral smudge might be forced to come into beautiful focus so that the sudden view could be identified, and the anonymous servant named. For the present, final, edition of *Speak, Memory* I have not only introduced basic changes and copious additions into the initial English text, but have availed myself of the corrections I made while turning it into Russian. This re-Englishing of a Russian re-version of what had been an English re-telling of Russian memories in the first place, proved to be a diabolical task, but some consolation was given me by the thought that such multiple metamorphosis, familiar to butterflies, had not been tried by any human before.

Among the anomalies of a memory, whose possessor and victim should never have tried to become an autobiographer, the worst is the inclination to equate in retrospect my age with that of the century. This has led to a series of remarkably consistent chronological blunders in the first version of this book. I was born in April 1899, and naturally, during the first third of, say, 1903, was roughly three years old; but in August of that year, the sharp "3" revealed to me (as described in "Perfect Past") should refer to the century's age, not to mine, which was "4" and as square and resilient as a rubber pillow. Similarly, in the early summer of 1906—the summer I began to collect butterflies—I was seven and not six as stated initially in the catastrophic second paragraph of Chapter 6. Mnemosyne, one must admit, has shown herself to be a very careless girl.

All dates are given in the New Style: we lagged twelve days behind the rest of the civilized world in the nineteenth century, and thirteen in the beginning of the twentieth. By the Old Style I was born on April 10, at daybreak, in the last year of the last century, and that was (if I could have been whisked across the border at once) April 22 in, say, Germany; but since all my birthdays were celebrated, with diminishing pomp, in the twentieth century, everybody, including myself, upon being shifted by revolution and expatriation from the Julian calendar to the Gregorian, used to add thirteen, instead of twelve days to the 10th of April. The error is serious. What is to be done? I find "April 23" under "birth date" in my most recent passport, which is also the birth date of

Shakespeare, my nephew Vladimir Sikorski, Shirley Temple and Hazel Brown (who, moreover, shares my passport). This, then, is the problem. Calculatory ineptitude prevents me from trying to solve it.

When after twenty years of absence I sailed back to Europe, I renewed ties that had been undone even before I had left it. At these family reunions, *Speak, Memory* was judged. Details of date and circumstance were checked, and it was found that in many cases I had erred, or had not examined deeply enough an obscure but fathomable recollection. Certain matters were dismissed by my advisers as legends or rumors or, if genuine, were proven to be related to events or periods other than those to which frail memory had attached them. My cousin Sergey Sergeevich Nabokov gave me invaluable information on the history of our family. Both my sisters angrily remonstrated against my description of the journey to Biarritz (beginning of Chapter Seven) and by pelting me with specific details convinced me I had been wrong in leaving them behind ("with nurses and aunts"!). What I still have not been able to rework through want of specific documentation, I have now preferred to delete for the sake of over-all truth. On the other hand, a number of facts relating to ancestors and other personages have come to light and have been incorporated in this final version of *Speak, Memory*. I hope to write some day a "Speak on, Memory," covering the years 1940–60 spent in America: the evaporation of certain volatiles and the melting of certain metals are still going on in my coils and crucibles.

The reader will find in the present work scattered references to my novels, but on the whole I felt that the trouble of writing them had been enough and that they should remain in the first stomach. My recent introductions to the

English translations of *Zashchita Luzhina*, 1930 (*The Defense*, Putnam, 1964), *Otchayanie*, 1936 (*Despair*, Putnam, 1966), *Priglashenie na kazn'*, 1938 (*Invitation to a Beheading*, Putnam, 1959), *Dar*, 1952, serialized 1937–38 (*The Gift*, Putnam, 1963) and *Soglyadatay*, 1938 (*The Eye*, Phaedra, 1965) give a sufficiently detailed, and racy, account of the creative part of my European past. For those who would like a fuller list of my publications, there is the detailed bibliography, worked out by Dieter E. Zimmer (*Vladimir Nabokov Bibliographie des Gesamtwerks*, Rowohlt, 1st ed. December, 1963; 2nd revised ed. May, 1964).

The two-mover described in the last chapter has been republished in *Chess Problems* by Lipton, Matthews & Rice (Faber, London 1963, p. 252). My most amusing invention, however, is a "White-retracts-move" problem which I dedicated to E. A. Znosko-Borovski, who published it, in the nineteen-thirties (1934?), in the émigré daily *Poslednie Novosti*, Paris. I do not recall the position lucidly enough to notate it here, but perhaps some lover of "fairy chess" (to which type of problem it belongs) will look it up some day in one of those blessed libraries where old newspapers are microfilmed, as all our memories should be. Reviewers read the first version more carelessly than they will this new edition: only one of them noticed my "vicious snap" at Freud in the first paragraph of Chapter Eight, section 2, and none discovered the name of a great cartoonist and a tribute to him in the last sentence of section 2, Chapter Eleven. It is most embarrassing for a writer to have to point out such things himself.

To avoid hurting the living or distressing the dead, certain proper names have been changed. These are set off by quotation marks in the index. Its main purpose is to list for my convenience some of the people and themes connected with my past years. Its presence will annoy the vulgar but may please the discerning, if only because

> Through the window of that index
> Climbs a rose
> And sometimes a gentle wind *ex*
> *Ponto* blows.

Vladimir Nabokov
January 5, 1966
Montreux

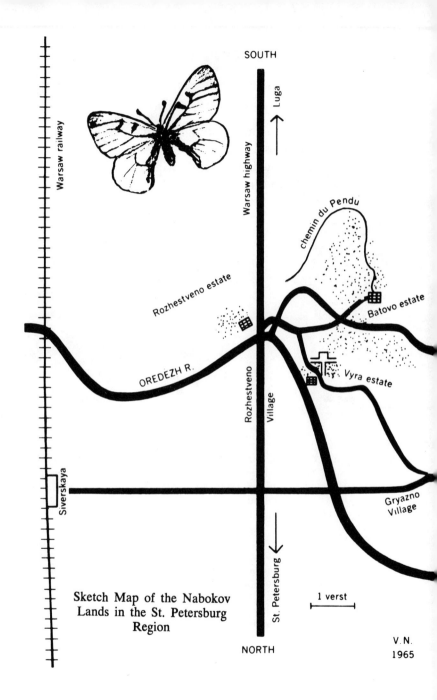

SOUTH

Warsaw railway

Warsaw highway

Luga

chemin du Pendu

Rozhestveno estate

Batovo estate

OREDEZH R.

Rozhestveno

Vyra estate

Village

Siverskaya

Gryazno Village

St. Petersburg

Sketch Map of the Nabokov
Lands in the St. Petersburg
Region

1 verst

NORTH

V. N.
1965

This photograph, taken in 1955 by an obliging American tourist, shows the Nabokov house, of pink granite with frescoes and other Italianate ornaments, in St. Petersburg, now Leningrad, 47, Morskaya, now Hertzen Street. Aleksandr Ivanovich Hertzen (1812–1870) was a famous liberal (whom this commemoration by a police state would hardly have gratified) as well as the talented author of *Bïloe i Dumï* (translatable as "Bygones and Meditations"), one of my father's favorite books. My room was on the third floor, above the oriel. The lindens lining the street did not exist. Those green upstarts now hide the second-floor east-corner window of the room where I was born. After nationalization the house accommodated the Danish mission, and later, a school of architecture. The little sedan at the curb belongs presumably to the photographer.

1

THE cradle rocks above an abyss, and common sense tells us that our existence is but a brief crack of light between two eternities of darkness. Although the two are identical twins, man, as a rule, views the prenatal abyss with more calm than the one he is heading for (at some forty-five hundred heartbeats an hour). I know, however, of a young chronophobiac who experienced something like panic when looking for the first time at homemade movies that had been taken a few weeks before his birth. He saw a world that was practically unchanged—the same house, the same people— and then realized that he did not exist there at all and that nobody mourned his absence. He caught a glimpse of his mother waving from an upstairs window, and that unfamiliar gesture disturbed him, as if it were some mysterious farewell. But what particularly frightened him was the sight of a brand-new baby carriage standing there on the porch, with the smug, encroaching air of a coffin; even that was empty, as if, in the reverse course of events, his very bones had disintegrated.

Such fancies are not foreign to young lives. Or, to put it otherwise, first and last things often tend to have an adoles-

cent note—unless, possibly, they are directed by some venerable and rigid religion. Nature expects a full-grown man to
accept the two black voids, fore and aft, as stolidly as he
accepts the extraordinary visions in between. Imagination,
the supreme delight of the immortal and the immature,
should be limited. In order to enjoy life, we should not enjoy
it too much.

I rebel against this state of affairs. I feel the urge to take
my rebellion outside and picket nature. Over and over again,
my mind has made colossal efforts to distinguish the faintest
of personal glimmers in the impersonal darkness on both
sides of my life. That this darkness is caused merely by the
walls of time separating me and my bruised fists from the free
world of timelessness is a belief I gladly share with the most
gaudily painted savage. I have journeyed back in thought—
with thought hopelessly tapering off as I went—to remote
regions where I groped for some secret outlet only to discover that the prison of time is spherical and without exits.
Short of suicide, I have tried everything. I have doffed my
identity in order to pass for a conventional spook and steal
into realms that existed before I was conceived. I have
mentally endured the degrading company of Victorian lady
novelists and retired colonels who remembered having, in
former lives, been slave messengers on a Roman road or
sages under the willows of Lhasa. I have ransacked my oldest
dreams for keys and clues—and let me say at once that I reject
completely the vulgar, shabby, fundamentally medieval world
of Freud, with its crankish quest for sexual symbols (something like searching for Baconian acrostics in Shakespeare's
works) and its bitter little embryos spying, from their natural
nooks, upon the love life of their parents.

Initially, I was unaware that time, so boundless at first
blush, was a prison. In probing my childhood (which is the

next best to probing one's eternity) I see the awakening of consciousness as a series of spaced flashes, with the intervals between them gradually diminishing until bright blocks of perception are formed, affording memory a slippery hold. I had learned numbers and speech more or less simultaneously at a very early date, but the inner knowledge that I was I and that my parents were my parents seems to have been established only later, when it was directly associated with my discovering their age in relation to mine. Judging by the strong sunlight that, when I think of that revelation, immediately invades my memory with lobed sun flecks through overlapping patterns of greenery, the occasion may have been my mother's birthday, in late summer, in the country, and I had asked questions and had assessed the answers I received. All this is as it should be according to the theory of recapitulation; the beginning of reflexive consciousness in the brain of our remotest ancestor must surely have coincided with the dawning of the sense of time.

Thus, when the newly disclosed, fresh and trim formula of my own age, four, was confronted with the parental formulas, thirty-three and twenty-seven, something happened to me. I was given a tremendously invigorating shock. As if subjected to a second baptism, on more divine lines than the Greek Catholic ducking undergone fifty months earlier by a howling, half-drowned half-Victor (my mother, through the half-closed door, behind which an old custom bade parents retreat, managed to correct the bungling archpresbyter, Father Konstantin Vetvenitski), I felt myself plunged abruptly into a radiant and mobile medium that was none other than the pure element of time. One shared it—just as excited bathers share shining seawater—with creatures that were not oneself but that were joined to one by time's common flow, an environment quite different from the spatial world, which not only man but apes and butterflies can perceive. At that instant, I became acutely aware that the twenty-seven-year-old being, in soft white and pink, holding my left hand, was my mother, and that the thirty-three-year-old being, in hard white and gold, holding my right hand, was my father. Between them, as they evenly progressed, I strutted, and trotted, and strutted again, from sun fleck to sun fleck, along the middle of a path, which I easily identify today with an alley of ornamental oaklings in the park of our country estate, Vyra, in the former Province of St. Petersburg, Russia. Indeed, from my present ridge of remote, isolated, almost uninhabited time, I see my diminutive self as celebrating, on that August day 1903, the birth of sentient life. If my left-hand-holder and my right-hand-holder had both been present before in my vague infant world, they had been so under the mask of a tender incognito; but now my father's attire, the resplendent uniform of the Horse Guards, with that smooth golden swell of cuirass burning upon his chest and back, came out like the sun, and for several years afterward I remained keenly interested in the age of my parents and kept myself informed about it, like a nervous passenger asking the time in order to check a new watch.

My father, let it be noted, had served his term of military training long before I was born, so I suppose he had that day put on the trappings of his old regiment as a festive joke. To a joke, then, I owe my first gleam of complete consciousness —which again has recapitulatory implications, since the first creatures on earth to become aware of time were also the first creatures to smile.

2

It was the primordial cave (and not what Freudian mystics might suppose) that lay behind the games I played when I was four. A big cretonne-covered divan, white with black trefoils, in one of the drawing rooms at Vyra rises in my mind, like some massive product of a geological upheaval before the beginning of history. History begins (with the promise of fair Greece) not far from one end of this divan, where a large potted hydrangea shrub, with pale blue blossoms and some greenish ones, half conceals, in a corner of the room, the pedestal of a marble bust of Diana. On the wall against which the divan stands, another phase of history is marked by a gray engraving in an ebony frame—one of those Napoleonic-battle pictures in which the episodic and the allegoric are the real adversaries and where one sees, all grouped together on the same plane of vision, a wounded drummer, a dead horse, trophies, one soldier about to bayonet another, and the invulnerable emperor posing with his generals amid the frozen fray.

With the help of some grown-up person, who would use first both hands and then a powerful leg, the divan would be moved several inches away from the wall, so as to form a narrow passage which I would be further helped to roof snugly with the divan's bolsters and close up at the ends with a couple of its cushions. I then had the fantastic pleasure of creeping through that pitch-dark tunnel, where I lingered a little to listen to the singing in my ears—that lonesome vibration so familiar to small boys in dusty hiding places—and then, in a burst of delicious panic, on rapidly thudding hands and knees I would reach the tunnel's far end, push its cushion away, and be welcomed by a mesh of sunshine on the parquet under the canework of a Viennese chair and two gamesome flies settling by turns. A dreamier and more delicate sensation was provided by another cave game, when upon awakening in the early morning I made a tent of my bedclothes and let my imagination play in a thousand dim

ways with shadowy snowslides of linen and with the faint
light that seemed to penetrate my penumbral covert from
some immense distance, where I fancied that strange, pale
animals roamed in a landscape of lakes. The recollection of
my crib, with its lateral nets of fluffy cotton cords, brings
back, too, the pleasure of handling a certain beautiful, delightfully solid, garnet-dark crystal egg left over from some
unremembered Easter; I used to chew a corner of the bedsheet until it was thoroughly soaked and then wrap the egg
in it tightly, so as to admire and re-lick the warm, ruddy
glitter of the snugly enveloped facets that came seeping
through with a miraculous completeness of glow and color.
But that was not yet the closest I got to feeding upon beauty.

How small the cosmos (a kangaroo's pouch would hold it),
how paltry and puny in comparison to human consciousness,
to a single individual recollection, and its expression in
words! I may be inordinately fond of my earliest impressions,
but then I have reason to be grateful to them. They led the
way to a veritable Eden of visual and tactile sensations. One
night, during a trip abroad, in the fall of 1903, I recall kneeling on my (flattish) pillow at the window of a sleeping car
(probably on the long-extinct Mediterranean Train de Luxe,
the one whose six cars had the lower part of their body
painted in umber and the panels in cream) and seeing with
an inexplicable pang, a handful of fabulous lights that beck-
oned to me from a distant hillside, and then slipped into a
pocket of black velvet: diamonds that I later gave away to
my characters to alleviate the burden of my wealth. I had
probably managed to undo and push up the tight tooled
blind at the head of my berth, and my heels were cold, but
I still kept kneeling and peering. Nothing is sweeter or
stranger than to ponder those first thrills. They belong to
the harmonious world of a perfect childhood and, as such,

possess a naturally plastic form in one's memory, which can be set down with hardly any effort; it is only starting with the recollections of one's adolescence that Mnemosyne begins to get choosy and crabbed. I would moreover submit that, in regard to the power of hoarding up impressions, Russian children of my generation passed through a period of genius, as if destiny were loyally trying what it could for them by giving them more than their share, in view of the cataclysm that was to remove completely the world they had known. Genius disappeared when everything had been stored, just as it does with those other, more specialized child prodigies—pretty, curly-headed youngsters waving batons or taming enormous pianos, who eventually turn into second-rate musicians with sad eyes and obscure ailments and something vaguely misshapen about their eunuchoid hindquarters. But even so, the individual mystery remains to tantalize the memoirist. Neither in environment nor in heredity can I find the exact instrument that fashioned me, the anonymous roller that pressed upon my life a certain intricate watermark whose unique design becomes visible when the lamp of art is made to shine through life's foolscap.

3

To fix correctly, in terms of time, some of my childhood recollections, I have to go by comets and eclipses, as historians do when they tackle the fragments of a saga. But in other cases there is no dearth of data. I see myself, for instance, clambering over wet black rocks at the seaside while Miss Norcott, a languid and melancholy governess, who thinks I am following her, strolls away along the curved beach with Sergey, my younger brother. I am wearing a toy bracelet. As I crawl over those rocks, I keep repeating, in a kind of zestful, copious, and deeply gratifying incantation, the English word "childhood," which sounds mysterious and new, and becomes stranger and stranger as it gets mixed up in my small, overstocked, hectic mind, with Robin Hood and Little Red Riding Hood, and the brown hoods of old hunchbacked fairies. There are dimples in the rocks, full of tepid seawater, and my magic muttering accompanies certain spells I am weaving over the tiny sapphire pools.

The place is of course Abbazia, on the Adriatic. The thing around my wrist, looking like a fancy napkin ring, made of semitranslucent, pale-green and pink, celluloidish stuff, is the fruit of a Christmas tree, which Onya, a pretty cousin, my coeval, gave me in St. Petersburg a few months before. I sentimentally treasured it until it developed dark streaks inside which I decided as in a dream were my hair cuttings which somehow had got into the shiny substance together with my tears during a dreadful visit to a hated hairdresser in nearby Fiume. On the same day, at a waterside café, my father happened to notice, just as we were being served, two Japanese officers at a table near us, and we immediately left—not without my hastily snatching a whole *bombe* of lemon sherbet, which I carried away secreted in my aching mouth. The year was 1904. I was five. Russia was fighting Japan. With hearty relish, the English illustrated weekly Miss Norcott subscribed to reproduced war pictures by Japanese artists that showed how the Russian locomotives—made singularly toylike by the Japanese pictorial style—would drown if our Army tried to lay rails across the treacherous ice of Lake Baikal.

But let me see. I had an even earlier association with that war. One afternoon at the beginning of the same year, in our St. Petersburg house, I was led down from the nursery into my father's study to say how-do-you-do to a friend of the family, General Kuropatkin. His thickset, uniform-encased

body creaking slightly, he spread out to amuse me a handful
of matches, on the divan where he was sitting, placed ten of
them end to end to make a horizontal line, and said, "This
is the sea in calm weather." Then he tipped up each pair so
as to turn the straight line into a zigzag—and that was "a
stormy sea." He scrambled the matches and was about to do,
I hoped, a better trick when we were interrupted. His aide-
de-camp was shown in and said something to him. With a
Russian, flustered grunt, Kuropatkin heavily rose from his
seat, the loose matches jumping up on the divan as his weight
left it. That day, he had been ordered to assume supreme
command of the Russian Army in the Far East.

This incident had a special sequel fifteen years later, when
at a certain point of my father's flight from Bolshevik-held
St. Petersburg to southern Russia he was accosted while crossing a bridge, by an old man who looked like a gray-bearded
peasant in his sheepskin coat. He asked my father for a light.
The next moment each recognized the other. I hope old
Kuropatkin, in his rustic disguise, managed to evade Soviet
imprisonment, but that is not the point. What pleases me is
the evolution of the match theme: those magic ones he had
shown me had been trifled with and mislaid, and his armies
had also vanished, and everything had fallen through, like
my toy trains that, in the winter of 1904–05, in Wiesbaden,
I tried to run over the frozen puddles in the grounds of the
Hotel Oranien. The following of such thematic designs
through one's life should be, I think, the true purpose of
autobiography.

4

The close of Russia's disastrous campaign in the Far East
was accompanied by furious internal disorders. Undaunted
by them, my mother, with her three children, returned to

St. Petersburg after almost a year of foreign resorts. This was
in the beginning of 1905. State matters required the presence
of my father in the capital; the Constitutionalist Democratic
Party, of which he was one of the founders, was to win a
majority of seats in the First Parliament the following year.
During one of his short stays with us in the country that summer, he ascertained, with patriotic dismay, that my brother
and I could read and write English but not Russian (except
KAKAO and MAMA). It was decided that the village schoolmaster should come every afternoon to give us lessons and
take us for walks.

With a sharp and merry blast from the whistle that was
part of my first sailor suit, my childhood calls me back into
that distant past to have me shake hands again with my
delightful teacher. Vasiliy Martïnovich Zhernosekov had a
fuzzy brown beard, a balding head, and china-blue eyes, one
of which bore a fascinating excrescence on the upper lid. The
first day he came he brought a boxful of tremendously appetizing blocks with a different letter painted on each side;
these cubes he would manipulate as if they were infinitely
precious things, which for that matter, they were (besides
forming splendid tunnels for toy trains). He revered my
father who had recently rebuilt and modernized the village
school. In old-fashioned token of free thought, he sported a
flowing black tie carelessly knotted in a bowlike arrangement.
When addressing me, a small boy, he used the plural of the
second person—not in the stiff way servants did, and not as
my mother would do in moments of intense tenderness,
when my temperature had gone up or I had lost a tiny train-
passenger (as if the singular were too thin to bear the load
of her love), but with the polite plainness of one man speaking to another whom he does not know well enough to use
"thou." A fiery revolutionary, he would gesture vehemently

on our country rambles and speak of humanity and freedom and the badness of warfare and the sad (but interesting, I thought) necessity of blowing up tyrants, and sometimes he would produce the then popular pacifist book *Doloy Oruzhie!* (a translation of Bertha von Suttner's *Die Waffen Nieder!*), and treat me, a child of six, to tedious quotations; I tried to refute them: at that tender and bellicose age I spoke up for bloodshed in angry defense of my world of toy pistols and Arthurian knights. Under Lenin's regime, when all non-Communist radicals were ruthlessly persecuted, Zhernosekov was sent to a hard-labor camp but managed to escape abroad, and died in Narva in 1939.

To him, in a way, I owe the ability to continue for another stretch along my private footpath which runs parallel to the road of that troubled decade. When, in July 1906, the Tsar unconstitutionally dissolved the Parliament, a number of its members, my father among them, held a rebellious session in Viborg and issued a manifesto that urged the people to resist the government. For this, more than a year and a half later they were imprisoned. My father spent a restful, if somewhat lonesome, three months in solitary confinement, with his books, his collapsible bathtub, and his copy of J. P. Muller's manual of home gymnastics. To the end of her days, my mother preserved the letters he managed to smuggle through to her—cheerful epistles written in pencil on toilet paper (these I have published in 1965, in the fourth issue of the Russian-language review *Vozdushnïe puti*, edited by Roman Grynberg in New York). We were in the country when he regained his liberty, and it was the village schoolmaster who directed the festivities and arranged the bunting (some of it frankly red) to greet my father on his way home from the railway station, under archivolts of fir needles and crowns of bluebottles, my father's favorite flower. We chil-

dren had gone down to the village, and it is when I recall
that particular day that I see with the utmost clarity the sun-
spangled river; the bridge, the dazzling tin of a can left by a
fisherman on its wooden railing; the linden-treed hill with its
rosy-red church and marble mausoleum where my mother's
dead reposed; the dusty road to the village; the strip of short,
pastel-green grass, with bald patches of sandy soil, between
the road and the lilac bushes behind which walleyed, mossy
log cabins stood in a rickety row; the stone building of the
new schoolhouse near the wooden old one; and, as we swiftly
drove by, the little black dog with very white teeth that
dashed out from among the cottages at a terrific pace but in
absolute silence, saving his voice for the brief outburst he
would enjoy when his muted spurt would at last bring him
close to the speeding carriage.

5

The old and the new, the liberal touch and the patriarchal
one, fatal poverty and fatalistic wealth got fantastically interwoven in that strange first decade of our century. Several
times during a summer it might happen that in the middle
of luncheon, in the bright, many-windowed, walnut-paneled
dining room on the first floor of our Vyra manor, Aleksey,
the butler, with an unhappy expression on his face, would
bend over and inform my father in a low voice (especially
low if we had company) that a group of villagers wanted to
see the *barin* outside. Briskly my father would remove his
napkin from his lap and ask my mother to excuse him. One
of the windows at the west end of the dining room gave upon
a portion of the drive near the main entrance. One could see
the top of the honeysuckle bushes opposite the porch. From

that direction the courteous buzz of a peasant welcome would reach us as the invisible group greeted my invisible father. The ensuing parley, conducted in ordinary tones, would not be heard, as the windows underneath which it took place were closed to keep out the heat. It presumably had to do with a plea for his mediation in some local feud, or with some special subsidy, or with the permission to harvest some bit of our land or cut down a coveted clump of our trees. If, as usually happened, the request was at once granted, there would be again that buzz, and then, in token of gratitude, the good *barin* would be put through the national ordeal of being rocked and tossed up and securely caught by a score or so of strong arms.

In the dining room, my brother and I would be told to go on with our food. My mother, a tidbit between finger and thumb, would glance under the table to see if her nervous and gruff dachshund was there. *"Un jour ils vont le laisser tomber,"* would come from Mlle Golay, a primly pessimistic old lady who had been my mother's governess and still dwelt with us (on awful terms with our own governesses). From my place at table I would suddenly see through one of the west windows a marvelous case of levitation. There, for an instant, the figure of my father in his wind-rippled white summer suit would be displayed, gloriously sprawling in midair, his limbs in a curiously casual attitude, his handsome, imperturbable features turned to the sky. Thrice, to the mighty heave-ho of his invisible tossers, he would fly up in this fashion, and the second time he would go higher than the first and then there he would be, on his last and loftiest flight, reclining, as if for good, against the cobalt blue of the summer noon, like one of those paradisiac personages who comfortably soar, with such a wealth of folds in their garments, on the vaulted ceil-

ing of a church while below, one by one, the wax tapers in
mortal hands light up to make a swarm of minute flames in
the mist of incense, and the priest chants of eternal repose,
and funeral lilies conceal the face of whoever lies there,
among the swimming lights, in the open coffin.

2

1

AS FAR back as I remember myself (with interest, with amusement, seldom with admiration or disgust), I have been subject to mild hallucinations. Some are aural, others are optical, and by none have I profited much. The fatidic accents that restrained Socrates or egged on Joaneta Darc have degenerated with me to the level of something one happens to hear between lifting and clapping down the receiver of a busy party-line telephone. Just before falling asleep, I often become aware of a kind of one-sided conversation going on in an adjacent section of my mind, quite independently from the actual trend of my thoughts. It is a neutral, detached, anonymous voice, which I catch saying words of no importance to me whatever—an English or a Russian sentence, not even addressed to me, and so trivial that I hardly dare give samples, lest the flatness I wish to convey be marred by a molehill of sense. This silly phenomenon seems to be the auditory counterpart of certain praedormitary visions, which I also know well. What I mean is not the bright mental image (as, for instance, the face of a beloved parent long dead) conjured up by a wing-stroke of the will; *that* is one of the bravest movements a human spirit can make. Nor am I alluding to the so-called *muscae volitantes*—shadows cast upon the retinal rods by motes in the vitreous humor, which are seen as transparent threads drifting across the visual field. Perhaps nearer to the hypnagogic mirages I am thinking of is the colored spot, the stab of an afterimage, with which the lamp one has just turned off wounds the palpebral night. However, a shock of this sort is not really a necessary starting point for the slow, steady development of the visions that pass before my closed eyes. They come and go, without the drowsy observer's participation, but are essentially different from dream pictures for he is still master of his senses. They are often grotesque. I am pestered by roguish profiles, by some coarse-featured and florid dwarf with a swelling nostril or ear. At times, however, my photisms take on a rather soothing *flou* quality, and then I see—projected, as it were, upon the inside of the eyelid—gray figures walking between beehives, or small black parrots gradually vanishing among mountain snows, or a mauve remoteness melting beyond moving masts.

On top of all this I present a fine case of colored hearing. Perhaps "hearing" is not quite accurate, since the color sensation seems to be produced by the very act of my orally forming a given letter while I imagine its outline. The long *a* of the English alphabet (and it is this alphabet I have in mind farther on unless otherwise stated) has for me the tint of weathered wood, but a French *a* evokes polished ebony. This black group also includes hard *g* (vulcanized rubber) and *r* (a sooty rag being ripped). Oatmeal *n*, noodle-limp *l*, and the ivory-backed hand mirror of *o* take care of the whites. I am puzzled by my French *on* which I see as the brimming tension-surface of alcohol in a small glass. Passing on to the blue group, there is steely *x*, thundercloud *z*, and huckleberry *k*. Since a subtle interaction exists between sound and shape,

I see *q* as browner than *k*, while *s* is not the light blue of *c*, but a curious mixture of azure and mother-of-pearl. Adjacent tints do not merge, and diphthongs do not have special colors of their own, unless represented by a single character in some other language (thus the fluffy-gray, three-stemmed Russian letter that stands for *sh*, a letter as old as the rushes of the Nile, influences its English representation).

I hasten to complete my list before I am interrupted. In the green group, there are alder-leaf *f*, the unripe apple of *p*, and pistachio *t*. Dull green, combined somehow with violet, is the best I can do for *w*. The yellows comprise various *e*'s and *i*'s, creamy *d*, bright-golden *y*, and *u*, whose alphabetical value I can express only by "brassy with an olive sheen." In the brown group, there are the rich rubbery tone of soft *g*, paler *j*, and the drab shoelace of *h*. Finally, among the reds, *b* has the tone called burnt sienna by painters, *m* is a fold of pink flannel, and today I have at last perfectly matched *v* with "Rose Quartz" in Maerz and Paul's *Dictionary of Color.* The word for rainbow, a primary, but decidedly muddy, rainbow, is in my private language the hardly pronounceable: *kzspygv*. The first author to discuss *audition colorée* was, as far as I know, an albino physician in 1812, in Erlangen.

The confessions of a synesthete must sound tedious and pretentious to those who are protected from such leakings and drafts by more solid walls than mine are. To my mother, though, this all seemed quite normal. The matter came up, one day in my seventh year, as I was using a heap of old alphabet blocks to build a tower. I casually remarked to her that their colors were all wrong. We discovered then that some of her letters had the same tint as mine and that, besides, she was optically affected by musical notes. These evoked no chromatisms in me whatsoever. Music, I regret to say, affects me merely as an arbitrary succession of more or less irritating sounds. Under certain emotional circumstances I can stand the spasms of a rich violin, but the concert piano and all wind instruments bore me in small doses and flay me in larger ones. Despite the number of operas I was exposed to every winter (I must have attended *Ruslan* and *Pikovaya Dama* at least a dozen times in the course of half as many years), my weak responsiveness to music was completely over-run by the visual torment of not being able to read over Pimen's shoulder or of trying in vain to imagine the hawk-moths in the dim bloom of Juliet's garden.

My mother did everything to encourage the general sensi-tiveness I had to visual stimulation. How many were the aquarelles she painted for me; what a revelation it was when she showed me the lilac tree that grows out of mixed blue and red! Sometimes, in our St. Petersburg house, from a secret compartment in the wall of her dressing room (and my birth room), she would produce a mass of jewelry for my bedtime amusement. I was very small then, and those flash-ing tiaras and chokers and rings seemed to me hardly inferior in mystery and enchantment to the illumination in the city during imperial fêtes, when, in the padded stillness of a frosty night, giant monograms, crowns, and other armorial designs, made of colored electric bulbs—sapphire, emerald, ruby—glowed with a kind of charmed constraint above snow-lined cornices on housefronts along residential streets.

2

My numerous childhood illnesses brought my mother and me still closer together. As a little boy, I showed an abnormal aptitude for mathematics, which I completely lost in my sin-gularly talentless youth. This gift played a horrible part in tussles with quinsy or scarlet fever, when I felt enormous spheres and huge numbers swell relentlessly in my aching brain. A foolish tutor had explained logarithms to me much too early, and I had read (in a British publication, the *Boy's Own Paper*, I believe) about a certain Hindu calculator who in exactly two seconds could find the seventeenth root of, say, 3529471145760275132301897342055866171392 (I am not sure I have got this right; anyway the root was 212). Such were the monsters that thrived on my delirium, and the only way to prevent them from crowding me out of myself was to kill them by extracting their hearts. But they were far too strong, and I would sit up and laboriously form garbled sentences as I tried to explain things to my mother. Beneath my delirium, she recognized sensations she had known herself, and her understanding would bring my expanding universe back to a Newtonian norm.

The future specialist in such dull literary lore as auto-plagiarism will like to collate a protagonist's experience in my novel *The Gift* with the original event. One day, after a long illness, as I lay in bed still very weak, I found myself basking in an unusual euphoria of lightness and repose. I knew my mother had gone to buy me the daily present that made those convalescences so delightful. What it would be this time I could not guess, but through the crystal of my strangely translucent state I vividly visualized her driving away down Morskaya Street toward Nevski Avenue. I distinguished the light sleigh drawn by a chestnut courser. I heard his snorting breath, the rhythmic clacking of his scrotum, and the lumps of frozen earth and snow thudding against the front of the sleigh. Before my eyes and before those of my mother loomed the hind part of the coachman, in his heavily padded blue robe, and the leather-encased watch (twenty minutes past two) strapped to the back of his belt, from under which curved the pumpkin-like folds of his huge stuffed rump. I saw my mother's seal furs and, as the icy speed in-creased, the muff she raised to her face—that graceful, winter-ride gesture of a St. Petersburg lady. Two corners of the voluminous spread of bearskin that covered her up to the waist were attached by loops to the two side knobs of the low back of her seat. And behind her, holding on to these knobs, a footman in a cockaded hat stood on his narrow sup-port above the rear extremities of the runners.

Still watching the sleigh, I saw it stop at Treumann's (writ-ing implements, bronze baubles, playing cards). Presently, my mother came out of this shop followed by the footman. He carried her purchase, which looked to me like a pencil. I was astonished that she did not carry so small an object her-self, and this disagreeable question of dimensions caused a faint renewal, fortunately very brief, of the "mind dilation effect" which I hoped had gone with the fever. As she was being tucked up again in the sleigh, I watched the vapor exhaled by all, horse included. I watched, too, the familiar pouting movement she made to distend the network of her close-fitting veil drawn too tight over her face, and as I write this, the touch of reticulated tenderness that my lips used to feel when I kissed her veiled cheek comes back to me—*flies* back to me with a shout of joy out of the snow-blue, blue-windowed (the curtains are not yet drawn) past.

A few minutes later, she entered my room. In her arms she held a big parcel. It had been, in my vision, greatly reduced in size—perhaps, because I subliminally corrected what logic warned me might still be the dreaded remnants of delirium's dilating world. Now the object proved to be a giant polygonal Faber pencil, four feet long and correspondingly thick. It had been hanging as a showpiece in the shop's window, and she presumed I had coveted it, as I coveted all things that were not quite purchasable. The shopman had been obliged to

ring up an agent, a "Doctor" Libner (as if the t
possessed indeed some pathological import). For a..
moment, I wondered whether the point was made of real
graphite. It was. And some years later I satisfied myself, by
drilling a hole in the side, that the lead went right through
the whole length—a perfect case of art for art's sake on the
part of Faber and Dr. Libner since the pencil was far too big
for use and, indeed, was not meant to be used.

"Oh, yes," she would say as I mentioned this or that unusual sensation. "Yes, I know all that," and with a somewhat
eerie ingenuousness she would discuss such things as double
sight, and little raps in the woodwork of tripod tables, and
premonitions, and the feeling of the *déjà vu*. A streak of sec-
tarianism ran through her direct ancestry. She went to church
only at Lent and Easter. The schismatic mood revealed itself
in her healthy distaste for the ritual of the Greek Catholic
Church and for its priests. She found a deep appeal in the
moral and poetical side of the Gospels, but felt no need in
the support of any dogma. The appalling insecurity of an
afterlife and its lack of privacy did not enter her thoughts.
Her intense and pure religiousness took the form of her having equal faith in the existence of another world and in the
impossibility of comprehending it in terms of earthly life.
All one could do was to glimpse, amid the haze and the
chimeras, something real ahead, just as persons endowed with
an unusual persistence of diurnal cerebration are able to perceive in their deepest sleep, somewhere beyond the throes of
an entangled and inept nightmare, the ordered reality of the
waking hour.

3

To love with all one's soul and leave the rest to fate, was the simple rule she heeded. *"Vot zapomni* [now remember],*"* she would say in conspiratorial tones as she drew my attention to this or that loved thing in Vyra—a lark ascending the curds-and-whey sky of a dull spring day, heat lightning taking pictures of a distant line of trees in the night, the palette of maple leaves on brown sand, a small bird's cuneate footprints on new snow. As if feeling that in a few years the tangible part of her world would perish, she cultivated an extraordinary consciousness of the various time marks distributed throughout our country place. She cherished her own past with the same retrospective fervor that I now do her image and my past. Thus, in a way, I inherited an exquisite simulacrum—the beauty of intangible property, unreal estate—and this proved a splendid training for the endurance of later losses. Her special tags and imprints became as dear and as sacred to me as they were to her. There was the room which in the past had been reserved for her mother's pet hobby, a chemical laboratory; there was the linden tree marking the spot, by the side of the road that sloped up toward the village of Gryazno (accented on the ultima), at the steepest bit where one preferred to take one's "bike by the horns" (*bïka za roga*) as my father, a dedicated cyclist, liked to say, and where he had proposed; and there was, in the so-called "old" park, the obsolete tennis court, now a region of moss, mole-heaps, and mushrooms, which had been the scene of gay rallies in the eighties and nineties (even her grim father would shed his coat and give the heaviest racket an appraisive shake) but which, by the time I was ten, nature had effaced with the thoroughness of a felt eraser wiping out a geometrical problem.

By then, an excellent modern court had been built at the end of the "new" part of the park by skilled workmen imported from Poland for that purpose. The wire mesh of an ample enclosure separated it from the flowery meadow that framed its clay. After a damp night the surface acquired a brownish gloss and the white lines would be repainted with liquid chalk from a green pail by Dmitri, the smallest and oldest of our gardeners, a meek, black-booted, red-shirted dwarf slowly retreating, all hunched up, as his paintbrush went down the line. A pea-tree hedge (the "yellow acacia" of northern Russia), with a midway opening, corresponding to the court's screen door, ran parallel to the enclosure and to a path dubbed *tropinka Sfinksov* ("path of the Sphingids") because of the hawkmoths visiting at dusk the fluffy lilacs along the border that faced the hedge and likewise broke in the middle. This path formed the bar of a great T whose vertical was the alley of slender oaks, my mother's coevals, that traversed (as already said) the new park through its entire length. Looking down that avenue from the base of the T near the drive one could make out quite distinctly the bright little gap five hundred yards away—or fifty years away from where I am now. Our current tutor or my father, when he stayed with us in the country, invariably had my brother for partner in our temperamental family doubles. "Play!" my mother would cry in the old manner as she put her little foot forward and bent her white-hatted head to ladle out an assiduous but feeble serve. I got easily cross with her, and she, with the ballboys, two barefooted peasant lads (Dmitri's pug-nosed grandson and the twin brother of pretty Polenka, the head coachman's daughter). The northern summer became tropical around harvest time. Scarlet Sergey would stick his racket between his knees and laboriously wipe his glasses. I see my butterfly net propped against the enclosure—just in case. Wallis Myers' book on lawn tennis lies open on a bench, and after every exchange my father (a first-rate player, with a cannonball service of the Frank Riseley type and a beautiful "lifting drive") pedantically inquires of my brother and me whether the "follow-through," that state of grace, has descended upon us. And sometimes a prodigious cloudburst would cause us to huddle under a shelter at the corner of the court while old Dmitri would be sent to fetch umbrellas and raincoats from the house. A quarter of an hour later he would reappear under a mountain of clothing in the vista of the long avenue which as he advanced would regain its leopard spots with the sun blazing anew and his huge burden unneeded.

She loved all games of skill and gambling. Under her expert hands, the thousand bits of a jigsaw puzzle gradually formed an English hunting scene; what had seemed to be the limb of a horse would turn out to belong to an elm and the hitherto unplaceable piece would snugly fill up a gap in the mottled background, affording one the delicate thrill of an abstract and yet tactile satisfaction. At one time, she was very fond of poker, which had reached St. Petersburg society via diplomatic circles, so that some of the combinations came with pretty French names—*brelan* for "three of a kind," *couleur* for "flush," and so on. The game in use was the regular "draw poker," with, occasionally, the additional tingle of jackpots and an omnivicarious joker. In town, she often played poker at the houses of friends until three in the morning, a society recreation in the last years before World War One; and later, in exile, she used to imagine (with the same wonder and dismay with which she recalled old Dmitri) the chauffeur Pirogov who still seemed to be waiting for her in the relentless frost of an unending night, although, in his case, rum-laced tea in a hospitable kitchen must have gone a long way to assuage those vigils.

One of her greatest pleasures in summer was the very Russian sport of *hodit' po gribï* (looking for mushrooms). Fried in butter and thickened with sour cream, her delicious finds appeared regularly on the dinner table. Not that the gustatory moment mattered much. Her main delight was in the quest, and this quest had its rules. Thus, no agarics were taken; all she picked were species belonging to the edible section of the genus *Boletus* (tawny *edulis*, brown *scaber*, red *aurantiacus*, and a few close allies), called "tube mushrooms" by some and coldly defined by mycologists as "terrestrial, fleshy, putrescent, centrally stipitate fungi." Their compact pilei—tight-fitting in infant plants, robust and appetizingly domed in ripe ones—have a smooth (not lamellate) undersurface and a neat, strong stem. In classical simplicity of form, boletes differ considerably from the "true mushroom," with its preposterous gills and effete stipal ring. It is, however, to the latter, to the lowly and ugly agarics, that nations with timorous taste buds limit their knowledge and appetite, so that to the Anglo-American lay mind the aristocratic boletes are, at best, reformed toadstools.

Rainy weather would bring out these beautiful plants in profusion under the firs, birches and aspens in our park, especially in its older part, east of the carriage road that divided the park in two. Its shady recesses would then harbor that special boletic reek which makes a Russian's nostrils dilate—a dark, dank, satisfying blend of damp moss, rich earth, rotting leaves. But one had to poke and peer for a goodish while among the wet underwood before something really nice, such as a family of bonneted baby *edulis* or the marbled variety of *scaber,* could be discovered and carefully teased out of the soil.

On overcast afternoons, all alone in the drizzle, my mother, carrying a basket (stained blue on the inside by somebody's whortleberries), would set out on a long collecting tour. Toward dinnertime, she could be seen emerging from the nebulous depths of a park alley, her small figure cloaked and hooded in greenish-brown wool, on which countless droplets of moisture made a kind of mist all around her. As she came nearer from under the dripping trees and caught sight of me, her face would show an odd, cheerless expression, which might have spelled poor luck, but which I knew was the tense, jealously contained beatitude of the successful hunter. Just before reaching me, with an abrupt, drooping movement of the arm and shoulder and a "Pouf!" of magnified exhaustion, she would let her basket sag, in order to stress its weight, its fabulous fullness.

Near a white garden bench, on a round garden table of iron, she would lay out her boletes in concentric circles to count and sort them. Old ones, with spongy, dingy flesh, would be eliminated, leaving the young and the crisp. For a moment, before they were bundled away by a servant to a place she knew nothing about, to a doom that did not interest her, she would stand there admiring them, in a glow of quiet contentment. As often happened at the end of a rainy day, the sun might cast a lurid gleam just before setting, and there, on the damp round table, her mushrooms would lie, very colorful, some bearing traces of extraneous vegetation—a grass blade sticking to a viscid fawn cap, or moss still clothing the bulbous base of a dark-stippled stem. And a tiny looper caterpillar would be there, too, measuring, like a child's finger and thumb, the rim of the table, and every now and then stretching upward to grope, in vain, for the shrub from which it had been dislodged.

4

Not only were the kitchen and the servants' hall never visited by my mother, but they stood as far removed from her consciousness as if they were the corresponding quarters in a hotel. My father had no inclination, either, to run the house. But he did order the meals. With a little sigh, he would open a kind of album laid by the butler on the dinner table after dessert and in his elegant, flowing hand write down the menu for the following day. He had a peculiar habit of letting his pencil or fountain pen vibrate just above the paper while he pondered the next ripple of words. My mother nodded a vague consent to his suggestions or made a wry face. Nominally, the housekeeping was in the hands of her former nurse, at that time a bleary, incredibly wrinkled old woman (born a slave around 1830) with the small face of a melancholy tortoise and big shuffling feet. She wore a nunnish brown dress and gave off a slight but unforgettable smell of coffee and decay. Her dreaded congratulation on our birthdays and namedays was the serfage kiss on the shoulder. Age had developed in her a pathological stinginess, especially in regard to sugar and preserves, so that by degrees, and with the sanction of my parents, other domestic arrangements, kept secret from her, had quietly come into force. Without knowing it (the knowledge would have broken her heart), she remained dangling as it were, from her own key ring, while my mother did her best to allay with soothing words the suspicions that now and then flitted across the old woman's weakening mind. Sole mistress of her moldy and remote little kingdom, which she thought was the real one (we would have starved had it been so), she was followed by the mocking glances of lackeys and maids as she steadily plodded through long corridors to store away half an apple or a couple of broken Petit-Beurre biscuits she had found on a plate.

Meanwhile, with a permanent staff of about fifty servants and no questions asked, our city household and country place were the scenes of a fantastic merry-go-round of theft. In this, according to nosy old aunts, whom nobody heeded but who proved to be right after all, the chief cook Nikolay Andreevich and the head gardener Egor, both staid-looking, bespectacled men with the hoary temples of trusty retainers, were the two masterminds. When confronted with stupendous and incomprehensible bills, or a sudden extinction of garden strawberries and hothouse peaches, my father, a jurist and a statesman, felt professionally vexed at not being able to cope with the economics of his own home; but every time a complicated case of larceny came to light, some legal doubt or scruple prevented him from doing anything about it. When common sense required the firing of a rascally servant, the man's little son would as likely as not fall desperately ill, and the resolution to get the best doctors in town for him would cancel all other considerations. So, with one thing and another, my father preferred to leave the whole housekeeping situation in a state of precarious equilibrium (not devoid of a certain quiet humor), with my mother deriving considerable comfort from the hope that her old nurse's illusory world would not be shattered.

My mother knew well how hurtful a broken illusion could be. The most trifling disappointment took on for her the dimensions of a major disaster. One Christmas Eve, in Vyra, not long before her fourth baby was to be born, she happened to be laid up with a slight ailment and made my brother and me (aged, respectively, five and six) promise not to look into the Christmas stockings that we would find hanging from our bedposts on the following morning but to bring them over to her room and investigate them there, so that she could watch and enjoy our pleasure. Upon awakening, I held a furtive conference with my brother, after which, with eager hands, each felt his delightfully crackling stocking, stuffed with small presents; these we cautiously fished out one by one, undid the ribbons, loosened the tissue paper, inspected everything by the weak light that came through a chink in the shutters, wrapped up the little things again, and crammed them back where they had been. I next recall our sitting on our mother's bed, holding those lumpy stockings and doing our best to give the performance she had wanted to see; but we had so messed up the wrappings, so amateurish were our renderings of enthusiastic surprise (I can see my brother casting his eyes upward and exclaiming, in imitation of our new French governess, *"Ah, que c'est beau!"*), that, after observing us for a moment, our audience burst into tears. A decade passed. World War One started. A crowd of patriots and my uncle Ruka stoned the German Embassy. *Peterburg* was sunk to *Petrograd* against all rules of nomenclatorial priority. Beethoven turned out to be Dutch. The newsreels showed photogenic explosions, the spasm of a cannon, Poincaré in his leathern leggings, bleak puddles, the poor little Tsarevich in Circassian uniform with dagger and cartridges, his tall sisters so dowdily dressed, long railway trains crammed with troops. My mother set up a private hospital for wounded soldiers. I remember her, in the fashionable nurse's gray-and-white uniform she abhorred, denouncing with the same childish tears the impenetrable meekness of those crippled peasants and the ineffectiveness of part-time compassion. And, still later, when in exile, reviewing the past, she would often accuse herself (unjustly as I see it now)

of having been less affected by the misery of man than by the
emotional load man dumps upon innocent nature—old trees,
old horses, old dogs.

Her particular fondness for brown dachshunds puzzled my
critical aunts. In the family albums illustrating her young
years, there was hardly a group that did not include one such
animal—usually with some part of its flexible body blurred
and always with the strange, paranoiac eyes dachshunds have
in snapshots. A couple of obese old-timers, Box I and Loulou,
still lolled in the sunshine on the porch when I was a child.
Sometime in 1904 my father bought at a dog show in Munich
a pup which grew into the bad-tempered but wonderfully
handsome Trainy (as I named him because of his being as
long and as brown as a sleeping car). One of the musical
themes of my childhood is Trainy's hysterical tongue, on the
trail of the hare he never got, in the depths of our Vyra park,
whence he would return at dusk (after my anxious mother
had stood whistling for a long time in the oak avenue) with
the old corpse of a mole in his jaws and burs in his ears.
Around 1915, his hind legs became paralyzed, and until he
was chloroformed, he would dismally drag himself over long,
glossy stretches of parquet floor like a *cul de jatte*. Then somebody gave us another pup, Box II, whose grandparents had
been Dr. Anton Chekhov's Quina and Brom. This final dachshund followed us into exile, and as late as 1930, in a suburb
of Prague (where my widowed mother spent her last years,
on a small pension provided by the Czech government), he
could be still seen going for reluctant walks with his mistress,
waddling far behind in a huff, tremendously old and furious with his long Czech muzzle of wire—an émigré dog in a
patched and ill-fitting coat.

During our last two Cambridge years, my brother and I
used to spend vacations in Berlin, where our parents with

the two girls and ten-year-old Kirill occupied one of those
large, gloomy, eminently bourgeois apartments that I have
let to so many émigré families in my novels and short stories.
On the night of March 28, 1922, around ten o'clock, in the
living room where as usual my mother was reclining on the
red-plush corner couch, I happened to be reading to her
Blok's verse on Italy—had just got to the end of the little
poem about Florence, which Blok compares to the delicate,
smoky bloom of an iris, and she was saying over her knitting,
"Yes, yes, Florence does look like a *dïmnïy iris,* how true! I
remember—" when the telephone rang.

After 1923, when she moved to Prague, and I lived in Germany and France, I was unable to visit her frequently; nor
was I with her at her death, which occurred on the eve of
World War Two. Whenever I did manage to go to Prague,
there was always that initial pang one feels just before time,
caught unawares, again dons its familiar mask. In the pitiable
lodgings she shared with her dearest companion, Evgeniya
Konstantinovna Hofeld (1884–1957), who had replaced, in
1914, Miss Greenwood (who, in her turn, had replaced Miss
Lavington) as governess of my two sisters (Olga, born January 5, 1903, and Elena, born March 31, 1906), albums, in
which, during the last years, she had copied out her favorite
poems, from Maykov to Mayakovski, lay around her on odds
and ends of decrepit, secondhand furniture. A cast of my
father's hand and a watercolor picture of his grave in the
Greek-Catholic cemetery of Tegel, now in East Berlin, shared
a shelf with émigré writers' books, so prone to disintegration
in their cheap paper covers. A soapbox covered with green
cloth supported the dim little photographs in crumbling
frames she liked to have near her couch. She did not really
need them, for nothing had been lost. As a company of traveling players carry with them everywhere, while they still re-

member their lines, a windy heath, a misty castle, an enchanted island, so she had with her all that her soul had stored. With great clarity, I can see her sitting at a table and serenely considering the laid-out cards of a game of solitaire: she leans on her left elbow and presses to her cheek the free thumb of her left hand, in which, close to her mouth, she holds a cigarette, while her right hand stretches toward the next card. The double gleam on her fourth finger is two marriage rings—her own and my father's, which, being too large for her, is fastened to hers by a bit of black thread.

Whenever in my dreams I see the dead, they always appear silent, bothered, strangely depressed, quite unlike their dear, bright selves. I am aware of them, without any astonishment, in surroundings they never visited during their earthly existence, in the house of some friend of mine they never knew. They sit apart, frowning at the floor, as if death were a dark taint, a shameful family secret. It is certainly not then—not in dreams—but when one is wide awake, at moments of robust joy and achievement, on the highest terrace of consciousness, that mortality has a chance to peer beyond its own limits, from the mast, from the past and its castle tower. And although nothing much can be seen through the mist, there is somehow the blissful feeling that one is looking in the right direction.

3

1

AN inexperienced heraldist resembles a medieval traveler who brings back from the East the faunal fantasies influenced by the domestic bestiary he possessed all along rather than by the results of direct zoological exploration. Thus, in the first version of this chapter, when describing the Nabokovs' coat of arms (carelessly glimpsed among some familial trivia many years before), I somehow managed to twist it into the fireside wonder of two bears posing with a great chessboard propped up between them. I have now looked it up, that blazon, and am disappointed to find that it boils down to a couple of lions—brownish and, perhaps, overshaggy beasts, but not really ursine—licking their chops, rampant, regardant, arrogantly demonstrating the unfortunate knight's shield, which is only one sixteenth of a checkerboard, of alternate tinctures, azure & gules, with a botonée cross, argent, in each rectangle. Above it one sees what remains of the knight: his tough helmet and inedible gorget, as well as one brave arm coming out of a foliate ornament, gules and azure, and still brandishing a short sword. *Za hrabrost'*, "for valour," says the scripture.

According to my father's first cousin Vladimir Viktorovich

Golubtsov, a lover of Russian antiquities, whom I consulted in 1930, the founder of our family was Nabok Murza (*floruit* 1380), a Russianized Tatar prince in Muscovy. My own first cousin, Sergey Sergeevich Nabokov, a learned genealogist, informs me that in the fifteenth century our ancestors owned land in the Moscow princedom. He refers me to a document (published by Yushkov in *Acts of the XIII-XVII Centuries,* Moscow, 1899) concerning a rural squabble which in the year 1494, under Ivan the Third, squire Kulyakin had with his neighbors, Filat, Evdokim, and Vlas, sons of Luka Nabokov. During the following centuries the Nabokovs were government officials and military men. My great-great-grandfather, General Aleksandr Ivanovich Nabokov (1749–1807), was, in the reign of Paul the First, chief of the Novgorod garrison regiment called "Nabokov's Regiment" in official documents. The youngest of his sons, my great-grandfather Nikolay Aleksandrovich Nabokov, was a young naval officer in 1817, when he participated, with the future admirals Baron von Wrangel and Count Litke, under the leadership of Captain (later Vice-Admiral) Vasiliy Mihaylovich Golovnin, in an expedition to map Nova Zembla (of all places) where "Nabokov's River" is named after my ancestor. The memory of the leader of the expedition is preserved in quite a number of place names, one of them being Golovnin's Lagoon, Seward Peninsula, W. Alaska, from where a butterfly, *Parnassius phoebus golovinus* (rating a big *sic*), has been described by Dr. Holland; but my great-grandfather has <u>nothing to show except</u> that <u>very blue, almost indigo blue, even indignantly blue,</u> little <u>river winding between wet rocks</u>; for he soon left the navy, *n'ayant pas le pied marin* (as says my cousin Sergey Sergeevich who informed me about him), and switched to the Moscow Guards. He married Anna Aleksandrovna Nazimov (sister of the Decembrist). I know nothing about his military career; whatever it was, he could not have competed with his brother, Ivan Aleksandrovich Nabokov (1787–1852), one of the heroes of the anti-Napoleon wars and, in his old age, commander of the Peter-and-Paul Fortress in St. Petersburg where (in 1849) one of his prisoners was the writer Dostoevski, author of *The Double,* etc., to whom the kind general lent books. Considerably more interesting, however, is the fact that he was married to Ekaterina Pushchin, sister of Ivan Pushchin, Pushkin's schoolmate and close friend. Careful, printers: two "chin" 's and one "kin."

The nephew of Ivan and the son of Nikolay was my paternal grandfather Dmitri Nabokov (1827–1904), Minister of Justice for eight years, under two Tsars. He married (September 24, 1859) Maria, the seventeen-year-old daughter of Baron Ferdinand Nicolaus Viktor von Korff (1805–1869), a German general in the Russian service.

In tenacious old families certain facial characteristics keep recurring as indicants and maker's marks. The Nabokov nose (e.g. my grandfather's) is of the Russian type with a soft round upturned tip and a gentle inslope in profile; the Korff nose (e.g. mine) is a handsome Germanic organ with a boldly boned bridge and a slightly tilted, distinctly grooved, fleshy end. The supercilious or surprised Nabokovs have rising eyebrows only proximally haired, thus fading toward the temples; the Korff eyebrow is more finely arched but likewise rather scanty. Otherwise the Nabokovs, as they recede through the picture gallery of time into the shadows, soon join the dim Rukavishnikovs of whom I knew only my mother and her brother Vasiliy, too small a sample for my present purpose. On the other hand, I see very clearly the women of the Korff line, beautiful, lily-and-rose girls, their high, flushed *pommettes,* pale blue eyes and that small beauty spot on one cheek, a patchlike mark, which my grandmother, my father, three or four of his siblings, some of my twenty-five cousins, my younger sister and my son Dmitri inherited in various stages of intensity as more or less distinct copies of the same print.

My German great-grandfather, Baron Ferdinand von Korff, who married Nina Aleksandrovna Shishkov (1819–1895), was born in Königsberg in 1805 and after a successful military career, died in 1869 in his wife's Volgan domain near Saratov. He was the grandson of Wilhelm Carl, Baron von Korff (1739–1799) and Eleonore Margarethe, Baroness von der Osten-Sacken (1731–1786), and the son of Nicolaus von Korff (d. 1812), a major in the Prussian army, and Antoinette Theodora Graun (d. 1859), who was the granddaughter of Carl Heinrich Graun, the composer.

Antoinette's mother, Elisabeth née Fischer (born 1760), was the daughter of Regina born Hartung (1732–1805), daughter of Johann Heinrich Hartung (1699–1765), head of a well-known publishing house in Königsberg. Elisabeth was a celebrated beauty. After divorcing her first husband, *Justiz-rat* Graun, the composer's son, in 1795, she married the minor poet Christian August von Stägemann, and was the "motherly friend," as my German source puts it, of a much better-known writer, Heinrich von Kleist (1777–1811), who, at thirty-three, had fallen passionately in love with her twelve-year-old daughter Hedwig Marie (later von Olfers). He is said to have called on the family, to say adieu before traveling to Wannsee—for the carrying out of an enthusiastic suicide pact with a sick lady—but was not admitted, it being laundry day in the Stägemann household. The number and diversity of contacts that my ancestors had with the world of letters are truly remarkable.

Carl Heinrich Graun, the great-grandfather of Ferdinand von Korff, *my* great-grandfather, was born in 1701, at Wahrenbrück, Saxony. His father, August Graun (born 1670), an exciseman (*"Königlicher Polnischer und Kurfürstlicher Sächsischer Akziseneinnehmer"*—the elector in question being his namesake, August II, King of Poland) came from a long line of parsons. His great-great-grandfather, Wolfgang Graun, was, in 1575, organist at Plauen (near Wahrenbrück), where a statue of his descendant, the composer, graces a public garden. Carl Heinrich Graun died at the age of fifty-eight, in 1759, in Berlin, where seventeen years earlier, the new opera house had opened with his *Caesar and Cleopatra*. He was one of the most eminent composers of his time, and even the greatest, according to local necrologists touched by his royal patron's grief. Graun is shown (posthumously) standing somewhat aloof, with folded arms, in Menzel's picture of Frederick the Great playing Graun's composition on the flute; reproductions of this kept following me through all the German lodgings I stayed in during my years of exile. I am told there is at the Sans-Souci Palace in Potsdam a contemporary painting representing Graun and his wife, Dorothea Rehkopp, sitting at the same clavecin. Musical encyclopedias often reproduce the portrait in the Berlin opera house where he looks very much like the composer Nikolay Dmitrievich Nabokov, my first cousin. An amusing little echo, to the tune of 250 dollars, from all those concerts under the painted ceilings of a guilded past, blandly reached me in heil-hitlering Berlin, in 1936, when the Graun family entail, basically a collection of pretty snuffboxes and other precious knickknacks, whose value after passing through many avatars in the Prussian state bank had dwindled to 43,000 reichsmarks (about 10,000 dollars), was distributed among the provident composer's descendants, the von Korff, von Wissmann and Nabokov clans (a fourth line, the Counts Asinari di San Marzano, had died out).

Two Baronesses von Korff have left their trace in the police records of Paris. One, born Anna-Christina Stegelman, daughter of a Swedish banker, was the widow of Baron Fromhold Christian von Korff, colonel in the Russian army, a great-granduncle of my grandmother. Anna-Christina was also the cousin or the sweetheart, or both, of another soldier, the famous Count Axel von Fersen; and it was she who, in Paris, in 1791, lent her passport and her brand-new custom-made traveling coach (a sumptuous affair on high red wheels, upholstered in white Utrecht velvet, with dark green curtains and all kinds of gadgets, then modern, such as a *vase de voyage*) to the royal family for their escape to Varennes, the Queen impersonating her, and the King, the tutor of the two children. The other police story involves a less dramatic masquerade.

With Carnival week nearing, in Paris, more than a century ago, the Count de Morny invited to a fancy ball at his house *"une noble dame que la Russie a prêtée cet hiver à la France"* (as reported by Henrys in the *Gazette du Palais* section of the *Illustration*, 1859, p. 251). This was Nina, Baroness von Korff, whom I have already mentioned; the eldest of her five daughters, Maria (1842–1926), was to marry in September of the same year, 1859, Dmitri Nikolaevich Nabokov (1827–1904), a friend of the family who was also in Paris at the time. In view of the ball, the lady ordered for Maria and Olga, flower-girl costumes, at two hundred and twenty francs each. Their cost, according to the glib *Illustration* reporter, represented six hundred and forty-three days *"de nourriture, de loyer et d'entretien du père Crépin* [food, rent and footwear]," which sounds odd. When the costumes were ready, Mme de Korff found them *"trop décolletés"* and refused to take them. The dressmaker sent her *huissier* (warrant officer), upon which there was a bad row, and my good great-grandmother (she was beautiful, passionate and, I am sorry to say, far less austere in her private morals than it would appear from her attitude toward low necklines) sued the dressmaker for damages.

She contended that the *demoiselles de magasin* who brought the dresses were "*des péronnelles* [saucy hussies]" who, in answer to her objecting that the dresses were cut too low for gentlewomen to wear, "*se sont permis d'exposer des théories égalitaires du plus mauvais goût* [dared to flaunt democratic ideas in the worst of taste]"; she said that it had been too late to have other fancy dresses made and that her daughters had not gone to the ball; she accused the *huissier* and his acolytes of sprawling on soft chairs while inviting the ladies to take hard ones; she also complained, furiously and bitterly, that the *huissier* had actually threatened to jail Monsieur Dmitri Nabokoff, "*Conseiller d'État, homme sage et plein de mesure* [a sedate, self-contained man]" only because the said gentleman had attempted to throw the *huissier* out of the window. It was not much of a case but the dressmaker lost it. She took back her dresses, refunded their cost and in addition paid a thousand francs to the plaintiff; on the other hand, the bill presented in 1791 to Christina by her carriage maker, a matter of five thousand nine hundred forty-four livres, had never been paid at all.

Dmitri Nabokov (the ending in *ff* was an old Continental fad), State Minister of Justice from 1878 to 1885, did what he could to protect, if not to strengthen, the liberal reforms of the sixties (trial by jury, for instance) against ferocious reactionary attacks. "He acted," says a biographer (Brockhaus' *Encyclopedia,* second Russian edition), "much like the captain of a ship in a storm who would throw overboard part of the cargo in order to save the rest." The epitaphical simile unwittingly echoes, I note, an epigraphical theme—my grandfather's earlier attempt to throw the law out of the window.

At his retirement, Alexander the Third offered him to choose between the title of count and a sum of money, presumably large—I do not know what exactly an earldom was worth in Russia, but contrary to the thrifty Tsar's hopes my grandfather (as also his uncle Ivan, who had been offered a similar choice by Nicholas the First) plumped for the more solid reward. (*"Encore un comte raté,"* dryly comments Sergey Sergeevich.) After that he lived mostly abroad. In the first years of this century his mind became clouded but he clung to the belief that as long as he remained in the Mediterranean region everything would be all right. Doctors took the opposite view and thought he might live longer in the climate of some mountain resort or in Northern Russia. There is an extraordinary story, which I have not been able to piece together adequately, of his escaping from his attendants somewhere in Italy. There he wandered about, denouncing, with King Lear-like vehemence, his children to grinning strangers, until he was captured in a wild rocky place by some matter-of-fact *carabinieri.* During the winter of 1903, my mother, the only person whose presence, in his moments of madness, the old man could bear, was constantly at his side in Nice. My brother and I, aged three and four respectively, were also there with our English governess; I remember the windowpanes rattling in the bright breeze and the amazing pain caused by a drop of hot sealing wax on my finger. Using a candle flame (diluted to a deceptive pallor by the sunshine that invaded the stone slabs on which I was kneeling), I had been engaged in transforming dripping sticks of the stuff into gluey, marvelously smelling, scarlet and blue and bronze-colored blobs. The next moment I was bellowing on the floor, and my mother had hurried to the rescue, and somewhere nearby my grandfather in a wheelchair was thumping the resounding flags with his cane. She had a hard time with him. He used improper language. He kept mistaking the attendant who rolled him along the Promenade des Anglais for Count Loris-Melikov, a (long-deceased) colleague of his in the ministerial cabinet of the eighties. *"Qui est cette femme—chassez-la!"* he would cry to my mother as he pointed a shaky finger at the Queen of Belgium or Holland who had stopped to inquire about his health. Dimly I recall running up to his chair to show him a pretty pebble, which he slowly examined and then slowly put into his mouth. I wish I had had more curiosity when, in later years, my mother used to recollect those times.

He would lapse for ever-increasing periods into an unconscious state; during one such lapse he was transferred to his pied-à-terre on the Palace Quay in St. Petersburg. As he gradually regained consciousness, my mother camouflaged his bedroom into the one he had had in Nice. Some similar pieces of furniture were found and a number of articles rushed from Nice by a special messenger, and all the flowers his hazy senses had been accustomed to were obtained, in their proper variety and profusion, and a bit of house wall that could be just glimpsed from the window was painted a brilliant white, so every time he reverted to a state of comparative lucidity he found himself safe on the illusory Riviera artistically staged by my mother; and there, on March 28, 1904, exactly eighteen years, day for day, before my father, he peacefully died.

He left four sons and five daughters. The eldest was Dmitri, who inherited the Nabokov majorat in the then Tsardom of Poland; his first wife was Lidia Eduardovna Falz-Fein, his second, Marie Redlich; next, came Sergey, governor of Mitau, who married Daria Nikolaevna Tuchkov, the great-great-granddaughter of Field Marshal Kutuzov, Prince of Smolensk, then came my father. The youngest was Konstantin, a confirmed bachelor. The sisters were: Natalia, wife of Ivan de Peterson, Russian consul at The Hague; Vera, wife of Ivan Pïhachev, sportsman and landowner; Nina, who divorced Baron Rausch von Traubenberg, military Governor of Warsaw, to marry Admiral Nikolay Kolomeytsev, hero of the Japanese war; Elizaveta, married to Henri, Prince Sayn-Wittgenstein-Berleburg, and after his death, to Roman Leikmann, former tutor of her sons; and Nadezhda, wife of Dmitri Vonlyarlyarski, whom she later divorced.

Uncle Konstantin was in the diplomatic service and, in the last stage of his career in London, conducted a bitter and unsuccessful struggle with Sablin as to which of them would head the Russian mission. His life was not particularly eventful, but he had had a couple of nice escapes from a fate less tame than the draft in a London hospital, which killed him in 1927. Once, in Moscow, on February 17, 1905, when an older friend, the Grand Duke Sergey, half a minute before the explosion, offered him a lift in his carriage, and my uncle said no, thanks, he'd rather walk, and away rolled the carriage to its fatal rendezvous with a terrorist's bomb; and the second time, seven years later, when he missed another appointment, this one with an iceberg, by chancing to return his *Titanic* ticket. We saw a good deal of him in London after we had escaped from Lenin's Russia. Our meeting at Victoria Station in 1919 is a vivid vignette in my mind: my father marching up to his prim brother with an unfolding bear hug; he, backing away and repeating: *"Mï v Anglii, mï v Anglii* [we are in England]." His charming little flat was full of souvenirs from India such as photographs of young British officers. He is the author of *The Ordeal of a Diplomat* (1921), easily obtainable in large public libraries, and of an English version of Pushkin's *Boris Godunov;* and he is portrayed, goatee and all (together with Count Witte, the two Japanese delegates and a benevolent Theodore Roosevelt), in a mural of the signing of the Portsmouth Treaty on the left side of the main entrance hall of the American Museum of Natural History—an eminently fit place to find my surname in golden Slavic characters, as I did the first time I passed there—with a fellow lepidopterist, who said "Sure, sure" in reply to my exclamation of recognition.

2

Diagrammatically, the three family estates on the Oredezh, fifty miles south of St. Petersburg, may be represented as three linked rings in a ten-mile chain running west-east across the Luga highway, with my mother's Vyra in the middle, her brother's Rozhestveno on the right, and my grandmother's Batovo on the left, the links being the bridges across the Oredezh (properly *Oredezh'*) which, in its winding, branching and looping course, bathed Vyra on either side.

Two other, much more distant, estates in the region were related to Batovo: my uncle Prince Wittgenstein's Druzhnoselie situated a few miles beyond the Siverski railway station, which was six miles northeast of our place; and my uncle Pïhachev's Mityushino, some fifty miles south on the way to Luga: I never once was there, but we fairly often drove the ten miles or so to the Wittgensteins and once (in August 1911) visited them at their other splendid estate, Kamenka, in the Province of Podolsk, S.W. Russia.

The estate of Batovo enters history in 1805 when it becomes the property of Anastasia Matveevna Rïleev, born Essen. Her son, Kondratiy Fyodorovich Rïleev (1795–1826), minor poet, journalist, and famous Decembrist, spent most of his summers in the region, addressed elegies to the Oredezh, and sang Prince Aleksey's castle, the jewel of its banks. Legend and logic, a rare but strong partnership, seem to indicate, as I have more fully explained in my notes to *Onegin,* that the Rïleev pistol duel with Pushkin, of which so little is known, took place in the Batovo park, between May 6 and 9 (Old Style), 1820. Pushkin, with two friends, Baron Anton Delvig and Pavel Yakovlev, who were accompanying him a little way on the first lap of his long journey from St. Petersburg to Ekaterinoslav, had quietly turned off the Luga highway, at Rozhestveno, crossed the bridge (hoof-thud changing to brief clatter), and followed the old rutty road westward to Batovo. There, in front of the manor house, Rïleev was eagerly awaiting them. He had just sent his wife, in her last month of pregnancy, to her estate near Voronezh, and was anxious to get the duel over—and, God willing, join her there. I can feel upon my skin and in my nostrils the delicious country roughness of the northern spring day which greeted Pushkin and his two seconds as they got out of their coach and penetrated into the linden avenue beyond the Batovo platbands, still virginally black. I see so plainly the three young men (the sum of their years equals my present age) following their host and two persons unknown, into the park. At that date small crumpled violets showed through the carpet of last year's dead leaves, and freshly emerged Orange-tips settled on the shivering dandelions. For one moment fate may have wavered between preventing a heroic rebel from heading for the gallows, and depriving Russia of *Eugene Onegin;* but then did neither.

A couple of decades after Rïleev's execution on the bastion of the Peter-and-Paul Fortress in 1826, Batovo was acquired from the state by my paternal grandmother's mother, Nina Aleksandrovna Shishkov, later Baroness von Korff, from

whom my grandfather purchased it around 1855. Two tutor-
and-governess-raised generations of Nabokovs knew a certain
trail through the woods beyond Batovo as *"Le Chemin du
Pendu,"* the favorite walk of The Hanged One, as Rïleev
was referred to in society: callously but also euphemistically
and wonderingly (gentlemen in those days were not often
hanged) in preference to The Decembrist or The Insurgent.
I can easily imagine young Rïleev in the green skeins of our
woods, walking and reading a book, a form of romantic am-
bulation in the manner of his era, as easily as I can visualize
the fearless lieutenant defying despotism on the bleak Senate
Square with his comrades and puzzled troops; but the name
of the long, "grown-up" *promenade* looked forward to by
good children, remained throughout boyhood unconnected
in our minds with the fate of the unfortunate master of
Batovo: my cousin Sergey Nabokov, who was born at Batovo
in *la Chambre du Revenant,* imagined a conventional ghost,
and I vaguely surmised with my tutor or governess that some
mysterious stranger had been found dangling from the aspen
upon which a rare hawkmoth bred. That Rïleev may have
been simply the "Hanged One" (*poveshennïy* or *visel'nik*) to
the local peasants, is not unnatural; but in the manorial families a bizarre taboo prevented, apparently, parents from identifying the ghost, as if a specific reference might introduce
a note of nastiness into the glamorous vagueness of the phrase
designating a picturesque walk in a beloved country place.
Still, I find it curious to realize that even my father, who had
so much information about the Decembrists and so much
more sympathy for them than his relatives, never once, as far
as I can recall, mentioned Kondratiy Rïleev during our rambles and bicycle rides in the environs. My cousin draws my
attention to the fact that General Rïleev, the poet's son, was

a close friend of Tsar Alexander II and of my grandfather, D. N. Nabokov, and that *on ne parle pas de corde dans la maison du pendu.*

From Batovo, the old rutty road (which we have followed with Pushkin and now retrace) ran east for a couple of miles to Rozhestveno. Just before the main bridge, one could either turn north in open country toward our Vyra and its two parks on each side of the road, or else continue east, down a steep hill past an old cemetery choked with raspberry and racemosa and cross the bridge toward my uncle's white-pillared house aloof on its hill.

The estate Rozhestveno, with a large village of the same name, extensive lands, and a manor house high above the Oredezh River, on the Luga (or Warsaw) highway, in the district of Tsarskoe Selo (now Pushkin), about fifty miles south from St. Petersburg (now Leningrad), had been known before the eighteenth century as the Kurovitz domain, in the old Koporsk district. Around 1715 it had been the property of Prince Aleksey, the unfortunate son of that archbully, Peter the First. Part of an *escalier dérobé* and something else I cannot recollect were preserved in the new anatomy of the building. I have touched that banister and have seen (or trod on?) the other, forgotten, detail. From that palace, along that highway leading to Poland and Austria, the prince had escaped only to be lured back from as far south as Naples to the paternal torture house by the Tsar's agent, Count Pyotr Andreevich Tolstoy, one-time ambassador in Constantinople (where he had obtained for his master the little blackamoor whose great-grandson was to be Pushkin). Rozhestveno later belonged, I believe, to a favorite of Alexander the First, and the manor had been partly rebuilt when my maternal grand-father acquired the domain around 1880, for his eldest son Vladimir who died at sixteen a few years later. His brother

Vasiliy inherited it in 1901 and spent there ten summers out of the fifteen that still remained to him. I particularly remember the cool and sonorous quality of the place, the checkerboard flagstones of the hall, ten porcelain cats on a shelf, a sarcophagus and an organ, the skylights and the upper galleries, the colored dusk of mysterious rooms, and carnations and crucifixes everywhere.

3

In his youth Carl Heinrich Graun had a fine tenor voice; one night, having to sing in an opera written by Schurmann, chapel-master of Brunswick, he got so disgusted with some airs in it that he replaced them by others of his own composition. Here I feel the shock of gleeful kinship; yet I prefer two other ancestors of mine, the young explorer already mentioned and that great pathologist, my mother's maternal grandfather, Nikolay Illarionovich Kozlov (1814–1889), first president of the Russian Imperial Academy of Medicine and author of such papers as "On the Development of the Idea of Disease" or "On the Coarctation of the Jugular Foramen in the Insane." At this convenient point, I may as well mention my own scientific papers, and especially my three favorite ones, "Notes on Neotropical Plebejinae" (*Psyche,* Vol. 52, Nos. 1–2 and 3–4, 1945), "A New Species of *Cyclargus* Nabokov" (*The Entomologist,* December 1948), and "The Nearctic Members of the Genus *Lycaeides* Hübner" (*Bulletin Mus. Comp. Zool.,* Harvard Coll., 1949), after which year I found it no longer physically possible to combine scientific research with lectures, belles-lettres, and *Lolita* (for she was on her way—a painful birth, a difficult baby).

The Rukavishnikov blazon is more modest, but also less conventional than the Nabokov one. The escutcheon is a stylized version of a *domna* (primitive blast furnace), in allusion, no doubt, to the smelting of the Uralian ores that my adventurous ancestors discovered. I wish to note that these Rukavishnikovs—Siberian pioneers, gold prospectors and mining engineers—were *not* related, as some biographers have carelessly assumed, to the no less wealthy Moscow merchants of the same name. *My* Rukavishnikovs belonged (since the eighteenth century) to the landed gentry of Kazan Province. Their mines were situated at Alopaevsk near Nizhni-Tagilsk, Province of Perm, on the Siberian side of the Urals. My father had twice traveled there on the former Siberian Express, a beautiful train of the Nord-Express family, which I planned to take soon, though rather on an entomological than mineralogical trip, but the revolution interfered with that project.

My mother, Elena Ivanovna (August 29, 1876—May 2, 1939), was the daughter of Ivan Vasilievich Rukavishnikov (1841–1901), landowner, justice of the peace, and philanthropist, son of a millionaire industrialist, and Olga Nikolaevna (1845–1901), daughter of Dr. Kozlov. My mother's parents both died of cancer within the same year, he in March, she in June. Of her seven siblings, five died in infancy, and of her two older brothers, Vladimir died at sixteen at Davos, in the eighteen-eighties, and Vasiliy in Paris, in 1916. Ivan Rukavishnikov had a terrible temper and my mother feared him. In my childhood all I knew about him were his portraits (his beard, the magisterial chain around his neck) and such attributes of his main hobby as decoy ducks and elk heads. A pair of especially large bears he had shot stood upright with redoubtably raised front paws in the iron-barred vestibule of our country house. Every summer I gauged my height by the ability to reach their fascinating claws—first those of the lower forelimbs, then those of the upper. Their bellies proved disappointingly hard, once your fingers (accustomed to palpate live dogs or toy animals) had sunk in their rough brown fur. Now and then they used to be taken out into a corner of the garden to be thoroughly whacked and aired, and poor Mademoiselle, approaching from the direction of the park, would utter a cry of alarm as she caught sight of two savage beasts waiting for her in the mobile shade of the trees. My father cared nothing for the shooting of game, greatly differing in this respect from his brother Sergey, a passionate sportsman who since 1908 was Master of the Hounds to His Majesty the Tsar.

One of my mother's happier girlhood recollections was having traveled one summer with her aunt Praskovia to the Crimea, where her paternal grandfather had an estate near Feodosia. Her aunt and she went for a walk with him and another old gentleman, the well-known seascape painter Ayvazovski. She remembered the painter saying (as he had said no doubt many times) that in 1836, at an exhibition of pictures in St. Petersburg, he had seen Pushkin, "an ugly little fellow with a tall handsome wife." That was more than half a century before, when Ayvazovski was an art student, and less than a year before Pushkin's death. She also remembered the touch nature added from its own palette—the white mark a bird left on the painter's gray top hat. The aunt Praskovia, walking beside her, was her mother's sister, who had married the celebrated syphilologist V. M. Tarnovski (1839–1906) and who herself was a doctor, the author of works on psychiatry, anthropology and social welfare. One evening at Ayvazovski's villa near Feodosia, Aunt Praskovia met at dinner the twenty-eight-year-old Dr. Anton Chekhov whom she somehow offended in the course of a medical conversation. She was a very learned, very kind, very elegant lady, and it is hard to imagine how exactly she could have provoked the incredibly coarse outburst Chekhov permits himself in a published letter of August 3, 1888, to his sister. Aunt Praskovia, or Aunt Pasha, as we called her, often visited us at Vyra. She had an enchanting way of greeting us, as she swept into the nursery with a sonorous *"Bonjour, les enfants!"* She died in 1910. My mother was at her bedside, and Aunt Pasha's last words were: "That's interesting. Now I understand. Everything is water, *vsyo—voda.*"

My mother's brother Vasiliy was in the diplomatic service, which he treated, however, far more lightly than my uncle Konstantin did. For Vasiliy Ivanovich it was not a career, but a more or less plausible setting. French and Italian friends, being unable to pronounce his long Russian surname, had boiled it down to "Ruka" (with the accent on the last syllable), and this suited him far better than did his Christian name. Uncle Ruka appeared to me in my childhood to belong to a world of toys, gay picture books, and cherry trees laden with glossy black fruit: he had glass-housed a whole orchard in a corner of his country estate, which was separated from ours by the winding river. During the summer, almost every day at lunchtime his carriage might be seen crossing the bridge and then speeding toward our house along a hedge of young firs. When I was eight or nine, he would invariably take me upon his knee after lunch and (while two young footmen were clearing the table in the empty dining room) fondle me, with crooning sounds and fancy endearments, and I felt embarrassed for my uncle by the presence of the servants and relieved when my father called him from the veranda: *"Basile, on vous attend."* Once, when I went to meet him at the station (I must have been eleven or twelve then) and watched him descend from the long international sleeping car, he gave me one look and said: "How sallow and plain [*jaune et laid*] you have become, my poor boy." On my fifteenth nameday, he took me aside and in his brusque, precise and somewhat old-fashioned French informed me that he was making me his heir. "And now you may go," he added, *"l'audience est finie. Je n'ai plus rien à vous dire."*

I remember him as a slender, neat little man with a dusky complexion, gray-green eyes flecked with rust, a dark, bushy mustache, and a mobile Adam's apple bobbing conspicuously above the opal and gold snake ring that held the knot of his tie. He also wore opals on his fingers and in his cuff links. A gold chainlet encircled his frail hairy wrist, and there was usually a carnation in the buttonhole of his dove-gray, mouse-gray or silver-gray summer suit. It was only in summer that I used to see him. After a brief stay in Rozhestveno he would go back to France or Italy, to his château (called Perpigna) near Pau, to his villa (called Tamarindo) near Rome, or to his beloved Egypt, from which he would send me picture postcards (palm trees and their reflections, sunsets, pharaohs with their hands on their knees) crossed by his thick scrawl. Then, in June again, when the fragrant *cheryomuha* (racemose old-world bird cherry or simply "racemosa" as I have baptized it in my work on "Onegin") was in foamy bloom, his private flag would be hoisted on his beautiful Rozhestveno house. He traveled with half-a-dozen enormous trunks, bribed the Nord-Express to make a special stop at our little country station, and with the promise of a marvelous present, on small, mincing feet in high-heeled white shoes would lead me mysteriously to the nearest tree and delicately pluck and proffer a leaf, saying, *"Pour mon neveu, la chose la plus belle au monde—une feuille verte."*

Or he would solemnly bring me from America the *Foxy Grandpa* series, and *Buster Brown*—a forgotten boy in a reddish suit: if one looked closely, one could see that the color was really a mass of dense red dots. Every episode ended in

a tremendous spanking for Buster, which was administered
by his wasp-waisted but powerful Ma, who used a slipper, a
hairbrush, a brittle umbrella, anything—even the bludgeon
of a helpful policeman—and drew puffs of dust from the seat
of Buster's pants. Since I had never been spanked, those pictures conveyed to me the impression of strange exotic torture
not different from, say, the burying of a popeyed wretch up
to his chin in the torrid sand of a desert, as represented in
the frontispiece of a Mayne Reid book.

4

Uncle Ruka seems to have led an idle and oddly chaotic
life. His diplomatic career was of the vaguest kind. He prided
himself, however, on being an expert in decoding ciphered
messages in any of the five languages he knew. We subjected
him to a test one day, and in a twinkle he turned the sequence
"5.13 24.11 13.16 9.13.5 5.13 24.11" into the opening words
of a famous monologue in Shakespeare.

Pink-coated, he rode to hounds in England or Italy; fur-
coated, he attempted to motor from St. Petersburg to Pau;
wearing an opera cloak, he almost lost his life in an airplane
crash on a beach near Bayonne. (When I asked him how did
the pilot of the smashed Voisin take it, Uncle Ruka thought
for a moment and then replied with complete assurance:
"*Il sanglotait assis sur un rocher.*") He sang barcaroles and
modish lyrics ("*Ils se regardent tous deux, en se mangeant des
yeux . . .*" "*Elle est morte en Février, pauvre Colinette! . . .*"
"*Le soleil rayonnait encore, j'ai voulu revoir les grands
bois . . .*" and dozens of others). He wrote music himself, of
the sweet, rippling sort, and French verse, curiously scan-
nable as English or Russian iambics, and marked by a

princely disregard for the comforts of the mute *e*'s. He was extremely good at poker.

Because he stammered and had difficulty in pronouncing labials, he changed his coachman's name from Pyotr to Lev; and my father (who was always a little sharp with him) accused him of a slaveowner's mentality. Apart from this, his speech was a fastidious combination of French, English and Italian, all of which he spoke with vastly more ease than he did his native tongue. When he resorted to Russian, it was invariably to misuse or garble some extremely idiomatic or even folksy expression, as when he would say at table with a sudden sigh (for there was always something amiss—a spell of hay fever, the death of a peacock, a lost borzoi): *"Je suis triste et seul comme une bylinka v pole* [as lonesome as a 'grass blade in the field']."

He insisted that he had an incurable heart ailment and that, when the seizures came, he could obtain relief only by lying supine on the floor. Nobody took him seriously, and after he did die of angina pectoris, all alone, in Paris, at the end of 1916, aged forty-five, it was with a quite special pang that one recalled those after-dinner incidents in the drawing room—the unprepared footman entering with the Turkish coffee, my father glancing (with quizzical resignation) at my mother, then (with disapproval) at his brother-in-law spread-eagled in the footman's path, then (with curiosity) at the funny vibration going on among the coffee things on the tray in the seemingly composed servant's cotton-gloved hands.

From other, stranger torments that beset him in the course of his short life, he sought relief—if I understand these matters rightly—in religion, first in certain Russian sectarian outlets, and eventually in the Roman Catholic Church. His was the kind of colorful neurosis that should have been accom-

panied by genius but in his case was not, hence the search
for a traveling shadow. In his youth he had been intensely
disliked by his father, a country gentleman of the old school
(bear hunting, a private theatre, a few fine Old Masters
among a good deal of trash), whose uncontrollable temper
was rumored to have been a threat to the boy's very life. My
mother told me later of the tension in the Vyra household
of her girlhood, of the atrocious scenes that took place in
Ivan Vasilievich's study, a gloomy corner room giving on an
old well with a rusty pumping wheel under five Lombardy
poplars. Nobody used that room except me. I kept my books
and spreading boards on its black shelves, and subsequently
induced my mother to have some of its furniture transferred
into my own sunny little study on the garden side, and
therein staggered, one morning, its tremendous desk with
nothing upon its waste of dark leather but a huge curved
paper knife, a veritable scimitar of yellow ivory carved from
a mammoth's tusk.

When Uncle Ruka died, at the end of 1916, he left me
what would amount nowadays to a couple of million dollars
and his country estate, with its white-pillared mansion on a
green, escarped hill and its two thousand acres of wildwood
and peatbog. The house, I am told, still stood there in 1940,
nationalized but aloof, a museum piece for any sightseeing
traveler who might follow the St. Petersburg–Luga highway
running below through the village Rozhestveno and across
the branching river. Because of its floating islands of water
lilies and algal brocade, the fair Oredezh had a festive air at
that spot. Farther down its sinuous course, where the sand
martins shot out of their holes in the steep red bank, it was
deeply suffused with the reflections of great, romantic firs
(the fringe of our Vyra); and still farther downstream, the
endless tumultuous flow of a water mill gave the spectator

(his elbows on the handrail) the sensation of receding endlessly, as if this were the stern of time itself.

5

The following passage is not for the general reader, but for
the particular idiot who, because he lost a fortune in some
crash, thinks he understands me.

My old (since 1917) quarrel with the Soviet dictatorship is
wholly unrelated to any question of property. My contempt
for the émigré who "hates the Reds" because they "stole" his
money and land is complete. The nostalgia I have been cher-
ishing all these years is a hypertrophied sense of lost childhood, not sorrow for lost banknotes.

And finally: I reserve for myself the right to yearn after
an ecological niche:

> . . . Beneath the sky
> Of my America to sigh
> For *one* locality in Russia.

The general reader may now resume.

6

I was nearing eighteen, then was over eighteen; love affairs
and verse-writing occupied most of my leisure; material questions left me indifferent, and, anyway, against the background
of our prosperity no inheritance could seem very conspicu-
ous; yet, upon looking back across the transparent abyss, I
find queer and somewhat unpleasant to reflect that during
the brief year that I was in the possession of that private
wealth, I was too much absorbed by the usual delights of
youth—youth that was rapidly losing its initial, non-usual

fervor—either to derive any special pleasure from the legacy
or to experience any annoyance when the Bolshevik Revolution abolished it overnight. This recollection gives me the
sense of having been ungrateful to Uncle Ruka; of having
joined in the general attitude of smiling condescension that
even those who liked him usually took toward him. It is with
the utmost repulsion that I force myself to recall the sarcastic
comments that Monsieur Noyer, my Swiss tutor (otherwise a
most kindly soul), used to make on my uncle's best composition, a *romance*, both the music and words of which he had
written. One day, on the terrace of his Pau castle, with the
amber vineyards below and the empurpled mountains in the
distance, at a time when he was harassed by asthma, palpita-
tions, shiverings, a Proustian excoriation of the senses, *se
débattant,* as it were, under the impact of the autumn colors
(described in his own words as the *"chapelle ardente de
feuilles aux tons violents"*), of the distant voices from the
valley, of a flight of doves striating the tender sky, he had
composed that one-winged *romance* (and the only person who
memorized the music and all the words was my brother Sergey, whom he hardly ever noticed, who also stammered, and
who is also now dead).

"*L'air transparent fait monter de la plaine...*" he would
sing in his high tenor voice, seated at the white piano in
our country house—and if I were at that moment hurrying
through the adjacent groves on my way home for lunch (soon
after seeing his jaunty straw hat and the black-velvet-clad
bust of his handsome coachman in Assyrian profile, with
scarlet-sleeved outstretched arms, skim rapidly along the rim
of the hedge separating the park from the drive) the plaintive
sounds

> *Un vol de tourterelles strie le ciel tendre,*
> *Les chrysanthèmes se parent pour la Toussaint*

reached me and my green butterfly net on the shady, tremulous trail, at the end of which was a vista of reddish sand and
the corner of our freshly repainted house, the color of young
fir cones, with the open drawing-room window whence the
wounded music came.

7

The act of vividly recalling a patch of the past is something
that I seem to have been performing with the utmost zest
all my life, and I have reason to believe that this almost
pathological keenness of the retrospective faculty is a heredi-
tary trait. There was a certain spot in the forest, a footbridge
across a brown brook, where my father would piously pause
to recall the rare butterfly that, on the seventeenth of August,
1883, his German tutor had netted for him. The thirty-year-
old scene would be gone through again. He and his brothers
had stopped short in helpless excitement at the sight of the
coveted insect poised on a log and moving up and down, as
though in alert respiration, its four cherry-red wings with a
pavonian eyespot on each. In tense silence, not daring to
strike himself, he had handed his net to Herr Rogge, who
was groping for it, his eyes fixed on the splendid fly. My
cabinet inherited that specimen a quarter of a century later.
One touching detail: its wings had "sprung" because it had
been removed from the setting board too early, too eagerly.

In a villa which in the summer of 1904 we rented with
my uncle Ivan de Peterson's family on the Adriatic (the name
was either "Neptune" or "Apollo"—I can still identify its
crenelated, cream-colored tower in old pictures of Abbazia),
aged five, mooning in my cot after lunch, I used to turn over
on my stomach and, carefully, lovingly, hopelessly, in an
artistically detailed fashion difficult to reconcile with the

ridiculously small number of seasons that had gone to form the inexplicably nostalgic image of "home" (that I had not seen since September 1903), I would draw with my forefinger on my pillow the carriage road sweeping up to our Vyra house, the stone steps on the right, the carved back of a bench on the left, the alley of oaklings beginning beyond the bushes of honeysuckle, and a newly shed horseshoe, a collector's item (much bigger and brighter than the rusty ones I used to find on the seashore), shining in the reddish dust of the drive. The recollection of that recollection is sixty years older than the latter, but far less unusual.

Once, in 1908 or 1909, Uncle Ruka became engrossed in some French children's books that he had come upon in our house; with an ecstatic moan, he found a passage he had loved in his childhood, beginning: *"Sophie n'était pas jolie..."* and many years later, my moan echoed his, when I rediscovered, in a chance nursery, those same "Bibliothèque Rose" volumes, with their stories about boys and girls who led in France an idealized version of the *vie de château* which my family led in Russia. The stories themselves (all those *Les Malheurs de Sophie, Les Petites Filles Modèles, Les Vacances*) are, as I see them now, an awful combination of preciosity and vulgarity; but in writing them the sentimental and smug Mme de Ségur, née Rostopchine, was Frenchifying the authentic surroundings of her Russian childhood which preceded mine by exactly one century. In my own case, when I come over Sophie's troubles again—her lack of eyebrows and love of thick cream—I not only go through the same agony and delight that my uncle did, but have to cope with an additional burden—the recollection I have of him, reliving his childhood with the help of those very books. I see again my schoolroom in Vyra, the blue roses of the wallpaper, the open window. Its reflection fills the oval mirror above the leathern couch where my uncle sits, gloating over a tattered book. A sense of security, of well-being, of summer warmth pervades my memory. That robust reality makes a ghost of the present. The mirror brims with brightness; a bumblebee has entered the room and bumps against the ceiling. Everything is as it should be, nothing will ever change, nobody will ever die.

Dmitri Nikolaevich Nabokov, the author's grandfather (1827–1904), Minister of Justice (1878–1885).

The author's paternal grandmother, Baroness Maria von Korff (1842–1926) in the late eighteen-fifties.

4

1

THE kind of Russian family to which I belonged—a kind now extinct—had, among other virtues, a traditional leaning toward the comfortable products of Anglo-Saxon civilization. Pears' Soap, tar-black when dry, topaz-like when held to the light between wet fingers, took care of one's morning bath. Pleasant was the decreasing weight of the English collapsible tub when it was made to protrude a rubber underlip and disgorge its frothy contents into the slop pail. "We could not improve the cream, so we improved the tube," said the English toothpaste. At breakfast, Golden Syrup imported from London would entwist with its glowing coils the revolving spoon from which enough of it had slithered onto a piece of Russian bread and butter. All sorts of snug, mellow things came in a steady procession from the English Shop on Nevski Avenue: fruitcakes, smelling salts, playing cards, picture puzzles, striped blazers, talcum-white tennis balls.

I learned to read English before I could read Russian. My first English friends were four simple souls in my grammar —Ben, Dan, Sam and Ned. There used to be a great deal of fuss about their identities and whereabouts—"Who is Ben?" "He is Dan," "Sam is in bed," and so on. Although it all

remained rather stiff and patchy (the compiler was handicapped by having to employ—for the initial lessons, at least—
words of not more than three letters), my imagination somehow managed to obtain the necessary data. Wan-faced, big-
limbed, silent nitwits, proud in the possession of certain tools
("Ben has an axe"), they now drift with a slow-motioned
slouch across the remotest backdrop of memory; and, akin
to the mad alphabet of an optician's chart, the grammar-book
lettering looms again before me.

The schoolroom was drenched with sunlight. In a sweating glass jar, several spiny caterpillars were feeding on nettle
leaves (and ejecting interesting, barrel-shaped pellets of olive-
green frass). The oilcloth that covered the round table smelled
of glue. Miss Clayton smelled of Miss Clayton. Fantastically,
gloriously, the blood-colored alcohol of the outside thermometer had risen to 24° Réaumur (86° Fahrenheit) in the shade.
Through the window one could see kerchiefed peasant girls
weeding a garden path on their hands and knees or gently
raking the sun-mottled sand. (The happy days when they
would be cleaning streets and digging canals for the State
were still beyond the horizon.) Golden orioles in the greenery
emitted their four brilliant notes: dee-del-dee-O!

Ned lumbered past the window in a fair impersonation of
the gardener's mate Ivan (who was to become in 1918 a member of the local Soviet). On later pages longer words appeared;
and at the very end of the brown, inkstained volume, a real,
sensible story unfolded its adult sentences ("One day Ted said
to Ann: Let us—"), the little reader's ultimate triumph and
reward. I was thrilled by the thought that some day I might
attain such proficiency. The magic has endured, and whenever a grammar book comes my way, I instantly turn to the
last page to enjoy a forbidden glimpse of the laborious stu-

dent's future, of that promised land where, at last, words are meant to mean what they mean.

2

Summer *soomerki*—the lovely Russian word for dusk. Time: a dim point in the first decade of this unpopular century. Place: latitude 59° north from your equator, longitude 100° east from my writing hand. The day would take hours to fade, and everything—sky, tall flowers, still water—would be kept in a state of infinite vesperal suspense, deepened rather than resolved by the doleful moo of a cow in a distant meadow or by the still more moving cry that came from some bird beyond the lower course of the river, where the vast expanse of a misty-blue sphagnum bog, because of its mystery and remoteness, the Rukavishnikov children had baptized America.

In the drawing room of our country house, before going to bed, I would often be read to in English by my mother. As she came to a particularly dramatic passage, where the hero was about to encounter some strange, perhaps fatal danger, her voice would slow down, her words would be spaced portentously, and before turning the page she would place upon it her hand, with its familiar pigeon-blood ruby and diamond ring (within the limpid facets of which, had I been a better crystal-gazer, I might have seen a room, people, lights, trees in the rain—a whole period of émigré life for which that ring was to pay).

There were tales about knights whose terrific but wonderfully aseptic wounds were bathed by damsels in grottoes. From a windswept clifftop, a medieval maiden with flying hair and a youth in hose gazed at the round Isles of the

Blessed. In "Misunderstood," the fate of Humphrey used to bring a more specialized lump to one's throat than anything in Dickens or Daudet (great devisers of lumps), while a shamelessly allegorical story, "Beyond the Blue Mountains," dealing with two pairs of little travelers—good Clover and Cowslip, bad Buttercup and Daisy—contained enough exciting details to make one forget its "message."

There were also those large, flat, glossy picture books. I particularly liked the blue-coated, red-trousered, coal-black Golliwogg, with underclothes buttons for eyes, and his meager harem of five wooden dolls. By the illegal method of cutting themselves frocks out of the American flag (Peg taking the motherly stripes, Sarah Jane the pretty stars) two of the dolls acquired a certain soft femininity, once their neutral articulations had been clothed. The Twins (Meg and Weg) and the Midget remained stark naked and, consequently, sexless.

We see them in the dead of night stealing out of doors to sling snowballs at one another until the chimes of a remote clock ("But Hark!" comments the rhymed text) send them back to their toybox in the nursery. A rude jack-in-the-box shoots out, frightening my lovely Sarah, and that picture I heartily disliked because it reminded me of children's parties at which this or that graceful little girl, who had bewitched me, happened to pinch her finger or hurt her knee, and would forthwith expand into a purple-faced goblin, all wrinkles and bawling mouth. Another time they went on a bicycle journey and were captured by cannibals; our unsuspecting travelers had been quenching their thirst at a palm-fringed pool when the tom-toms sounded. Over the shoulder of my past I admire again the crucial picture: the Golliwogg, still on his knees by the pool but no longer drinking; his hair stands on end and the normal black of his face has changed to a weird ashen hue. There was also the motorcar book (Sarah Jane, always my favorite, sporting a long green veil), with the usual sequel—crutches and bandaged heads.

And, yes—the airship. Yards and yards of yellow silk went to make it, and an additional tiny balloon was provided for the sole use of the fortunate Midget. At the immense altitude to which the ship reached, the aeronauts huddled together for warmth while the lost little soloist, still the object of my intense envy notwithstanding his plight, drifted into an abyss of frost and stars—alone.

3

I next see my mother leading me bedward through the enormous hall, where a central flight of stairs swept up and up, with nothing but hothouse-like panes of glass between the upper landing and the light green evening sky. One would lag back and shuffle and slide a little on the smooth stone floor of the hall, causing the gentle hand at the small of one's back to propel one's reluctant frame by means of indulgent pushes. Upon reaching the stairway, my custom was to get to the steps by squirming under the handrail between the newel post and the first banister. With every new summer, the process of squeezing through became more difficult; nowadays, even my ghost would get stuck.

Another part of the ritual was to ascend with closed eyes. "Step, step, step," came my mother's voice as she led me up— and sure enough, the surface of the next tread would receive the blind child's confident foot; all one had to do was lift it a little higher than usual, so as to avoid stubbing one's toe against the riser. This slow, somewhat somnambulistic ascension in self-engendered darkness held obvious delights. The keenest of them was not knowing when the last step would

come. At the top of the stairs, one's foot would be automatically lifted to the deceptive call of "Step," and then, with
a momentary sense of exquisite panic, with a wild contrac-
tion of muscles, would sink into the phantasm of a step,
padded, as it were, with the infinitely elastic stuff of its own
nonexistence.

It is surprising what method there was in my bedtime
dawdling. True, the whole going-up-the-stairs business now
reveals certain transcendental values. Actually, however, I
was merely playing for time by extending every second to its
utmost. This would still go on when my mother turned me
over, to be undressed, to Miss Clayton or Mademoiselle.

There were five bathrooms in our country house, and a
medley of venerable washstands (one of these I would seek
out in its dark nook whenever I had been crying, so as to feel
on my swollen face which I was ashamed to show, the healing
touch of its groping jet while I stepped on the rusty pedal).
Regular baths were taken in the evening. For morning ablutions, the round, rubber English tubs were used. Mine was
about four feet in diameter, with a knee-high rim. Upon the
lathered back of the squatting child, a jugful of water was
carefully poured by an aproned servant. Its temperature
varied with the hydrotherapeutic notions of successive mentors. There was that bleak period of dawning puberty, when
an icy deluge was decreed by our current tutor, who happened to be a medical student. On the other hand, the temperature of one's evening bath remained pleasantly constant
at 28° Réaumur (95° Fahrenheit) as measured by a large
kindly thermometer whose wooden sheathing (with a bit of
damp string in the eye of the handle) allowed it to share in
the buoyancy of celluloid goldfishes and little swans.

The toilets were separate from the bathrooms, and the
oldest among them was a rather sumptuous but gloomy affair

with some fine panelwork and a tasseled rope of red velvet, which, when pulled, produced a beautifully modulated, discreetly muffled gurgle and gulp. From that corner of the house, one could see Hesperus and hear the nightingales, and it was there that, later, I used to compose my youthful verse, dedicated to unembraced beauties, and morosely survey, in a dimly illuminated mirror, the immediate erection of a strange castle in an unknown Spain. As a small child, however, I was assigned a more modest arrangement, rather casually situated in a narrow recess between a wicker hamper and the door leading to the nursery bathroom. This door I liked to keep ajar; through it I drowsily looked at the shimmer of steam above the mahogany bath, at the fantastic flotilla of swans and skiffs, at myself with a harp in one of the boats, at a furry moth pinging against the reflector of the kerosene lamp, at the stained-glass window beyond, at its two halberdiers consisting of colored rectangles. Bending from my warm seat, I liked to press the middle of my brow, its ophryon to be precise, against the smooth comfortable edge of the door and then roll my head a little, so that the door would move to and fro while its edge remained all the time in soothing contact with my forehead. A dreamy rhythm would permeate my being. The recent "Step, step, step," would be taken up by a dripping faucet. And, fruitfully combining rhythmic pattern with rhythmic sound, I would unravel the labyrinthian frets on the linoleum, and find faces where a crack or a shadow afforded a *point de repère* for the eye. I appeal to parents: never, never say, "Hurry up," to a child.

The final stage in the course of my vague navigation would come when I reached the island of my bed. From the veranda or drawing room, where life was going on without me, my mother would come up for the warm murmur of her goodnight kiss. Closed inside shutters, a lighted candle, Gentle

Jesus, meek and mild, something-something little child, the child kneeling on the pillow that presently would engulf his humming head. English prayers and the little icon featuring a sun-tanned Greek Catholic saint formed an innocent association upon which I look back with pleasure; and above the icon, high up on the wall, where the shadow of something (of the bamboo screen between bed and door?) undulated in the warm candlelight, a framed aquarelle showed a dusky path winding through one of those eerily dense European beechwoods, where the only undergrowth is bindweed and the only sound one's thumping heart. In an English fairy tale my mother had once read to me, a small boy stepped out of his bed into a picture and rode his hobbyhorse along a painted path between silent trees. While I knelt on my pillow in a mist of drowsiness and talc-powdered well-being, half sitting on my calves and rapidly going through my prayer, I imagined the motion of climbing into the picture above my bed and plunging into that enchanted beechwood—which I did visit in due time.

4

A bewildering sequence of English nurses and governesses, some of them wringing their hands, others smiling at me enigmatically, come out to meet me as I re-enter my past.

There was dim Miss Rachel, whom I remember mainly in terms of Huntley and Palmer biscuits (the nice almond rocks at the top of the blue-papered tin box, the insipid cracknels at the bottom) which she unlawfully shared with me after my teeth had been brushed. There was Miss Clayton, who, when I slumped in my chair, would poke me in the middle vertebrae and then smilingly throw back her own shoulders to show what she wanted of me: she told me a nephew of hers at my age (four) used to breed caterpillars, but those she collected for me in an open jar with nettles all walked away one morning, and the gardener said they had hanged themselves. There was lovely, black-haired, aquamarine-eyed Miss Norcott, who lost a white kid glove at Nice or Beaulieu, where I vainly looked for it on the shingly beach among the colored pebbles and the glaucous lumps of sea-changed bottle glass. Lovely Miss Norcott was asked to leave at once, one night at Abbazia. She embraced me in the morning twilight of the nursery, pale-mackintoshed and weeping like a Babylonian willow, and that day I remained inconsolable, despite the hot chocolate that the Petersons' old Nanny had made especially for me and the special bread and butter, on the smooth surface of which my aunt Nata, adroitly capturing my attention, drew a daisy, then a cat, and then the little mermaid whom I had just been reading about with Miss Norcott and crying over, too, so I started to cry again. There was myopic little Miss Hunt, whose short stay with us in Wiesbaden came to an end the day my brother and I—aged four and five, respectively—managed to evade her nervous vigilance by boarding a steamer that took us quite a way down the Rhine before recapture. There was pink-nosed Miss Robinson. There was Miss Clayton again. There was one awful person who read to me Marie Corelli's *The Mighty Atom*. There were still others. At a certain point they faded out of my life. French and Russian took over; and what little time remained for the speaking of English was devoted to occasional sessions with two gentlemen, Mr. Burness and Mr. Cummings, neither of whom dwelt with us. They are associated in my mind with winters in St. Petersburg, where we had a house on the Morskaya Street.

Mr. Burness was a large Scotsman with a florid face, light-blue eyes and lank, straw-colored hair. He spent his mornings teaching at a language school and then crammed into the afternoon more private lessons than the day could well hold. Traveling, as he did, from one part of the town to another and having to depend on the torpid trot of dejected *izvozchik* (cab) horses to get him to his pupils, he would be, with luck, only a quarter of an hour late for his two o'clock lesson (wherever that was), but would arrive after five for his four o'clock one. The tension of waiting for him and hoping that, for once, his superhuman doggedness might balk before the gray wall of some special snowstorm was the kind of feeling that one trusts never to meet with in mature life (but that I did experience again when circumstances forced me, in my turn, to give lessons and when, in my furnished rooms in Berlin, I awaited a certain stone-faced pupil, who would *always* turn up despite the obstacles I mentally piled in his way).

The very darkness that was gathering outside seemed a waste product of Mr. Burness' efforts to reach our house. Presently the valet would come to drop the blue voluminous blinds and draw the flowered window draperies. The ticktock of the grandfather's clock in the schoolroom gradually assumed a dreary, nagging intonation. The tightness of my shorts in the groin and the rough touch of ribbed black stockings rubbing against the tender inside of my bent legs would mingle with the dull pressure of a humble need, the satisfaction of which I kept postponing. Nearly an hour would pass and there would be no sign of Mr. Burness. My brother would go to his room and play some practice piece on the piano and then plunge and replunge into some of the melodies that I loathed—the instruction to the artificial flowers in *Faust* (. . . *dites-lui qu'elle est belle* . . .) or Vladimir Lenski's wail (. . . *Koo-dah, koo-dah, koo-dah vï udalilis'*). I would leave the upper floor, where we children dwelt, and slowly slide along the balustrade down to the second story, where my parents' rooms were situated. As often as not, they used to be out at that time, and in the gathering dusk the place acted upon my young senses in a curiously teleological way, as if this accumulation of familiar things in the dark were doing its utmost to form the definite and permanent image that repeated exposure did finally leave in my mind.

The sepia gloom of an arctic afternoon in midwinter invaded the rooms and was deepening to an oppressive black. A bronze angle, a surface of glass or polished mahogany here and there in the darkness, reflected the odds and ends of light from the street, where the globes of tall street lamps along its middle line were already diffusing their lunar glow. Gauzy shadows moved on the ceiling. In the stillness, the dry sound of a chrysanthemum petal falling upon the marble of a table made one's nerves twang.

My mother's boudoir had a convenient oriel for looking out on the Morskaya in the direction of the Maria Square. With lips pressed against the thin fabric that veiled the windowpane I would gradually taste the cold of the glass through the gauze. From that oriel, some years later, at the outbreak of the Revolution, I watched various engagements and saw my first dead man: he was being carried away on a stretcher, and from one dangling leg an ill-shod comrade kept trying to pull off the boot despite pushes and punches from the stretchermen—all this at a goodish trot. But in the days of Mr. Burness' lessons there was nothing to watch save the dark, muffled street and its receding line of loftily suspended lamps, around which the snowflakes passed and repassed with a graceful, almost deliberately slackened motion, as if to show how the trick was done and how simple it was. From another angle, one might see a more generous stream of snow in a brighter, violet-tinged nimbus of gaslight, and then the jutting enclosure where I stood would seem to drift slowly up and up, like a balloon. At last one of the phantom sleighs gliding along the street would come to a stop, and with gawky haste Mr. Burness in his fox-furred *shapka* would make for our door.

From the schoolroom, whither I had preceded him, I would hear his vigorous footsteps crashing nearer and nearer, and, no matter how cold the day was, his good, ruddy face would be sweating abundantly as he strode in. I remember the terrific energy with which he pressed on the spluttering pen as he wrote down, in the roundest of round hands, the tasks to be prepared for the next day. Usually at the end of the lesson a certain limerick was asked for and granted, the point of the performance being that the word "screamed" in it was to be involuntarily enacted by oneself every time Mr. Burness gave a formidable squeeze to the hand he held in his beefy paw as he recited the lines:

> There was a young lady from Russia
> Who (squeeze) whenever you'd crush her.
> She (squeeze) and she (squeeze) . . .

by which time the pain would have become so excruciating that we never got any farther.

5

The quiet, bearded gentleman with a stoop, old-fashioned Mr. Cummings, who taught me, in 1907 or 1908, to draw, had been my mother's drawing master also. He had come to Russia in the early nineties as foreign correspondent and illustrator for the London *Graphic*. Marital misfortunes were rumored to obscure his life. A melancholy sweetness of manner made up for the meagerness of his talent. He wore an ulster unless the weather was very mild, when he would switch to the kind of greenish-brown woolen cloak called a *loden*.

I was captivated by his use of the special eraser he kept in his waistcoat pocket, by the manner in which he held the page taut, and afterwards flicked off, with the back of his fingers, the "gutticles of the percha" (as he said). Silently, sadly, he illustrated for me the marble laws of perspective: long, straight strokes of his elegantly held, incredibly sharp pencil caused the lines of the room he created out of nothing (abstract walls, receding ceiling and floor) to come together in one remote hypothetical point with tantalizing and sterile accuracy. Tantalizing, because it made me think of railway tracks, symmetrically and trickily converging before the bloodshot eyes of my favorite mask, a grimy engine driver; sterile, because that room remained unfurnished and quite empty, being devoid even of the neutral statues one finds in the uninteresting first hall of a museum.

The rest of the picture gallery made up for its gaunt vestibule. Mr. Cummings was a master of the sunset. His little watercolors, purchased at different times for five or ten roubles apiece by members of our household, led a somewhat precarious existence, shifting, as they did, to more and more obscure nooks and finally getting completely eclipsed by some sleek porcelain beast or a newly framed photograph. After I had learned not only to draw cubes and cones but to shade properly with smooth, merging slants such parts of them as had to be made to turn away forever, the kind old gentleman contented himself with painting under my enchanted gaze his own wet little paradises, variations of one landscape: a summer evening with an orange sky, a pasture ending in the black fringe of a distant forest, and a luminous river, repeating the sky and winding away and away.

Later on, from around 1910 to 1912, the well-known "impressionist" (a term of the period) Yaremich took over; a humorless and formless person, he advocated a "bold" style, blotches of dull color, smears of sepia and olive-brown, by means of which I had to reproduce on huge sheets of gray paper, humanoid shapes that we modeled of plasticine and placed in "dramatic" positions against a backcloth of velvet with all kinds of folds and shadow effects. It was a depressing combination of at least three different arts, all approximative, and finally I rebelled.

He was replaced by the celebrated Dobuzhinski who liked to give me his lessons on the *piano nobile* of our house, in one of its pretty reception rooms downstairs, which he entered in a particularly noiseless way as if afraid to startle me from my verse-making stupor. He made me depict from memory, in the greatest possible detail, objects I had certainly seen thousands of times without visualizing them properly: a street lamp, a postbox, the tulip design on the stained glass of our own front door. He tried to teach me to find the geometrical coordinations between the slender twigs of a leafless boulevard tree, a system of visual give-and-takes, requiring a precision of linear expression, which I failed to achieve in my youth, but applied gratefully, in my adult instar, not only to the drawing of butterfly genitalia during my seven years at the Harvard Museum of Comparative Zoology, when immersing myself in the bright wellhole of a microscope to record in India ink this or that new structure; but also, perhaps, to certain camera-lucida needs of literary composition. Emotionally, however, I am still more indebted to the earlier color treats given me by my mother and her former teacher. How readily Mr. Cummings would sit down on a stool, part behind with both hands his—what? was he wearing a frock coat? I see only the gesture—and proceed to open the black tin paintbox. I loved the nimble way he had of soaking his paintbrush in multiple color to the accompaniment of a rapid clatter produced by the enamel containers wherein the rich reds and yellows that the brush dimpled were appetizingly cupped; and having thus collected its honey, it would cease to hover and poke, and, by two or three sweeps of its lush tip, would drench the "Vatmanski" paper with an even spread of orange sky, across which, while that sky was still dampish, a long purple-black cloud would be laid. "And that's all, dearie," he would say. "That's all there is to it."

On one occasion, I had him draw an express train for me. I watched his pencil ably evolve the cowcatcher and elaborate headlights of a locomotive that looked as if it had been acquired secondhand for the Trans-Siberian line after it had done duty at Promontory Point, Utah, in the sixties. Then came five disappointingly plain carriages. When he had quite finished them, he carefully shaded the ample smoke coming from the huge funnel, cocked his head, and, after a moment of pleased contemplation, handed me the drawing. I tried to look pleased, too. He had forgotten the tender.

A quarter of a century later, I learned two things: that Burness, by then dead, had been well known in Edinburgh as a scholarly translator of the Russian romantic poems that had been the altar and frenzy of my boyhood; and that my humble drawing master, whose age I used to synchronize with that of granduncles and old family servants, had married a young Estonian girl about the time I myself married. When I learned these later developments, I experienced a queer shock; it was as if life had impinged upon my creative rights by wriggling on beyond the subjective limits so elegantly and economically set by childhood memories that I thought I had signed and sealed.

"And what about Yaremich?" I asked M. V. Dobuzhinski, one summer afternoon in the nineteen forties, as we strolled through a beech forest in Vermont. "Is he remembered?"

"Indeed, he is," replied Mstislav Valerianovich. "He was exceptionally gifted. I don't know what kind of teacher he was, but I do know that *you* were the most hopeless pupil I ever had."

5

I HAVE often noticed that after I had bestowed on the characters of my novels some treasured item of my past, it would pine away in the artificial world where I had so abruptly placed it. Although it lingered on in my mind, its personal warmth, its retrospective appeal had gone and, presently, it became more closely identified with my novel than with my former self, where it had seemed to be so safe from the intrusion of the artist. Houses have crumbled in my memory as soundlessly as they did in the mute films of yore, and the portrait of my old French governess, whom I once lent to a boy in one of my books, is fading fast, now that it is engulfed in the description of a childhood entirely unrelated to my own. The man in me revolts against the fictionist, and here is my desperate attempt to save what is left of poor Mademoiselle.

A large woman, a very stout woman, Mademoiselle rolled into our existence in December 1905 when I was six and my brother five. There she is. I see so plainly her abundant dark hair, brushed up high and covertly graying; the three wrinkles on her austere forehead; her beetling brows; the steely eyes behind the black-rimmed pince-nez; that vestigial mustache; that blotchy complexion, which in moments of wrath develops an additional flush in the region of the third, and amplest, chin so regally spread over the frilled mountain of her blouse. And now she sits down, or rather she tackles the job of sitting down, the jelly of her jowl quaking, her prodigious posterior, with the three buttons on the side, lowering itself warily; then, at the last second, she surrenders her bulk to the wicker armchair, which, out of sheer fright, bursts into a salvo of crackling.

We had been abroad for about a year. After spending the summer of 1904 in Beaulieu and Abbazia, and several months in Wiesbaden, we left for Russia in the beginning of 1905. I fail to remember the month. One clue is that in Wiesbaden I had been taken to its Russian church—the first time I had been to church anywhere—and that might have been in the Lenten season (during the service I asked my mother what were the priest and deacon talking about; she whispered back in English that they were saying we should all love one another but I understood she meant that those two gorgeous personages in cone-shaped shining robes were telling each other they would always remain good friends). From Frankfurt we arrived in Berlin in a snowstorm, and next morning caught the Nord-Express, which thundered in from Paris. Twelve hours later it reached the Russian frontier. Against the background of winter, the ceremonial change of cars and engines acquired a strange new meaning. An exciting sense of *rodina*, "motherland," was for the first time organically mingled with the comfortably creaking snow, the deep footprints across it, the red gloss of the engine stack, the birch logs piled high, under their private layer of transportable snow, on the red tender. I was not quite six, but that year abroad, a year of difficult decisions and liberal hopes, had exposed a small Russian boy to grown-up conversations. He

The author's maternal grandmother, Olga Nikolaevna Rukavishnikov, born Kozlov (1845–1901), St. Petersburg, around
1885.

The author's father, Vladimir Dmitrievich Nabokov (1870–1922),
as a schoolboy around 1885 with his three brothers (from *left*
to *right* Dmitri, Konstantin, and Sergey). My father was about
to graduate from the Third Gymnasium and enter the university
at an astonishingly early age. Uncle Konstantin, at eleven or
twelve, was still being educated at home. Uncle Dmitri and
Uncle Sergey were *pravoveds*, i.e. scholars of the fashionable
Imperial School of Jurisprudence.

could not help being affected in some way of his own by a mother's nostalgia and a father's patriotism. In result, that particular return to Russia, my first *conscious* return, seems to me now, sixty years later, a rehearsal—not of the grand homecoming that will never take place, but of its constant dream in my long years of exile.

The summer of 1905 in Vyra had not yet evolved lepidoptera. The village schoolmaster took us for instructive walks ("What you hear is the sound of a scythe being sharpened"; "That field there will be given a rest next season"; "Oh, just a small bird—no special name"; "If that peasant is drunk, it is because he is poor"). Autumn carpeted the park with varicolored leaves, and Miss Robinson showed us the beautiful device—which the Ambassador's Boy, a familiar character in her small world, had enjoyed so much the preceding autumn —of choosing on the ground and arranging on a big sheet of paper such maple leaves as would form an almost complete spectrum (minus the blue—a big disappointment!), green shading into lemon, lemon into orange and so on through the reds to purples, purplish browns, reddish again and back through lemon to green (which was getting quite hard to find except as a part, a last brave edge). The first frosts hit the asters and still we did not move to town.

That winter of 1905–1906, when Mademoiselle arrived from Switzerland, was the only one of my childhood that I spent in the country. It was a year of strikes, riots and police-inspired massacres, and I suppose my father wished to keep his family away from the city, in our quiet country place, where his popularity with the peasants might mitigate, as he correctly surmised, the risks of unrest. It was also a particularly severe winter, producing as much snow as Mademoiselle might have expected to find in the hyperborean gloom of remote Muscovy. When she alighted at the little Siverski

station, from which she still had to travel half-a-dozen miles
by sleigh to Vyra, I was not there to greet her; but I do so
now as I try to imagine what she saw and felt at that last stage
of her fabulous and ill-timed journey. Her Russian vocabulary consisted, I know, of one short word, the same solitary
word that years later she was to take back to Switzerland.
This word, which in her pronunciation may be phonetically
rendered as "giddy-eh" (actually it is *gde* with *e* as in "yet"),
meant "Where?" And that was a good deal. Uttered by her
like the raucous cry of some lost bird, it accumulated such
interrogatory force that it sufficed for all her needs. "Giddy-
eh? Giddy-eh?" she would wail, not only to find out her
whereabouts but also to express supreme misery: the fact that
she was a stranger, shipwrecked, penniless, ailing, in search
of the blessed land where at last she would be understood.

I can visualize her, by proxy, as she stands in the middle
of the station platform, where she has just alighted, and
vainly my ghostly envoy offers her an arm that she cannot
see. ("There I was, abandoned by all, *comme la Comtesse
Karenine,*" she later complained, eloquently, if not quite
correctly.) The door of the waiting room opens with a shuddering whine peculiar to nights of intense frost; a cloud of
hot air rushes out, almost as profuse as the steam from the
panting engine; and now our coachman Zahar takes over—a
burly man in sheepskin with the leather outside, his huge
gloves protruding from his scarlet sash into which he has
stuffed them. I hear the snow crunching under his felt boots
while he busies himself with the luggage, the jingling har-
ness, and then his own nose, which he eases by means of a
dexterous tweak-and-shake of finger and thumb as he trudges
back around the sleigh. Slowly, with grim misgivings, *"Mad-
mazelya,"* as her helper calls her, climbs in, clutching at him
in mortal fear lest the sleigh move off before her vast form

is securely encased. Finally, she settles down with a grunt and thrusts her fists into her skimpy plush muff. At the juicy smack of their driver's lips the two black horses, Zoyka and Zinka, strain their quarters, shift hooves, strain again; and then Mademoiselle gives a backward jerk of her torso as the heavy sleigh is wrenched out of its world of steel, fur, flesh, to enter a frictionless medium where it skims along a spectral road that it seems barely to touch.

For one moment, thanks to the sudden radiance of a lone lamp where the station square ends, a grossly exaggerated shadow, also holding a muff, races beside the sleigh, climbs a billow of snow, and is gone, leaving Mademoiselle to be swallowed up by what she will later allude to, with awe and gusto, as *"le steppe."* There, in the limitless gloom, the changeable twinkle of remote village lights seems to her to be the yellow eyes of wolves. She is cold, she is frozen stiff, frozen "to the center of her brain"—for she soars with the wildest hyperbole when not tagging after the most pedestrian dictum. Every now and then, she looks back to make sure that a second sleigh, bearing her trunk and hatbox, is following—always at the same distance, like those companionable phantoms of ships in polar waters which explorers have described. And let me not leave out the moon—for surely there must be a moon, the full, incredibly clear disc that goes so well with Russian lusty frosts. So there it comes, steering out of a flock of small dappled clouds, which it tinges with a vague iridescence; and, as it sails higher, it glazes the runner tracks left on the road, where every sparkling lump of snow is emphasized by a swollen shadow.

Very lovely, very lonesome. But what am I doing in this stereoscopic dreamland? How did I get here? Somehow, the two sleighs have slipped away, leaving behind a passportless spy standing on the blue-white road in his New England

snowboots and stormcoat. The vibration in my ears is no
longer their receding bells, but only my old blood singing.
All is still, spellbound, enthralled by the moon, fancy's rear-
vision mirror. The snow is real, though, and as I bend to it
and scoop up a handful, sixty years crumble to glittering
frost-dust between my fingers.

2

A large, alabaster-based kerosene lamp is steered into the
gloaming. Gently it floats and comes down; the hand of
memory, now in a footman's white glove, places it in the
center of a round table. The flame is nicely adjusted, and a
rosy, silk-flounced lamp shade, with inset glimpses of rococo
winter sports, crowns the readjusted (cotton wool in Casimir's
ear) light. Revealed: a warm, bright, stylish ("Russian Empire") drawing room in a snow-muffled house—soon to be
termed *le château*—built by my mother's grandfather, who,
being afraid of fires, had the staircase fashioned of iron, so
that when the house did get burned to the ground, sometime
after the Soviet Revolution, those fine-wrought steps, with
the sky shining through their openwork risers, remained
standing, all alone but still leading up.

Some more about that drawing room, please. The gleaming white moldings of the furniture, the embroidered roses
of its upholstery. The white piano. The oval mirror. Hanging on taut cords, its pure brow inclined, it strives to retain
the falling furniture and a slope of bright floor that keep
slipping from its embrace. The chandelier pendants. These
emit a delicate tinkling (things are being moved in the upstairs room where Mademoiselle will dwell). Colored pencils.
Their detailed spectrum advertised on the box but never
completely represented by those inside. We are sitting at

a round table, my brother and I and Miss Robinson, who now and then looks at her watch: roads must be dreadful with all that snow; and anyway many professional hardships lie in wait for the vague French person who will replace her.

Now the colored pencils in action. The green one, by a mere whirl of the wrist, could be made to produce a ruffled tree, or the eddy left by a submerged crocodile. The blue one drew a simple line across the page—and the horizon of all seas was there. A nondescript blunt one kept getting into one's way. The brown one was always broken, and so was the red, but sometimes, just after it had snapped, one could still make it serve by holding it so that the loose tip was propped, none too securely, by a jutting splinter. The little purple fellow, a special favorite of mine, had got worn down so short as to become scarcely manageable. The white one alone, that lanky albino among pencils, kept its original length, or at least did so until I discovered that, far from being a fraud leaving no mark on the page, it was the ideal implement since I could imagine whatever I wished while I scrawled.

Alas, these pencils, too, have been distributed among the characters in my books to keep fictitious children busy; they are not quite my own now. Somewhere, in the apartment house of a chapter, in the hired room of a paragraph, I have also placed that tilted mirror, and the lamp, and the chandelier drops. Few things are left, many have been squandered. Have I given away Box I (son and husband of Loulou, the housekeeper's pet), that old brown dachshund fast asleep on the sofa? No, I think he is still mine. His grizzled muzzle, with the wart at the puckered corner of the mouth, is tucked into the curve of his hock, and from time to time a deep sigh distends his ribs. He is so old and his sleep is so thickly padded with dreams (about chewable slippers and a few last

smells) that he does not stir when faint bells jingle outside.
Then a pneumatic door heaves and clangs in the vestibule.
She has come after all; I had so hoped she would not.

3

Another dog, the sweet-tempered sire of a ferocious family,
a Great Dane not allowed in the house, played a pleasant part
in an adventure that took place on one of the following days,
if not the very day after. It so happened that my brother and
I were left completely in charge of the newcomer. As I recon-
stitute it now, my mother had probably gone, with her maid
and young Trainy, to St. Petersburg (a distance of some fifty
miles) where my father was deeply involved in the grave political events of that winter. She was pregnant and very nervous.
Miss Robinson, instead of staying to break in Mademoiselle,
had gone too—back to that ambassador's family, about which
we had heard from her as much as they would about us. In
order to prove that this was no way of treating us, I immediately formed the project of repeating the exciting performance of a year before when we escaped from poor Miss Hunt
in Wiesbaden. This time the countryside all around was a
wilderness of snow, and it is hard to imagine what exactly
could have been the goal of the journey I planned. We had
just returned from our first afternoon walk with Mademoiselle and I was seething with frustration and hatred. With a
little prompting, I had meek Sergey share some of my anger.
To keep up with an unfamiliar tongue (all we knew in the
way of French were a few household phrases), and on top of
it to be crossed in all our fond habits, was more than one
could bear. The *bonne promenade* she had promised us had
turned out to be a tedious stroll near the house where the
snow had been cleared and the icy ground sprinkled with

sand. She had had us wear things we never used to wear, even on the frostiest day—horrible gaiters and hoods that hampered our every movement. She had restrained us when I induced Sergey to explore the creamy, smooth swellings of snow that had been flower beds in summer. She had not allowed us to walk under the organ-pipelike system of huge icicles that hung from the eaves and gloriously burned in the low sun. And she had rejected as *ignoble* one of my favorite pastimes (devised by Miss Robinson)—lying prone on a little plush sledge with a bit of rope tied to its front and a hand in a leathern mitten pulling me along a snow-covered path, under white trees, and Sergey, not lying but sitting on a second sledge, upholstered in red plush, attached to the rear of my blue one, and the heels of two felt boots, right in front of my face, walking quite fast with toes slightly turned in, now this, now that sole skidding on a raw patch of ice. (The hand and the feet belonged to Dmitri, our oldest and shortest gardener, and the path was the avenue of oaklings which seems to have been the main artery of my infancy.)

I explained to my brother a wicked plan and persuaded him to accept it. As soon as we came back from that walk, we left Mademoiselle puffing on the steps of the vestibule and dashed indoors, giving her the impression that we were about to conceal ourselves in some remote room. Actually, we trotted on till we reached the other side of the house, and then, through a veranda, emerged into the garden again. The above-mentioned Great Dane was in the act of fussily adjusting himself to a nearby snowdrift, but while deciding which hindleg to lift, he noticed us and at once joined us at a joyful gallop.

The three of us followed a fairly easy trail and after plodding through deeper snow, reached the road that led to the village. Meanwhile the sun had set. Dusk came with uncanny suddenness. My brother declared he was cold and tired, but I urged him on and finally made him ride the dog (the only member of the party to be still enjoying himself). We had gone more than two miles, and the moon was fantastically shiny, and my brother, in perfect silence, had begun to fall, every now and then, from his mount when Dmitri with a lantern overtook us and led us home. "Giddy-eh, giddy-eh?" Mademoiselle was frantically shouting from the porch. I brushed past her without a word. My brother burst into tears, and gave himself up. The Great Dane, whose name was Turka, returned to his interrupted affairs in connection with serviceable and informative snowdrifts around the house.

4

In our childhood we know a lot about hands since they live and hover at the level of our stature; Mademoiselle's were unpleasant because of the froggy gloss on their tight skin besprinkled with brown ecchymotic spots. Before her time no stranger had ever stroked my face. Mademoiselle, as soon as she came, had taken me completely aback by patting my cheek in sign of spontaneous affection. All her mannerisms come back to me when I think of her hands. Her trick of peeling rather than sharpening a pencil, the point held toward her stupendous and sterile bosom swathed in green wool. The way she had of inserting her little finger into her ear and vibrating it very rapidly. The ritual observed every time she gave me a fresh copybook. Always panting a little, her mouth slightly open and emitting in quick succession a series of asthmatic puffs, she would open the copybook to make a margin in it; that is, she would sharply imprint a vertical line with her thumbnail, fold in the edge of the page, press, release, smooth it out with the heel of her hand, after which the book would be briskly twisted around and placed before me ready for use. A new pen followed; she would moisten the glistening nib with susurrous lips before dipping it into the baptismal ink font. Then, delighting in every limb of every limpid letter (especially so because the preceding copybook had ended in utter sloppiness), with exquisite care I would inscribe the word *Dictée* while Mademoiselle hunted through her collection of spelling tests for a good, hard passage.

5

Meanwhile the setting has changed. The berimed tree and the high snowdrift with its xanthic hole have been removed by a silent property man. The summer afternoon is alive with steep clouds breasting the blue. Eyed shadows move on the garden paths. Presently, lessons are over and Mademoiselle is reading to us on the veranda where the mats and plaited chairs develop a spicy, biscuity smell in the heat. On the white window ledges, on the long window seats covered with faded calico, the sun breaks into geometrical gems after passing through rhomboids and squares of stained glass. This is the time when Mademoiselle is at her very best.

What a number of volumes she read through to us on that veranda! Her slender voice sped on and on, never weakening, without the slightest hitch or hesitation, an admirable reading machine wholly independent of her sick bronchial tubes. We got it all: *Les Malheurs de Sophie, Le Tour du Monde en Quatre Vingts Jours, Le Petit Chose, Les Misérables, Le Comte de Monte Cristo,* many others. There she sat, distilling her reading voice from the still prison of her person. Apart from the lips, one of her chins, the smallest but true one, was the only mobile detail of her Buddha-like bulk. The black-rimmed pince-nez reflected eternity. Occasionally a fly would settle on her stern forehead and its three wrinkles would instantly leap up all together like three runners over three hurdles. But nothing whatever changed in the expression of her face—the face I so often tried to depict in my sketchbook, for its impassive and simple symmetry offered a far greater temptation to my stealthy pencil than the bowl of flowers or the decoy duck on the table before me, which I was supposedly drawing.

Presently my attention would wander still farther, and it was then, perhaps, that the rare purity of her rhythmic voice accomplished its true purpose. I looked at a tree and the stir of its leaves borrowed that rhythm. Egor was pottering among the peonies. A wagtail took a few steps, stopped as if it had remembered something—and then walked on, enacting its name. Coming from nowhere, a Comma butterfly settled on the threshold, basked in the sun with its angular fulvous wings spread, suddenly closed them just to show the tiny initial chalked on their dark underside, and as suddenly darted away. But the most constant source of enchantment during those readings came from the harlequin pattern of colored panes inset in a whitewashed framework on either side of the veranda. The garden when viewed through these magic glasses grew strangely still and aloof. If one looked through blue glass, the sand turned to cinders while inky trees swam in a tropical sky. The yellow created an amber world infused with an extra strong brew of sunshine. The red made the foliage drip ruby dark upon a pink footpath. The green soaked greenery in a greener green. And when, after such richness, one turned to a small square of normal, savorless glass, with its lone mosquito or lame daddy longlegs, it was like taking a draught of water when one is not thirsty, and one saw a matter-of-fact white bench under familiar trees.

But of all the windows this is the pane through which in later years parched nostalgia longed to peer.

Mademoiselle never found out how potent had been the even flow of her voice. The subsequent claims she put forward were quite different. "Ah," she sighed, *"comme on s'aimait*—didn't we love each other! Those good old days in the *château!* The dead wax doll we once buried under the oak! [No—a wool-stuffed Golliwogg.] And that time you and Serge ran away and left me stumbling and howling in the depths of the forest! [Exaggerated.] *Ah, la fessée que je vous ai flanquée*—My, what a spanking I gave you! [She did try to slap me once but the attempt was never repeated.] *Votre tante, la Princesse,* whom you struck with your little fist because she had been rude to me! [Do not remember.] And the way you whispered to me your childish troubles! [Never!] And the nook in my room where you loved to snuggle because you felt so warm and secure!"

Mademoiselle's room, both in the country and in town, was a weird place to me—a kind of hothouse sheltering a thick-leaved plant imbued with a heavy, enuretic odor. Although next to ours, when we were small, it did not seem to belong to our pleasant, well-aired home. In that sickening mist, reeking, among other woolier effluvia, of the brown smell of oxidized apple peel, the lamp burned low, and strange objects glimmered upon the writing desk: a lacquered box with licorice sticks, black segments of which she would hack off with her penknife and put to melt under her tongue; a picture postcard of a lake and a castle with mother-of-pearl spangles for windows; a bumpy ball of tightly rolled bits of silver paper that came from all those chocolates she used to consume at night; photographs of the nephew who had died, of his mother who had signed her picture *Mater Dolorosa,*

and of a certain Monsieur de Marante who had been forced
by his family to marry a rich widow.

Lording it over the rest was one in a fancy frame incrusted
with garnets; it showed, in three-quarter view, a slim young
brunette clad in a close-fitting dress, with brave eyes and
abundant hair. "A braid as thick as my arm and reaching
down to my ankles!" was Mademoiselle's melodramatic com-
ment. For this had been she—but in vain did my eyes probe
her familiar form to try and extract the graceful creature it
had engulfed. Such discoveries as my awed brother and I did
make merely increased the difficulties of that task; and the
grown-ups who during the day beheld a densely clothed
Mademoiselle never saw what we children saw when, roused
from her sleep by one of us shrieking himself out of a bad
dream, disheveled, candle in hand, a gleam of gilt lace on
the blood-red dressing gown that could not quite wrap her
quaking mass, the ghastly Jézabel of Racine's absurd play
stomped barefooted into our bedroom.

All my life I have been a poor go-to-sleeper. People in
trains, who lay their newspaper aside, fold their silly arms,
and immediately, with an offensive familiarity of demeanor,
start snoring, amaze me as much as the uninhibited chap
who cozily defecates in the presence of a chatty tubber, or
participates in huge demonstrations, or joins some union in
order to dissolve in it. Sleep is the most moronic fraternity
in the world, with the heaviest dues and the crudest rituals.
It is a mental torture I find debasing. The strain and drain
of composition often force me, alas, to swallow a strong pill
that gives me an hour or two of frightful nightmares or even
to accept the comic relief of a midday snooze, the way a senile
rake might totter to the nearest euthanasium; but I simply
cannot get used to the nightly betrayal of reason, humanity,
genius. No matter how great my weariness, the wrench of

parting with consciousness is unspeakably repulsive to me.
I loathe Somnus, that black-masked headsman binding me to
the block; and if in the course of years, with the approach
of a far more thorough and still more risible disintegration,
which nowanights, I confess, detracts much from the routine
terrors of sleep, I have grown so accustomed to my bedtime
ordeal as almost to swagger while the familiar ax is coming
out of its great velvet-lined double-bass case, initially I had
no such comfort or defense: I had nothing—except one token
light in the potentially refulgent chandelier of Mademoiselle's bedroom, whose door, by our family doctor's decree
(I salute you, Dr. Sokolov!), remained slightly ajar. Its vertical line of lambency (which a child's tears could transform
into dazzling rays of compassion) was something I could cling
to, since in absolute darkness my head would swim and my
mind melt in a travesty of the death struggle.

Saturday night used to be or ought to have been a pleasurable prospect, because that was the night Mademoiselle,
who belonged to the classical school of hygiene and regarded
our *toquades anglaises* as merely a source of colds, indulged
in the perilous luxury of a weekly bath, thus granting a
longer lease to my tenuous gleam. But then a subtler torment
set in.

We have moved now to our town house, an Italianate construction of Finnish granite, built by my grandfather circa
1885, with floral frescoes above the third (upper) story and a
second-floor oriel, in St. Peterburg (now Leningrad), 47,
Morskaya (now Hertzen Street). The children occupied the
third floor. In 1908, the year selected here, I still shared a
nursery with my brother. The bathroom assigned to Mademoiselle was at the end of a Z-shaped corridor some twenty
heartbeats' distance from my bed, and between dreading her
premature return from the bathroom to her lighted bedroom

next to our nursery and envying my brother's regular little wheeze behind the japanned screen separating us, I could never really put my additional time to profit by deftly getting to sleep while a chink in the dark still bespoke a speck of myself in nothingness. At length they would come, those inexorable steps, plodding along the passage and causing some fragile glass object, which had been secretly sharing my vigil, to vibrate in dismay on its shelf.

Now she has entered her room. A brisk interchange of light values tells me that the candle on her bed table takes over the job of the ceiling cluster of bulbs, which, having run up with a couple of clicks two additional steps of natural, and then supernatural, brightness, clicks off altogether. My line of light is still there, but it has grown old and wan, and flickers whenever Mademoiselle makes her bed creak by moving. For I still hear her. Now it is a silvery rustle spelling "Suchard"; now the trk-trk-trk of a fruit knife cutting the pages of *La Revue des Deux Mondes*. A period of decline has started: she is reading Bourget. Not one word of his will survive him. Doom is nigh. I am in acute distress, desperately trying to coax sleep, opening my eyes every few seconds to check the faded gleam, and imagining paradise as a place where a sleepless neighbor reads an endless book by the light of an eternal candle.

The inevitable happens: the pince-nez case shuts with a snap, the review shuffles onto the marble of the bed table, and gustily Mademoiselle's pursed lips blow; the first attempt fails, a groggy flame squirms and ducks; then comes a second lunge, and light collapses. In that pitchy blackness I lose my bearings, my bed seems to be slowly drifting, panic makes me sit up and stare; finally my dark-adapted eyes sift out, among entoptic floaters, certain more precious blurrings that roam in aimless amnesia until, half-remembering, they settle down as the dim folds of window curtains behind which street lights are remotely alive.

How utterly foreign to the troubles of the night were those exciting St. Petersburg mornings when the fierce and tender, damp and dazzling arctic spring bundled away broken ice down the sea-bright Neva! It made the roofs shine. It painted the slush in the streets a rich purplish-blue shade which I have never seen anywhere since. On those glorious days *on allait se promener en équipage*—the old-world expression current in our set. I can easily refeel the exhilarating change from the thickly padded, knee-length *polushubok,* with the hot beaver collar, to the short navy-blue coat with its anchor-patterned brass buttons. In the open landau I am joined by the valley of a lap rug to the occupants of the more interesting back seat, majestic Mademoiselle, and triumphant, tear-bedabbled Sergey, with whom I have just had a row at home. I am kicking him slightly, now and then, under our common cover, until Mademoiselle sternly tells me to stop. We drift past the show windows of Fabergé whose mineral monstrosities, jeweled troykas poised on marble ostrich eggs, and the like, highly appreciated by the imperial family, were emblems of grotesque garishness to ours. Church bells are ringing, the first Brimstone flies up over the Palace Arch, in another month we shall return to the country; and as I look up I can see, strung on ropes from housefront to housefront high above the street, great, tensely smooth, semitransparent banners billowing, their three wide bands—pale red, pale blue, and merely pale—deprived by the sun and the flying cloud-shadows of any too blunt connection with a national holiday, but undoubtedly celebrating now, in the city of memory, the essence of that spring day, the swish of the mud, the beginning of mumps, the ruffled exotic bird with one bloodshot eye on Mademoiselle's hat.

6

She spent seven years with us, lessons getting rarer and rarer and her temper worse and worse. Still, she seemed like a rock of grim permanence when compared to the ebb and flow of English governesses and Russian tutors passing through our large household. She was on bad terms with all of them. In summer seldom less than fifteen people sat down for meals and when, on birthdays, this number rose to thirty or more, the question of place at table became a particularly burning one for Mademoiselle. Uncles and aunts and cousins would arrive on such days from neighboring estates, and the village doctor would come in his dogcart, and the village schoolmaster would be heard blowing his nose in the cool hall, where he passed from mirror to mirror with a greenish, damp, creaking bouquet of lilies of the valley or a sky-colored, brittle one of cornflowers in his fist.

If Mademoiselle found herself seated too far at the end of the huge table, and especially if she lost precedence to a certain poor relative who was almost as fat as she (*"Je suis une sylphide à côté d'elle,"* Mademoiselle would say with a shrug of contempt), then her sense of injury caused her lips to twitch in a would-be ironical smile—and when a naïve neighbor would smile back, she would rapidly shake her head, as if coming out of some very deep meditation, with the remark: *"Excusez-moi, je souriais à mes tristes pensées."*

And as though nature had not wished to spare her anything that makes one supersensitive, she was hard of hearing. Sometimes at table we boys would suddenly become aware of two big tears crawling down Mademoiselle's ample cheeks. "Don't mind me," she would say in a small voice, and she kept on eating till the unwiped tears blinded her; then, with a heartbroken hiccough she would rise and blunder out of the dining room. Little by little the truth would come out. The general talk had turned, say, on the subject of the warship my uncle commanded, and she had perceived in this a sly dig at her Switzerland that had no navy. Or else it was because she fancied that whenever French was spoken, the game consisted in deliberately preventing her from directing and adorning the conversation. Poor lady, she was always in such a nervous hurry to seize control of intelligible table talk before it bolted back into Russian that no wonder she bungled her cue.

"And your Parliament, sir, how is it getting along?" she would suddenly burst out brightly from her end of the table, challenging my father, who, after a harassing day, was not exactly eager to discuss troubles of the state with a singularly unreal person who neither knew nor cared anything about them. Thinking that someone had referred to music, "But Silence, too, may be beautiful," she would bubble. "Why, one evening, in a desolate valley of the Alps, I actually *heard* Silence." Sallies like these, especially when growing deafness led her to answer questions none had put, resulted in a painful hush, instead of touching off the rockets of a sprightly *causerie*.

And, really, her French was so lovely! Ought one to have minded the shallowness of her culture, the bitterness of her temper, the banality of her mind, when that pearly language of hers purled and scintillated, as innocent of sense as the alliterative sins of Racine's pious verse? My father's library, not her limited lore, taught me to appreciate authentic poetry; nevertheless, something of her tongue's limpidity and luster has had a singularly bracing effect upon me, like those sparkling salts that are used to purify the blood. This is why it makes me so sad to imagine now the anguish Mademoiselle must have felt at seeing how lost, how little valued was

the nightingale voice which came from her elephantine body.
She stayed with us long, much too long, obstinately hoping
for some miracle that would transform her into a kind of
Madame de Rambouillet holding a gilt-and-satin *salon* of
poets, princes and statesmen under her brilliant spell.

She would have gone on hoping had it not been for one
Lenski, a young Russian tutor, with mild myopic eyes and
strong political opinions, who had been engaged to coach us
in various subjects and participate in our sports. He had had
several predecessors, none of whom Mademoiselle had liked,
but he, as she put it, was *"le comble."* While venerating my
father, Lenski could not quite stomach certain aspects of our
household, such as footmen and French, which last he considered an aristocratic convention of no use in a liberal's
home. On the other hand, Mademoiselle decided that if
Lenski answered her point-blank questions only with short
grunts (which he tried to Germanize for want of a better language), it was not because he could not understand French,
but because he wished to insult her in front of everybody.

I can hear and see Mademoiselle requesting him in dulcet
tones, but with an ominous quiver of her upper lip, to pass
her the bread; and, likewise, I can hear and see Lenski
Frenchlessly and unflinchingly going on with his soup; finally,
with a slashing *"Pardon, monsieur,"* Mademoiselle would
swoop right across his plate, snatch up the breadbasket, and
recoil again with a *"Merci!"* so charged with irony that Lenski's downy ears would turn the hue of geraniums. "The
brute! The cad! The Nihilist!" she would sob later in her
room—which was no longer next to ours though still on the
same floor.

If Lenski happened to come tripping downstairs while,
with an asthmatic pause every ten steps or so, she was working her way up (for the little hydraulic elevator of our house

in St. Petersburg would constantly, and rather insultingly, refuse to function), Mademoiselle maintained that he had viciously bumped into her, pushed her, knocked her down, and we already could see him trampling her prostrate body. More and more frequently she would leave the table, and the dessert she would have missed was diplomatically sent up in her wake. From her remote room she would write a sixteen-page letter to my mother, who, upon hurrying upstairs, would find her dramatically packing her trunk. And then, one day, she was allowed to go on with her packing.

7

She returned to Switzerland. World War One came, then the Revolution. In the early twenties, long after our correspondence had fizzled out, by a fluke move of life in exile I chanced to visit Lausanne with a college friend of mine, so I thought I might as well look up Mademoiselle, if she were still alive.

She was. Stouter than ever, quite gray and almost totally deaf, she welcomed me with a tumultuous outburst of affection. Instead of the Château de Chillon picture, there was now one of a garish troika. She spoke as warmly of her life in Russia as if it were her own lost homeland. Indeed, I found in the neighborhood quite a colony of such old Swiss governesses. Huddled together in a constant seething of competitive reminiscences, they formed a small island in an environment that had grown alien to them. Mademoiselle's bosom friend was now mummy-like Mlle Golay, my mother's former governess, still prim and pessimistic at eighty-five; she had remained in our family long after my mother had married, and her return to Switzerland had preceded only by a couple of years that of Mademoiselle, with whom she had not been on speaking terms when both had been living under our roof. One is always at home in one's past, which partly explains those pathetic ladies' posthumous love for a remote and, to be perfectly frank, rather appalling country, which they never had really known and in which none of them had been very content.

As no conversation was possible because of Mademoiselle's deafness, my friend and I decided to bring her next day the appliance which we gathered she could not afford. She adjusted the clumsy thing improperly at first, but no sooner had she done so than she turned to me with a dazzled look of moist wonder and bliss in her eyes. She swore she could hear every word, every murmur of mine. She could not for, having my doubts, I had not spoken. If I had, I would have told her to thank my friend, who had paid for the instrument. Was it, then, silence she heard, that Alpine Silence she had talked about in the past? In that past, she had been lying to herself; now she was lying to me.

Before leaving for Basle and Berlin, I happened to be walking along the lake in the cold, misty night. At one spot a lone light dimly diluted the darkness and transformed the mist into a visible drizzle. *"Il pleut toujours en Suisse"* was one of those casual comments which, formerly, had made Mademoiselle weep. Below, a wide ripple, almost a wave, and something vaguely white attracted my eye. As I came quite close to the lapping water, I saw what it was—an aged swan, a large, uncouth, dodo-like creature, making ridiculous efforts to hoist himself into a moored boat. He could not do it. The heavy, impotent flapping of his wings, their slippery sound against the rocking and plashing boat, the gluey glistening of the dark swell where it caught the light—all seemed for a moment laden with that strange significance which sometimes in dreams is attached to a finger pressed to mute lips and then pointed at something the dreamer has no time to distinguish before waking with a start. But although I soon forgot that dismal night, it was, oddly enough, that night, that compound image—shudder and swan and swell—which first came to my mind when a couple of years later I learned that Mademoiselle had died.

She had spent all her life in feeling miserable; this misery was her native element; its fluctuations, its varying depths, alone gave her the impression of moving and living. What bothers me is that a sense of misery, and nothing else, is not enough to make a permanent soul. My enormous and morose Mademoiselle is all right on earth but impossible in eternity. Have I really salvaged her from fiction? Just before the rhythm I hear falters and fades, I catch myself wondering whether, during the years I knew her, I had not kept utterly missing something in her that was far more she than her chins or her ways or even her French—something perhaps akin to that last glimpse of her, to the radiant deceit she had used in order to have me depart pleased with my own kindness, or to that swan whose agony was so much closer to artistic truth than a drooping dancer's pale arms; something, in short, that I could appreciate only after the things and beings that I had most loved in the security of my childhood had been turned to ashes or shot through the heart.

There is an appendix to Mademoiselle's story. When I first wrote it I did not know about certain amazing survivals. Thus, in 1960, my London cousin Peter de Peterson told me that their English nanny, who had seemed old to me in 1904 in Abbazia, was by now over ninety and in good health; neither was I aware that the governess of my father's two youngest sisters, Mlle Bouvier (later Mme Conrad), survived my father by almost half a century. She had entered their household in 1889 and stayed six years, being the last in a series of governesses. A pretty little keepsake drawn in 1895 by Ivan de Peterson, Peter's father, shows various events of life at Batovo vignetted over an inscription in my father's hand: *A celle qui a toujours su se faire aimer et qui ne saura jamais se faire oublier;* signatures have been appended by four young male Nabokovs and three of their sisters, Natalia, Elizaveta, and Nadezhda, as well as by Natalia's husband, their little son Mitik, two girl cousins, and Ivan Aleksandrovich Tihotski, the Russian tutor. Sixty-five years later, in Geneva, my sister Elena discovered Mme Conrad, now in her tenth decade. The ancient lady, skipping one generation, naïvely mistook Elena for our mother, then a girl of eighteen, who used to drive up with Mlle Golay from Vyra to Batovo, in those distant times whose long light finds so many ingenious ways to reach me.

6

O N a summer morning, in the legendary Russia of my boyhood, my first glance upon awakening was for the chink between the white inner shutters. If it disclosed a watery pallor, one had better not open them at all, and so be spared the sight of a sullen day sitting for its picture in a puddle. How resentfully one would deduce, from a line of dull light, the leaden sky, the sodden sand, the gruel-like mess of broken brown blossoms under the lilacs—and that flat, fallow leaf (the first casualty of the season) pasted upon a wet garden bench!

But if the chink was a long glint of dewy brilliancy, then I made haste to have the window yield its treasure. With one blow, the room would be cleft into light and shade. The foliage of birches moving in the sun had the translucent green tone of grapes, and in contrast to this there was the dark velvet of fir trees against a blue of extraordinary intensity, the like of which I rediscovered only many years later, in the montane zone of Colorado.

From the age of seven, everything I felt in connection with a rectangle of framed sunlight was dominated by a single passion. If my first glance of the morning was for the sun, my first thought was for the butterflies it would engender. The original event had been banal enough. On the honeysuckle, overhanging the carved back of a bench just opposite the main entrance, my guiding angel (whose wings, except for the absence of a Florentine limbus, resemble those of Fra Angelico's Gabriel) pointed out to me a rare visitor, a splendid, pale-yellow creature with black blotches, blue crenels, and a cinnabar eyespot above each chrome-rimmed black tail. As it probed the inclined flower from which it hung, its powdery body slightly bent, it kept restlessly jerking its great wings, and my desire for it was one of the most intense I have ever experienced. Agile Ustin, our town-house janitor, who for a comic reason (explained elsewhere) happened to be that summer in the country with us, somehow managed to catch it in my cap, after which it was transferred, cap and all, to a wardrobe, where domestic naphthalene was fondly expected by Mademoiselle to kill it overnight. On the following morning, however, when she unlocked the wardrobe to take something out, my Swallowtail, with a mighty rustle, flew into her face, then made for the open window, and presently was but a golden fleck dipping and dodging and soaring eastward, over timber and tundra, to Vologda, Viatka and Perm, and beyond the gaunt Ural range to Yakutsk and Verkhne Kolymsk, and from Verkhne Kolymsk, where it lost a tail, to the fair Island of St. Lawrence, and across Alaska to Dawson, and southward along the Rocky Mountains—to be finally overtaken and captured, after a forty-year race, on an immigrant dandelion under an endemic aspen near Boulder. In a letter from Mr. Brune to Mr. Rawlins, June 14, 1735, in the Bodleian collection, he states that one Mr. Vernon followed a butterfly nine miles before he could catch him (*The Recreative Review or Eccentricities of Literature and Life*, Vol. 1, p. 144, London, 1821).

Soon after the wardrobe affair I found a spectacular moth, marooned in a corner of a vestibule window, and my mother dispatched it with ether. In later years, I used many killing agents, but the least contact with the initial stuff would always cause the porch of the past to light up and attract that blundering beauty. Once, as a grown man, I was under ether during appendectomy, and with the vividness of a decalcomania picture I saw my own self in a sailor suit mounting a freshly emerged Emperor moth under the guidance of a Chinese lady who I knew was my mother. It was all there, brilliantly reproduced in my dream, while my own vitals were being exposed: the soaking, ice-cold absorbent cotton pressed to the insect's lemurian head; the subsiding spasms of its body; the satisfying crackle produced by the pin penetrating the hard crust of its thorax; the careful insertion of the point of the pin in the cork-bottomed groove of the spreading board; the symmetrical adjustment of the thick, strong-veined wings under neatly affixed strips of semitransparent paper.

2

I must have been eight when, in a storeroom of our country house, among all kinds of dusty objects, I discovered some wonderful books acquired in the days when my mother's mother had been interested in natural science and had had a famous university professor of zoology (Shimkevich) give private lessons to her daughter. Some of these books were mere curios, such as the four huge brown folios of Albertus Seba's work (*Locupletissimi Rerum Naturalium Thesauri Accurata Descriptio . . .*), printed in Amsterdam around 1750. On their coarse-grained pages I found woodcuts of serpents and butterflies and embryos. The fetus of an Ethiopian female child hanging by the neck in a glass jar used to give me a nasty shock every time I came across it; nor did I much care for the stuffed hydra on plate CII, with its seven lion-toothed turtleheads on seven serpentine necks and its strange, bloated body which bore buttonlike tubercules along the sides and ended in a knotted tail.

Other books I found in that attic, among herbariums full of alpine columbines, and blue palemoniums, and Jove's campions, and orange-red lilies, and other Davos flowers, came closer to my subject. I took in my arms and carried downstairs glorious loads of fantastically attractive volumes: Maria Sibylla Merian's (1647–1717) lovely plates of Surinam insects, and Esper's noble *Die Schmetterlinge* (Erlangen, 1777), and Boisduval's *Icones Historiques de Lépidoptères Nouveaux ou Peu Connus* (Paris, begun in 1832). Still more exciting were the products of the latter half of the century— Newman's *Natural History of British Butterflies and Moths*, Hofmann's *Die Gross-Schmetterlinge Europas*, the Grand Duke Nikolay Mihailovich's *Mémoires* on Asiatic lepidoptera (with incomparably beautiful figures painted by Kavrigin, Rybakov, Lang), Scudder's stupendous work on the *Butterflies of New England*.

Retrospectively, the summer of 1905, though quite vivid in many ways, is not animated yet by a single bit of quick flutter or colored fluff around or across the walks with the village schoolmaster: the Swallowtail of June, 1906, was still in the larval stage on a roadside umbellifer; but in the course of that month I became acquainted with a score or so of common things, and Mademoiselle was already referring to a certain forest road that culminated in a marshy meadow full of Small Pearl-bordered Fritillaries (thus called in my first unforgettable and unfadingly magical little manual, Richard South's *The Butterflies of the British Isles* which had just come out at the time) as *le chemin des papillons bruns*. The following year I became aware that many of our butterflies and moths did not occur in England or Central Europe, and more complete atlases helped me to determine them. A severe illness (pneumonia, with fever up to 41° centigrade), in the beginning of 1907, mysteriously abolished the rather monstrous gift of numbers that had made of me a child prodigy during a few months (today I cannot multiply 13 by 17 without pencil and paper; I can add them up, though, in a trice, the teeth of the three fitting in neatly); but the butterflies survived. My mother accumulated a library and a museum around my bed, and the longing to describe a new species completely replaced that of discovering a new prime number. A trip to Biarritz, in August 1907, added new wonders (though not as lucid and numerous as they were to be in 1909). By 1908, I had gained absolute control over the European lepidoptera as known to Hofmann. By 1910, I had dreamed my way through the first volumes of Seitz's prodigious picture book *Die Gross-Schmetterlinge der Erde,* had purchased a number of rarities recently described, and was voraciously reading entomological periodicals, especially English and Russian ones. Great upheavals were taking place in the development of systematics. Since the middle of the century, Continental lepidopterology had been, on the whole, a simple and stable affair, smoothly run by the Germans. Its high priest, Dr. Staudinger, was also the head of the largest firm of insect dealers. Even now, half a century after his death, German lepidopterists have not quite managed to shake off the hypnotic spell occasioned by his authority. He was still alive when his school began to lose ground as a scientific force in the world. While he and his followers stuck to specific and generic names sanctioned by long usage and were content to classify butterflies by characters visible to the naked eye, English-speaking authors were introducing nomenclatorial changes as a result of a strict application of the law of priority and taxonomic changes based on the microscopic study of organs. The Germans did their best to ignore the new trends and continued to cherish the philately-like side of entomology. Their solicitude for the "average collector who should not be made to dissect" is comparable to the way nervous publishers of popular novels pamper the "average reader"—who should not be made to think.

There was another more general change, which coincided with my ardent adolescent interest in butterflies and moths. The Victorian and Staudingerian kind of species, hermetic and homogeneous, with sundry (alpine, polar, insular, etc.) "varieties" affixed to it from the outside, as it were, like inci-dental appendages, was replaced by a new, multiform and fluid kind of species, organically *consisting* of geographical races or subspecies. The evolutional aspects of the case were thus brought out more clearly, by means of more flexible methods of classification, and further links between butter-flies and the central problems of nature were provided by biological investigations.

The mysteries of mimicry had a special attraction for me. Its phenomena showed an artistic perfection usually asso-ciated with man-wrought things. Consider the imitation of oozing poison by bubblelike macules on a wing (complete with pseudo-refraction) or by glossy yellow knobs on a chry-salis ("Don't eat me—I have already been squashed, sampled and rejected"). Consider the tricks of an acrobatic caterpillar (of the Lobster Moth) which in infancy looks like bird's dung, but after molting develops scrabbly hymenopteroid appendages and baroque characteristics, allowing the extraor-dinary fellow to play two parts at once (like the actor in Oriental shows who *becomes* a pair of intertwisted wrestlers): that of a writhing larva and that of a big ant seemingly harrowing it. When a certain moth resembles a certain wasp in shape and color, it also walks and moves its antennae in a waspish, unmothlike manner. When a butterfly has to look like a leaf, not only are all the details of a leaf beautifully rendered but markings mimicking grub-bored holes are generously thrown in. "Natural selection," in the Darwinian sense, could not explain the miraculous coincidence of imitative aspect and imitative behavior, nor could one appeal to the theory of "the struggle for life" when a protective device was carried to a point of mimetic subtlety, exuberance, and luxury far in excess of a predator's power of appreciation. I discovered in nature the nonutilitarian delights that I sought in art. Both were a form of magic, both were a game of intricate enchantment and deception.

3

I have hunted butterflies in various climes and disguises: as a pretty boy in knickerbockers and sailor cap; as a lanky cosmopolitan expatriate in flannel bags and beret; as a fat hatless old man in shorts. Most of my cabinets have shared the fate of our Vyra house. Those in our town house and the small addendum I left in the Yalta Museum have been destroyed, no doubt, by carpet beetles and other pests. A collection of South European stuff that I started in exile vanished in Paris during World War Two. All my American captures from 1940 to 1960 (several thousands of specimens including great rarities and types) are in the Mus. of Comp. Zoology, the Am. Nat. Hist. Mus., and the Cornell Univ. Mus. of Entomology, where they are safer than they would be in Tomsk or Atomsk. Incredibly happy memories, quite comparable, in fact, to those of my Russian boyhood, are associated with my research work at the MCZ, Cambridge, Mass.

(1941–1948). No less happy have been the many collecting trips taken almost every summer, during twenty years, through most of the states of my adopted country.

In Jackson Hole and in the Grand Canyon, on the mountain slopes above Telluride, Colo., and on a celebrated pine barren near Albany, N.Y., dwell, and will dwell, in generations more numerous than editions, the butterflies I have described as new. Several of my finds have been dealt with by other workers; some have been named after me. One of these, Nabokov's Pug (*Eupithecia nabokovi* McDunnough), which I boxed one night in 1943 on a picture window of James Laughlin's Alta Lodge in Utah, fits most philosophically into the thematic spiral that began in a wood on the Oredezh around 1910—or perhaps even earlier, on that Nova Zemblan river a century and a half ago.

Few things indeed have I known in the way of emotion or appetite, ambition or achievement, that could surpass in richness and strength the excitement of entomological exploration. From the very first it had a great many intertwinkling facets. One of them was the acute desire to be alone, since any companion, no matter how quiet, interfered with the concentrated enjoyment of my mania. Its gratification admitted of no compromise or exception. Already when I was ten, tutors and governesses knew that the morning was mine and cautiously kept away.

In this connection, I remember the visit of a schoolmate, a boy of whom I was very fond and with whom I had excellent fun. He arrived one summer night—in 1913, I think—from a town some twenty-five miles away. His father had recently perished in an accident, the family was ruined and the stouthearted lad, not being able to afford the price of a railway ticket, had bicycled all those miles to spend a few days with me.

On the morning following his arrival, I did everything I could to get out of the house for my morning hike without his knowing where I had gone. Breakfastless, with hysterical haste, I gathered my net, pill boxes, killing jar, and escaped through the window. Once in the forest, I was safe; but still I walked on, my calves quaking, my eyes full of scalding tears, the whole of me twitching with shame and self-disgust, as I visualized my poor friend, with his long pale face and black tie, moping in the hot garden—patting the panting dogs for want of something better to do, and trying hard to justify my absence to himself.

Let me look at my demon objectively. With the exception of my parents, no one really understood my obsession, and it was many years before I met a fellow sufferer. One of the first things I learned was not to depend on others for the growth of my collection. One summer afternoon, in 1911, Mademoiselle came into my room, book in hand, started to say she wanted to show me how wittily Rousseau denounced zoology (in favor of botany), and by then was too far gone in the gravitational process of lowering her bulk into an armchair to be stopped by my howl of anguish: on that seat I had happened to leave a glass-lidded cabinet tray with long, lovely series of the Large White. Her first reaction was one of stung vanity: her weight, surely, could not be accused of damaging what in fact it had demolished; her second was to console me: *Allons donc, ce ne sont que des papillons de potager!*—which only made matters worse. A Sicilian pair recently purchased from Staudinger had been crushed and bruised. A huge Biarritz example was utterly mangled. Smashed, too, were some of my choicest local captures. Of these, an aberration resembling the Canarian race of the species might have been mended with a few drops of glue; but a precious gynandromorph, left side male, right side female, whose abdomen could not be traced and whose wings had come off, was lost forever: one might reattach the wings but one could not prove that all four belonged to that headless thorax on its bent pin. Next morning, with an air of great mystery, poor Mademoiselle set off for St. Petersburg and came back in the evening bringing me ("something better than your cabbage butterflies") a banal Urania moth mounted on plaster. "How you hugged me, how you danced with joy!" she exclaimed ten years later in the course of inventing a brand-new past.

Our country doctor, with whom I had left the pupae of a rare moth when I went on a journey abroad, wrote me that everything had hatched finely; but in reality a mouse had got at the precious pupae, and upon my return the deceitful old man produced some common Tortoiseshell butterflies, which, I presume, he had hurriedly caught in his garden and popped into the breeding cage as plausible substitutes (so *he* thought). Better than he, was an enthusiastic kitchen boy who would sometimes borrow my equipment and come back two hours later in triumph with a bagful of seething invertebrate life and several additional items. Loosening the mouth of the net which he had tied up with a string, he would pour out his cornucopian spoil—a mass of grasshoppers, some sand, the two parts of a mushroom he had thriftily plucked on the way home, more grasshoppers, more sand, and one battered Small White.

In the works of major Russian poets I can discover only two lepidopteral images of genuinely sensuous quality: Bunin's impeccable evocation of what is certainly a Tortoiseshell:

> And there will fly into the room
> A colored butterfly in silk
> To flutter, rustle and pit-pat
> On the blue ceiling . . .

The author's father and mother, Elena Ivanovna Nabokov, born Rukavishnikov (1876–1939), in 1900, on the garden terrace at Vyra, their estate in the Province of St. Petersburg. The birches and firs of the park behind my parents belong to the same back-drop of past summers as the foliage of photograph facing p. 192.

My brother Sergey and I, aged one and two, respectively (and looking like the same infant, wigless and wigged), in December 1901, in Biarritz. We had, I suppose, come there from Pau where we were living that winter. A shining wet roof—that is all I remember from that first trip to the South of France. It was followed by other trips, two to Biarritz (autumn 1907 and 1909) and two to the Riviera (late autumn 1903 and early summer 1904).

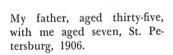

My father, aged thirty-five, with me aged seven, St. Petersburg, 1906.

and Fet's "Butterfly" soliloquizing:

> Whence have I come and whither am I hasting
> Do not inquire;
> Now on a graceful flower I have settled
> And now respire.

In French poetry one is struck by Musset's well-known lines (in *Le Saule*):

> *Le phalène doré dans sa course légère*
> *Traverse les prés embaumés*

which is an absolutely exact description of the crepuscular flight of the male of the geometrid called in England the Orange moth; and there is Fargue's fascinatingly apt phrase (in *Les Quatres Journées*) about a garden which, at nightfall, *se glace de bleu comme l'aile du grand Sylvain* (the Poplar Admirable). And among the very few genuine lepidopterological images in English poetry, my favorite is Browning's

> On our other side is the straight-up rock;
> And a path is kept 'twixt the gorge and it
> By boulder-stones where lichens mock
> The marks on a moth, and small ferns fit
> Their teeth to the polished block
>
> ("By the Fire-side")

It is astounding how little the ordinary person notices butterflies. "None," calmly replied that sturdy Swiss hiker with Camus in his rucksack when purposely asked by me for the benefit of my incredulous companion if he had seen any butterflies while descending the trail where, a moment before, you and I had been delighting in swarms of them. It is also true that when I call up the image of a particular path remembered in minute detail but pertaining to a summer before that of 1906, preceding, that is, the date on my first locality label, and never revisited, I fail to make out one wing, one wingbeat, one azure flash, one moth-gemmed flower, as if an evil spell had been cast on the Adriatic coast making all its "leps" (as the slangier among us say) invisible. Exactly thus an entomologist may feel some day when plodding beside a jubilant, and already helmetless botanist amid the hideous flora of a parallel planet, with not a single insect in sight; and thus (in odd proof of the odd fact that whenever possible the scenery of our infancy is used by an economically minded producer as a ready-made setting for our adult dreams) the seaside hilltop of a certain recurrent nightmare of mine, whereinto I smuggle a collapsible net from my waking state, is gay with thyme and melilot, but incomprehensibly devoid of all the butterflies that should be there.

I also found out very soon that a "lepist" indulging in his quiet quest was apt to provoke strange reactions in other creatures. How often, when a picnic had been arranged, and I would be self-consciously trying to get my humble implements unnoticed into the tar-smelling charabanc (a tar preparation was used to keep flies away from the horses) or the tea-smelling Opel convertible (benzine forty years ago smelled that way), some cousin or aunt of mine would remark: "Must you *really* take that net with you? Can't you enjoy yourself like a normal boy? Don't you think you are spoiling everybody's pleasure?" Near a sign NACH BODENLAUBE, at Bad Kissingen, Bavaria, just as I was about to join for a long walk my father and majestic old Muromtsev (who, four years before, in 1906, had been President of the first Russian Parliament), the latter turned his marble head toward me, a vulnerable boy of eleven, and said with his famous solemnity: "Come with us by all means, but do not chase butterflies, child. It spoils the rhythm of the walk." On a path above the Black Sea, in the Crimea, among shrubs in waxy bloom, in March 1918, a bow-legged Bolshevik sentry attempted to arrest me for signaling (with my net, he said) to a British warship. In the summer of 1929, every time I walked through a village in the Eastern Pyrenees, and happened to look back, I would see in my wake the villagers frozen in the various attitudes my passage had caught them in, as if I were Sodom and they Lot's wife. A decade later, in the Maritime Alps, I once noticed the grass undulate in a serpentine way behind me because a fat rural policeman was wriggling after me on his belly to find out if I were not trapping songbirds. America has shown even more of this morbid interest in my retiary activities than other countries have—perhaps because I was in my forties when I came there to live, and the older the man, the queerer he looks with a butterfly net in his hand. Stern farmers have drawn my attention to NO FISHING signs; from cars passing me on the highway have come wild howls of derision; sleepy dogs, though unmindful of the worst bum, have perked up and come at me, snarling; tiny tots have pointed me out to their puzzled mamas; broad-minded vacationists have asked me whether I was catching bugs for bait; and one morning on a wasteland, lit by tall yuccas in bloom, near Santa Fe, a big black mare followed me for more than a mile.

4

When, having shaken off all pursuers, I took the rough, red road that ran from our Vyra house toward field and forest, the animation and luster of the day seemed like a tremor of sympathy around me.

Very fresh, very dark Arran Browns, which emerged only every second year (conveniently, retrospection has fallen here into line), flitted among the firs or revealed their red markings and checkered fringes as they sunned themselves on the roadside bracken. Hopping above the grass, a diminutive Ringlet called Hero dodged my net. Several moths, too, were flying—gaudy sun lovers that sail from flower to flower like painted flies, or male insomniacs in search of hidden females, such as that rust-colored Oak Eggar hurtling across the shrubbery. I noticed (one of the major mysteries of my childhood) a soft pale green wing caught in a spider's web (by then I knew what it was: part of a Large Emerald). The tremendous larva of the Goat Moth, ostentatiously segmented, flat-headed, flesh-colored and glossily flushed, a strange creature "as naked as a worm" to use a French comparison, crossed my path in frantic search for a place to pupate (the awful pressure of metamorphosis, the aura of a disgraceful fit in a public place). On the bark of that birch tree, the stout one near the park wicket, I had found last spring a dark aberration of Sievers' Carmelite (just another gray moth to the reader). In the ditch, under the bridgelet, a bright-yellow Silvius Skipper hobnobbed with a dragonfly (just a blue libellula to me). From a flower head two male Coppers rose to a tremendous height, fighting all the way up—and then, after a while, came the downward flash of one of them returning to his thistle. These were familiar insects, but at any moment something better might cause me to stop with a quick intake of breath. I remember one day when I warily brought my net closer and closer to an uncommon Hairstreak that had daintily settled on a sprig. I could clearly see the white W on its chocolate-brown underside. Its wings were closed and the inferior ones were rubbing against each other in a curious circular motion—possibly producing some small, blithe crepitation pitched too high for a human ear to catch. I had long wanted that particular species, and, when near enough, I struck. You have heard champion tennis players moan after muffing an easy shot. You may have seen the face of the world-famous grandmaster Wilhelm Edmundson when, during a simultaneous display in a Minsk café, he lost his rook, by an absurd oversight, to the local amateur and pediatrician, Dr. Schach, who eventually won. But that day nobody (except my older self) could see me shake out a piece of twig from an otherwise empty net and stare at a hole in the tarlatan.

5

Near the intersection of two carriage roads (one, well-kept, running north-south in between our "old" and "new" parks, and the other, muddy and rutty, leading, if you turned west, to Batovo) at a spot where aspens crowded on both sides of a dip, I would be sure to find in the third week of June great blue-black nymphalids striped with pure white, gliding and wheeling low above the rich clay which matched the tint of their undersides when they settled and closed their wings. Those were the dung-loving males of what the old Aurelians used to call the Poplar Admirable, or, more exactly, they belonged to its Bucovinan subspecies. As a boy of nine, not knowing that race, I noticed how much our North Russian specimens differed from the Central European form figured in Hofmann, and rashly wrote to Kuznetsov, one of the greatest Russian, or indeed world, lepidopterists of all time, naming my new subspecies *"Limenitis populi rossica."* A long month later he returned my description and aquarelle of *"rossica* Nabokov" with only two words scribbled on the back of my letter: *"bucovinensis* Hormuzaki." How I hated Hormuzaki! And how hurt I was when in one of Kuznetsov's later papers I found a gruff reference to "schoolboys who keep naming minute varieties of the Poplar Nymph!" Undaunted, however, by the *populi* flop, I "discovered" the following year a "new" moth. That summer I had been collecting assiduously on moonless nights, in a glade of the park, by spreading a bedsheet over the grass and its annoyed glow-worms, and casting upon it the light of an acytelene lamp (which, six years later, was to shine on Tamara). Into that arena of radiance, moths would come drifting out of the solid blackness around me, and it was in that manner, upon that magic sheet, that I took a beautiful *Plusia* (now *Phytometra*) which, as I saw at once, differed from its closest ally by its mauve-and-maroon (instead of golden-brown) fore-wings, and narrower bractea mark and was not recognizably figured in any of my books. I sent its description and picture to Richard South, for publication in *The Entomologist*. He did not know it either, but with the utmost kindness checked it in the British Museum collection—and found it had been described long ago as *Plusia excelsa* by Kretschmar. I received the sad news, which was most sympathetically worded ("... should be congratulated for obtaining ... very rare Volgan thing ... admirable figure ...") with the utmost stoicism; but many years later, by a pretty fluke (I know I should not point out these plums to people), I got even with the first discoverer of *my* moth by giving his own name to a blind man in a novel.

Let me also evoke the hawkmoths, the jets of my boyhood! Colors would die a long death on June evenings. The lilac shrubs in full bloom before which I stood, net in hand, displayed clusters of a fluffy gray in the dusk—the ghost of purple. A moist young moon hung above the mist of a neighboring meadow. In many a garden have I stood thus in later years—in Athens, Antibes, Atlanta—but never have I waited with such a keen desire as before those darkening lilacs. And suddenly it would come, the low buzz passing from flower to flower, the vibrational halo around the streamlined body of an olive and pink Hummingbird moth poised in the air above the corolla into which it had dipped its long tongue. Its handsome black larva (resembling a diminutive cobra when it puffed out its ocellated front segments) could be found on dank willow herb two months later. Thus every hour and season had its delights. And, finally, on cold, or even frosty, autumn nights, one could sugar for moths by painting tree trunks with a mixture of molasses, beer, and rum. Through the gusty blackness, one's lantern would illumine the stickily glistening furrows of the bark and two or three large moths upon it imbibing the sweets, their nervous wings half open butterfly fashion, the lower ones exhibiting their incredible crimson silk from beneath the lichen-gray primaries. *"Catocala adultera!"* I would triumphantly shriek in the direction of the lighted windows of the house as I stumbled home to show my captures to my father.

6

The "English" park that separated our house from the hayfields was an extensive and elaborate affair with labyrinthine paths, Turgenevian benches, and imported oaks among the endemic firs and birches. The struggle that had gone on since my grandfather's time to keep the park from reverting to the wild state always fell short of complete success. No gardener could cope with the hillocks of frizzly black earth that the pink hands of moles kept heaping on the tidy sand of the main walk. Weeds and fungi, and ridgelike tree roots crossed and recrossed the sun-flecked trails. Bears had been eliminated in the eighties, but an occasional moose still visited the grounds. On a picturesque boulder, a little mountain ash and a still smaller aspen had climbed, holding hands, like two clumsy, shy children. Other, more elusive trespassers— lost picnickers or merry villagers—would drive our hoary gamekeeper Ivan crazy by scrawling ribald words on the benches and gates. The disintegrating process continues still, in a different sense, for when, nowadays, I attempt to follow in memory the winding paths from one given point to another, I notice with alarm that there are many gaps, due to oblivion or ignorance, akin to the terra-incognita blanks map makers of old used to call "sleeping beauties."

Beyond the park, there were fields, with a continuous shimmer of butterfly wings over a shimmer of flowers—daisies, bluebells, scabious, and others—which now rapidly pass by me in a kind of colored haze like those lovely, lush meadows, never to be explored, that one sees from the diner on a transcontinental journey. At the end of this grassy wonderland, the forest rose like a wall. There I roamed, scanning the tree trunks (the enchanted, the silent part of a tree) for certain tiny moths, called Pugs in England—delicate little creatures that cling in the daytime to speckled surfaces, with which their flat wings and turned-up abdomens blend. There, at the bottom of that sea of sunshot greenery, I slowly spun round the great boles. Nothing in the world would have seemed sweeter to me than to be able to add, by a stroke of luck, some remarkable new species to the long list of Pugs already named by others. And my pied imagination, ostensibly, and almost grotesquely, groveling to my desire (but all the time, in ghostly conspiracies behind the scenes, coolly planning the most distant events of my destiny), kept providing me with hallucinatory samples of small print: "... the only specimen so far known ..." "... the only specimen known of *Eupithecia petropolitanata* was taken by a Russian schoolboy ..." "... by a young Russian collector ..." "... by myself in the Government of St. Petersburg, Tsarskoe Selo District, in 1910 ... 1911 ... 1912 ... 1913 ..." And then, thirty years later, that blessed black night in the Wasatch Range.

At first—when I was, say, eight or nine—I seldom roamed farther than the fields and woods between Vyra and Batovo. Later, when aiming at a particular spot half-a-dozen miles or more distant, I would use a bicycle to get there with my net strapped to the frame; but not many forest paths were passable on wheels; it was possible to ride there on horseback, of course, but, because of our ferocious Russian tabanids, one could not leave a horse haltered in a wood for any length of time: my spirited bay almost climbed up the tree it was tied to one day trying to elude them: big fellows with watered-silk eyes and tiger bodies, and gray little runts with an even more painful proboscis, but much more sluggish: to dispatch two or three of these dingy tipplers with one crush of the gloved hand as they glued themselves to the neck of my mount afforded me a wonderful empathic relief (which a dipterist might not appreciate). Anyway, on my butterfly hunts I always preferred hiking to any other form of locomotion (except, naturally, a flying seat gliding leisurely over the plant mats and rocks of an unexplored mountain, or hovering just above the flowery roof of a rain forest); for when you walk, especially in a region you have studied well, there is an exquisite pleasure in departing from one's itinerary to visit, here and there by the wayside, this glade, that glen, this or that combination of soil and flora—to drop in, as it were, on a familiar butterfly in his particular habitat, in order to see if he has emerged, and if so, how he is doing.

There came a July day—around 1910, I suppose—when I felt the urge to explore the vast marshland beyond the Oredezh. After skirting the river for three or four miles, I found a rickety footbridge. While crossing over, I could see the huts of a hamlet on my left, apple trees, rows of tawny pine logs lying on a green bank, and the bright patches made on the turf by the scattered clothes of peasant girls, who,

stark naked in shallow water, romped and yelled, heeding me
as little as if I were the discarnate carrier of my present
reminiscences.

On the other side of the river, a dense crowd of small,
bright blue male butterflies that had been tippling on the
rich, trampled mud and cow dung through which I trudged
rose all together into the spangled air and settled again as
soon as I had passed.

After making my way through some pine groves and alder
scrub I came to the bog. No sooner had my ear caught the
hum of diptera around me, the guttural cry of a snipe overhead, the gulping sound of the morass under my foot, than
I knew I would find here quite special arctic butterflies,
whose pictures, or, still better, nonillustrated descriptions I
had worshiped for several seasons. And the next moment I
was among them. Over the small shrubs of bog bilberry with
fruit of a dim, dreamy blue, over the brown eye of stagnant
water, over moss and mire, over the flower spikes of the fragrant bog orchid (the *nochnaya fialka* of Russian poets), a
dusky little Fritillary bearing the name of a Norse goddess
passed in low, skimming flight. Pretty Cordigera, a gemlike
moth, buzzed all over its uliginose food plant. I pursued
rose-margined Sulphurs, gray-marbled Satyrs. Unmindful of
the mosquitoes that furred my forearms, I stooped with a
grunt of delight to snuff out the life of some silver-studded
lepidopteron throbbing in the folds of my net. Through the
smells of the bog, I caught the subtle perfume of butterfly
wings on my fingers, a perfume which varies with the species
—vanilla, or lemon, or musk, or a musty, sweetish odor difficult to define. Still unsated, I pressed forward. At last I saw
I had come to the end of the marsh. The rising ground
beyond was a paradise of lupines, columbines, and pent-
stemons. Mariposa lilies bloomed under Ponderosa pines.

In the distance, fleeting cloud shadows dappled the dull green of slopes above timber line, and the gray and white of Longs Peak.

I confess I do not believe in time. I like to fold my magic carpet, after use, in such a way as to superimpose one part of the pattern upon another. Let visitors trip. And the highest enjoyment of timelessness—in a landscape selected at random —is when I stand among rare butterflies and their food plants. This is ecstasy, and behind the ecstasy is something else, which is hard to explain. It is like a momentary vacuum into which rushes all that I love. A sense of oneness with sun and stone. A thrill of gratitude to whom it may concern—to the contrapuntal genius of human fate or to tender ghosts humoring a lucky mortal.

A family group taken in our garden at Vyra by a St. Petersburg photographer in August 1908, between my father's recent return from prison and his departure on the following day, with my mother, for Stresa. The round thing on the tree trunk is an archery target. My mother has placed photophobic Trainy upon the iron table mentioned in connection with mushrooms in Chapter 2. My paternal grandmother is holding, in a decorative but precarious cluster, my two little sisters whom she never held in real life: Olga on her knee, Elena against her shoulder. The dark depth of the oldest part of our park provides the background. The lady in black is my mother's maternal aunt, Praskovia Nikolaevna Tarnovski, born Kozlov (1848–1910), who was to look after us and our mentors during our parents' trip to Italy. My brother Sergey is linked to her left elbow; her other hand supports me. I am perched on the bench arm, hating my collar and Stresa.

7

1

IN the early years of this century, a travel agency on Nevski Avenue displayed a three-foot-long model of an oak-brown international sleeping car. In delicate verisimilitude it completely outranked the painted tin of my clockwork trains. Unfortunately it was not for sale. One could make out the blue upholstery inside, the embossed leather lining of the compartment walls, their polished panels, inset mirrors, tulip-shaped reading lamps, and other maddening details. Spacious windows alternated with narrower ones, single or geminate, and some of these were of frosted glass. In a few of the compartments, the beds had been made.

The then great and glamorous Nord-Express (it was never the same after World War One when its elegant brown became a nouveau-riche blue), consisting solely of such international cars and running but twice a week, connected St. Petersburg with Paris. I would have said: directly with Paris, had passengers not been obliged to change from one train to a superficially similar one at the Russo-German frontier (Verzhbolovo-Eydtkuhnen), where the ample and lazy Russian sixty-and-a-half-inch gauge was replaced by the fifty-six-and-a-half-inch standard of Europe and coal succeeded birch logs.

In the far end of my mind I can unravel, I think, at least five such journeys to Paris, with the Riviera or Biarritz as their ultimate destination. In 1909, the year I now single out, our party consisted of eleven people and one dachshund. Wearing gloves and a traveling cap, my father sat reading a book in the compartment he shared with our tutor. My brother and I were separated from them by a washroom. My mother and her maid Natasha occupied a compartment adjacent to ours. Next came my two small sisters, their English governess, Miss Lavington, and a Russian nurse. The odd one of our party, my father's valet, Osip (whom a decade later, the pedantic Bolsheviks were to shoot, because he appropriated our bicycles instead of turning them over to the nation), had a stranger for companion.

Historically and artistically, the year had started with a political cartoon in *Punch:* goddess England bending over goddess Italy, on whose head one of Messina's bricks has landed—probably, the worst picture *any* earthquake has ever inspired. In April of that year, Peary had reached the North Pole. In May, Shalyapin had sung in Paris. In June, bothered by rumors of new and better Zeppelins, the United States War Department had told reporters of plans for an aerial Navy. In July, Blériot had flown from Calais to Dover (with a little additional loop when he lost his bearings). It was late August now. The firs and marshes of Northwestern Russia sped by, and on the following day gave way to German pinewoods and heather.

At a collapsible table, my mother and I played a card game called *durachki*. Although it was still broad daylight, our cards, a glass and, on a different plane, the locks of a suitcase were reflected in the window. Through forest and field, and in sudden ravines, and among scuttling cottages, those discarnate gamblers kept steadily playing on for steadily sparkling stakes. It was a long, very long game: on this gray winter morning, in the looking glass of my bright hotel room, I see shining the same, the very same, locks of that now seventy-year-old valise, a highish, heavyish *nécessaire de voyage* of pigskin, with "H.N." elaborately interwoven in thick silver under a similar coronet, which had been bought in 1897 for my mother's wedding trip to Florence. In 1917 it transported from St. Petersburg to the Crimea and then to London a handful of jewels. Around 1930, it lost to a pawnbroker its expensive receptacles of crystal and silver leaving empty the cunningly contrived leathern holders on the inside of the lid. But that loss has been amply recouped during the thirty years it then traveled with me—from Prague to Paris, from St. Nazaire to New York and through the mirrors of more than two hundred motel rooms and rented houses, in forty-six states. The fact that of our Russian heritage the hardiest survivor proved to be a traveling bag is both logical and emblematic.

"Ne budet-li, tï ved' ustal [Haven't you had enough, aren't you tired]?" my mother would ask, and then would be lost in thought as she slowly shuffled the cards. The door of the compartment was open and I could see the corridor window, where the wires—six thin black wires—were doing their best to slant up, to ascend skywards, despite the lightning blows dealt them by one telegraph pole after another; but just as all six, in a triumphant swoop of pathetic elation, were about to reach the top of the window, a particularly vicious blow would bring them down, as low as they had ever been, and they would have to start all over again.

When, on such journeys as these, the train changed its pace to a dignified amble and all but grazed housefronts and shop signs, as we passed through some big German town, I used to feel a twofold excitement, which terminal stations could not provide. I saw a city, with its toylike trams, linden trees and brick walls, enter the compartment, hobnob with the mirrors, and fill to the brim the windows on the corridor side. This informal contact between train and city was one part of the thrill. The other was putting myself in the place of some passer-by who, I imagined, was moved as I would be moved myself to see the long, romantic, auburn cars, with their intervestibular connecting curtains as black as bat wings and their metal lettering copper-bright in the low sun, unhurriedly negotiate an iron bridge across an everyday thoroughfare and then turn, with all windows suddenly ablaze, around a last block of houses.

There were drawbacks to those optical amalgamations. The wide-windowed dining car, a vista of chaste bottles of mineral water, miter-folded napkins, and dummy chocolate bars (whose wrappers—Cailler, Kohler, and so forth—enclosed nothing but wood), would be perceived at first as a cool haven beyond a consecution of reeling blue corridors; but as the meal progressed toward its fatal last course, and more and more dreadfully one equilibrist with a full tray would back against our table to let another equilibrist pass with another full tray, I would keep catching the car in the act of being recklessly sheathed, lurching waiters and all, in the landscape, while the landscape itself went through a complex system of motion, the daytime moon stubbornly keeping abreast of one's plate, the distant meadows opening fanwise, the near trees sweeping up on invisible swings toward the track, a parallel rail line all at once committing suicide by anastomosis, a bank of nictitating grass rising, rising, rising, until the little witness of mixed velocities was made to disgorge his portion of *omelette aux confitures de fraises*.

It was at night, however, that the *Compagnie Internationale des Wagons-Lits et des Grands Express Européens* lived up to the magic of its name. From my bed under my brother's bunk (Was he asleep? Was he there at all?), in the semidarkness of our compartment, I watched things, and parts of things, and shadows, and sections of shadows cautiously moving about and getting nowhere. The woodwork gently creaked and crackled. Near the door that led to the toilet, a dim garment on a peg and, higher up, the tassel of the blue, bivalved nightlight swung rhythmically. It was hard to correlate those halting approaches, that hooded stealth, with the headlong rush of the outside night, which I knew *was* rushing by, spark-streaked, illegible.

I would put myself to sleep by the simple act of identifying myself with the engine driver. A sense of drowsy well-being invaded my veins as soon as I had everything nicely arranged—the carefree passengers in their rooms enjoying the ride I was giving them, smoking, exchanging knowing smiles, nodding, dozing; the waiters and cooks and train guards (whom I had to place somewhere) carousing in the diner; and myself, goggled and begrimed, peering out of the engine cab at the tapering track, at the ruby or emerald point in the black distance. And then, in my sleep, I would see something totally different—a glass marble rolling under a grand piano or a toy engine lying on its side with its wheels still working gamely.

A change in the speed of the train sometimes interrupted the current of my sleep. Slow lights were stalking by; each, in passing, investigated the same chink, and then a luminous compass measured the shadows. Presently, the train stopped with a long-drawn Westinghousian sigh. Something (my brother's spectacles, as it proved next day) fell from above. It was marvelously exciting to move to the foot of one's bed, with part of the bedclothes following, in order to undo cautiously the catch of the window shade, which could be made

to slide only halfway up, impeded as it was by the edge of the
upper berth.

Like moons around Jupiter, pale moths revolved about a
lone lamp. A dismembered newspaper stirred on a bench.
Somewhere on the train one could hear muffled voices, somebody's comfortable cough. There was nothing particularly interesting in the portion of station platform before me, and
still I could not tear myself away from it until it departed
of its own accord.

Next morning, wet fields with misshapen willows along the
radius of a ditch or a row of poplars afar, traversed by a horizontal band of milky-white mist, told one that the train was
spinning through Belgium. It reached Paris at 4 P.M., and
even if the stay was only an overnight one, I had always time
to purchase something—say, a little brass *Tour Eiffel,* rather
roughly coated with silver paint—before we boarded, at noon
on the following day, the Sud-Express which, on its way to
Madrid, dropped us around 10 P.M. at the La Négresse station of Biarritz, a few miles from the Spanish frontier.

2

Biarritz still retained its quiddity in those days. Dusty
blackberry bushes and weedy *terrains à vendre* bordered the
road that led to our villa. The Carlton was still being built.
Some thirty-six years had to elapse before Brigadier General
Samuel McCroskey would occupy the royal suite of the Hôtel
du Palais, which stands on the site of a former palace, where
in the sixties, that incredibly agile medium, Daniel Home, is
said to have been caught stroking with his bare foot (in imitation of a ghost hand) the kind, trustful face of Empress
Eugénie. On the promenade near the Casino, an elderly

flower girl, with carbon eyebrows and a painted smile, nimbly slipped the plump torus of a carnation into the buttonhole of an intercepted stroller whose left jowl accentuated its royal fold as he glanced down sideways at the coy insertion of the flower.

The rich-hued Oak Eggars questing amid the brush were quite unlike ours (which did not breed on oak, anyway), and here the Speckled Woods haunted not woods, but hedges and had tawny, not pale-yellowish, spots. Cleopatra, a tropical-looking, lemon-and-orange Brimstone, languorously flopping about in gardens, had been a sensation in 1907 and was still a pleasure to net.

Along the back line of the *plage,* various seaside chairs and stools supported the parents of straw-hatted children who were playing in front on the sand. I could be seen on my knees trying to set a found comb aflame by means of a magnifying glass. Men sported white trousers that to the eye of today would look as if they had comically shrunk in the washing; ladies wore, that particular season, light coats with silk-faced lapels, hats with big crowns and wide brims, dense embroidered white veils, frill-fronted blouses, frills at their wrists, frills on their parasols. The breeze salted one's lips. At a tremendous pace a stray Clouded Yellow came dashing across the palpitating *plage.*

Additional movement and sound were provided by venders hawking *cacahuètes,* sugared violets, pistachio ice cream of a heavenly green, cachou pellets, and huge convex pieces of dry, gritty, waferlike stuff that came from a red barrel. With a distinctness that no later superpositions have dimmed, I see that waffleman stomp along through deep mealy sand, with the heavy cask on his bent back. When called, he would sling it off his shoulder by a twist of its strap, bang it down on the sand in a Tower of Pisa position, wipe his face with his sleeve, and proceed to manipulate a kind of arrow-and-dial arrangement with numbers on the lid of the cask. The arrow rasped and whirred around. Luck was supposed to fix the size of a sou's worth of wafer. The bigger the piece, the more I was sorry for him.

The process of bathing took place on another part of the beach. Professional bathers, burly Basques in black bathing suits, were there to help ladies and children enjoy the terrors of the surf. Such a *baigneur* would place the *client* with his back to the incoming wave and hold him by the hand as the rising, rotating mass of foamy, green water violently descended from behind, knocking one off one's feet with a mighty wallop. After a dozen of these tumbles, the *baigneur*, glistening like a seal, would lead his panting, shivering, moistly snuffling charge landward, to the flat foreshore, where an unforgettable old woman with gray hairs on her chin promptly chose a bathing robe from several hanging on a clothesline. In the security of a little cabin, one would be helped by yet another attendant to peel off one's soggy, sand-heavy bathing suit. It would plop onto the boards, and, still shivering, one would step out of it and trample on its bluish, diffuse stripes. The cabin smelled of pine. The attendant, a hunchback with beaming wrinkles, brought a basin of steaming-hot water, in which one immersed one's feet. From him I learned, and have preserved ever since in a glass cell of my memory, that "butterfly" in the Basque language is *misericoletea*—or at least it sounded so (among the seven words I have found in dictionaries the closest approach is *micheletea*).

3

On the browner and wetter part of the *plage,* that part which at low tide yielded the best mud for castles, I found myself digging, one day, side by side with a little French girl called Colette.

She would be ten in November, I had been ten in April. Attention was drawn to a jagged bit of violet mussel shell upon which she had stepped with the bare sole of her narrow long-toed foot. No, I was not English. Her greenish eyes seemed flecked with the overflow of the freckles that covered her sharp-featured face. She wore what might now be termed a playsuit, consisting of a blue jersey with rolled-up sleeves and blue knitted shorts. I had taken her at first for a boy and then had been puzzled by the bracelet on her thin wrist and the corkscrew brown curls dangling from under her sailor cap.

She spoke in birdlike bursts of rapid twitter, mixing governess English and Parisian French. Two years before, on the same *plage,* I had been much attached to Zina, the lovely, sun-tanned, bad-tempered little daughter of a Serbian naturopath—she had, I remember (absurdly, for she and I were only eight at the time), a *grain de beauté* on her apricot skin just below the heart, and there was a horrible collection of chamber pots, full and half-full, and one with surface bubbles, on the floor of the hall in her family's boardinghouse lodgings which I visited early one morning to be given by her as she was being dressed, a dead hummingbird moth found by the cat. But when I met Colette, I knew at once that this was the real thing. Colette seemed to me so much stranger than all my other chance playmates at Biarritz! I somehow acquired the feeling that she was less happy than I, less loved. A bruise on her delicate, downy forearm gave rise to awful conjectures. "He pinches as bad as my mummy," she said, speaking of a crab. I evolved various schemes to save her from her parents, who were *"des bourgeois de Paris"* as I heard somebody tell my mother with a slight shrug. I interpreted the disdain in my own fashion, as I knew that those people had come all the way from Paris in their blue-and-yellow limousine (a fashionable adventure in those days) but had drably sent Colette with her dog and governess by an ordinary coach-train. The dog was a female fox terrier with bells on her collar and a most waggly behind. From sheer exuberance, she would lap up salt water out of Colette's toy pail. I remember the sail, the sunset and the lighthouse pictured on that pail, but I cannot recall the dog's name, and this bothers me.

During the two months of our stay at Biarritz, my passion for Colette all but surpassed my passion for Cleopatra. Since my parents were not keen to meet hers, I saw her only on the beach; but I thought of her constantly. If I noticed she had been crying, I felt a surge of helpless anguish that brought tears to my own eyes. I could not destroy the mosquitoes that had left their bites on her frail neck, but I could, and did, have a successful fistfight with a red-haired boy who had been rude to her. She used to give me warm handfuls of hard candy. One day, as we were bending together over a starfish, and Colette's ringlets were tickling my ear, she suddenly turned toward me and kissed me on the cheek. So great was my emotion that all I could think of saying was, "You little monkey."

I had a gold coin that I assumed would pay for our elopement. Where did I want to take her? Spain? America? The mountains above Pau? *"Là-bas, là-bas, dans la montagne,"* as I had heard Carmen sing at the opera. One strange night, I lay awake, listening to the recurrent thud of the ocean and planning our flight. The ocean seemed to rise and grope in the darkness and then heavily fall on its face.

Of our actual getaway, I have little to report. My memory retains a glimpse of her obediently putting on rope-soled canvas shoes, on the lee side of a flapping tent, while I stuffed a folding butterfly net into a brown-paper bag. The next glimpse is of our evading pursuit by entering a pitch-dark *cinéma* near the Casino (which, of course, was absolutely out of bounds). There we sat, holding hands across the dog, which now and then gently jingled in Colette's lap, and were shown a jerky, drizzly, but highly exciting bullfight at San Sebastián. My final glimpse is of myself being led along the promenade by Linderovski. His long legs move with a kind of ominous briskness and I can see the muscles of his grimly set jaw working under the tight skin. My bespectacled brother, aged nine, whom he happens to hold with his other hand, keeps trotting out forward to peer at me with awed curiosity, like a little owl.

Among the trivial souvenirs acquired at Biarritz before leaving, my favorite was not the small bull of black stone and not the sonorous seashell but something which now seems almost symbolic—a meerschaum penholder with a tiny peephole of crystal in its ornamental part. One held it quite close to one's eye, screwing up the other, and when one had got rid of the shimmer of one's own lashes, a miraculous photographic view of the bay and of the line of cliffs ending in a lighthouse could be seen inside.

And now a delightful thing happens. The process of re-creating that penholder and the microcosm in its eyelet stimulates my memory to a last effort. I try again to recall the name of Colette's dog—and, triumphantly, along those remote beaches, over the glossy evening sands of the past, where each footprint slowly fills up with sunset water, here it comes, here it comes, echoing and vibrating: Floss, Floss, Floss!

Colette was back in Paris by the time we stopped there for a day before continuing our homeward journey; and there, in a fawn park under a cold blue sky, I saw her (by arrangement between our mentors, I believe) for the last time. She carried a hoop and a short stick to drive it with, and everything about her was extremely proper and stylish in an autumnal, Parisian, *tenue-de-ville-pour-fillettes* way. She took from her governess and slipped into my brother's hand a farewell present, a box of sugar-coated almonds, meant, I knew, solely for me; and instantly she was off, tap-tapping her glinting hoop through light and shade, around and around a fountain choked with dead leaves, near which I stood. The leaves mingle in my memory with the leather of her shoes and gloves, and there was, I remember, some detail in her attire (perhaps a ribbon on her Scottish cap, or the pattern of her stockings) that reminded me then of the rainbow spiral in a glass marble. I still seem to be holding that wisp of iridescence, not knowing exactly where to fit it, while she runs with her hoop ever faster around me and finally dissolves among the slender shadows cast on the graveled path by the interlaced arches of its low looped fence.

8

1

I AM going to show a few slides, but first let me indicate the where and the when of the matter. My brother and I were born in St. Petersburg, the capital of Imperial Russia, he in the middle of March, 1900, and I eleven months earlier. The English and French governesses we had in our childhood were eventually assisted, and finally superseded, by Russian-speaking tutors, most of them graduate students at the capital's university. This tutorial era started about 1906 and lasted for almost a full decade, overlapping, from 1911 on, our high-school years. Each tutor, in turn, dwelt with us—at our St. Petersburg house during the winter, and the rest of the time either at our country estate, fifty miles from the city, or at the foreign resorts we often visited in the fall. Three years was the maximum it took me (I was better at such things than my brother) to wear out any one of those hardy young men.

In choosing our tutors, my father seems to have hit upon the ingenious idea of engaging each time a representative of another class or race, so as to expose us to all the winds that swept over the Russian Empire. I doubt that it was a completely deliberate scheme on his part, but in looking back

I find the pattern curiously clear, and the images of those tutors appear within memory's luminous disc as so many magic-lantern projections.

The admirable and unforgettable village schoolmaster who in the summer of 1905 taught us Russian spelling used to come for only a few hours a day and thus does not really belong to the present series. He helps, however, to join its beginning and its end, since my final recollection of him refers to the Easter vacation in 1915, which my brother and I spent with my father and one Volgin—the last, and worst tutor—skiing in the snow-smothered country around our estate under an intense, almost violet sky. Our old friend invited us to his lodgings in the icicle-eaved school building for what he called a snack; actually it was a complex and lovingly planned meal. I can still see his beaming face and the beautifully simulated delight with which my father welcomed a dish (hare roasted in sour cream) that I knew he happened to detest. The room was overheated. My thawing ski boots were not as waterproof as they were supposed to be. My eyes, still smarting from the dazzling snows, kept trying to decipher, on the near wall, a so-called "typographical" portrait of Tolstoy. Like the tail of the mouse on a certain page in *Alice in Wonderland,* it was wholly composed of printed matter. A complete Tolstoy story ("Master and Man") had gone to make its author's bearded face, which, incidentally, our host's features somewhat resembled. We were just on the point of attacking the unfortunate hare, when the door flew open and Hristofor, a blue-nosed footman in a woman's woolen kerchief, ushered in sideways, with an idiotic smile, a huge luncheon basket packed with viands and wines that my tactless grandmother (who was wintering at Batovo) had thought necessary to send us, in case the schoolmaster's fare proved insufficient. Before our host had time to feel hurt,

my father sent the untouched hamper back, with a brief note
that probably puzzled the well-meaning old lady as most of
his actions puzzled her. In a flowing silk gown and net mitts,
a period piece rather than a live person, she spent most of her
life on a couch, fanning herself with an ivory fan. A box of
boules de gomme, or a glass of almond milk were always
within her reach, as well as a hand mirror, for she used to
repowder her face, with a large pink puff, every hour or so,
the little mole on her cheekbone showing through all that
flour, like a currant. Notwithstanding the languid aspects of
her usual day, she remained an extraordinarily hardy woman
and made a point of sleeping near a wide-open window all
year round. One morning, after a nightlong blizzard, her
maid found her lying under a layer of sparkling snow which
had swept over her bed and her, without infringing upon the
healthy glow of her sleep. If she loved anybody, it was only
her youngest daughter, Nadezhda Vonlyarlyarski, for whose
sake she suddenly sold Batovo in 1916, a deal which benefited
no one at that dusking-tide of imperial history. She complained to all our relatives about the dark forces that had
seduced her gifted son into scorning the kind of "brilliant"
career in the Tsar's service his forefathers had pursued. What
she found especially hard to understand was that my father,
who, she knew, thoroughly appreciated all the pleasures of
great wealth, could jeopardize its enjoyment by becoming a
Liberal, thus helping to bring on a revolution that would,
in the long run, as she correctly foresaw, leave him a pauper.

2

Our spelling master was a carpenter's son. In the magic-
lantern sequence that follows, my first slide shows a young
man we called Ordo, the enlightened son of a Greek Catho-

lic deacon. On walks with my brother and me in the cool summer of 1907, he wore a Byronic black cloak with a silver S-shaped clasp. In the deep Batovo woods, at a spot near a brook where the ghost of a hanged man was said to appear, Ordo would give a rather profane and foolish performance for which my brother and I clamored every time we passed there. Bending his head and flapping his cloak in weird, vampiric fashion he would slowly cavort around a lugubrious aspen. One wet morning during that ritual he dropped his cigarette case and while helping to look for it, I discovered two freshly emerged specimens of the Amur hawkmoth, rare in our region—lovely, velvety, purplish-gray creatures—in tranquil copulation, clinging with chinchilla-coated legs to the grass at the foot of the tree. In the fall of that same year, Ordo accompanied us to Biarritz, and a few weeks later abruptly departed, leaving a present we had given him, a Gillette safety razor, on his pillow, with a pinned note. It seldom happens that I do not quite know whether a recollection is my own or has come to me secondhand, but in this case I do waver, especially because, much later, my mother, in her reminiscent moods, used to refer with amusement to the flame she had unknowingly kindled. I seem to remember a door ajar into a drawing room, and there, in the middle of the floor, Ordo, our Ordo, crouching on his knees and wringing his hands in front of my young, beautiful, and dumbfounded mother. The fact that I seem to see, out of the corner of my mind's eye, the undulations of a romantic cloak around Ordo's heaving shoulders suggests my having transferred something of the earlier forest dance to that blurred room in our Biarritz apartment (under the windows of which, in a roped-off section of the square, a huge custard-colored balloon was being inflated by Sigismond Lejoyeux, a local aeronaut).

Next came a Ukrainian, an exuberant mathematician with a dark mustache and a sparkling smile. He spent part of the winter of 1907–1908 with us. He, too, had his accomplishments, among which a vanishing-coin trick was particularly fetching. *A coin, placed on a sheet of paper, is covered with a tumbler and forthwith disappears.* Take an ordinary drinking glass. Paste neatly over its mouth a round piece of paper. The paper should be ruled (or otherwise patterned)—this will enhance the illusion. Place upon a similarly ruled sheet a small coin (a silver twenty-kopek piece will do). Briskly slip the tumbler over the coin, taking care to have both sets of rules or patterns tally. Coincidence of pattern is one of the wonders of nature. The wonders of nature were beginning to impress me at that early age. On one of his Sundays off, the poor conjuror collapsed in the street and was shoved by the police into a cold cell with a dozen drunks. Actually, he suffered from a heart condition, of which he died a few years later.

The next picture looks as if it had come on the screen upside down. It shows our third tutor standing on his head. He was a large, formidably athletic Lett, who walked on his hands, lifted enormous weights, juggled with dumbbells and in a trice could fill a large room with a garrison's worth of sweat reek. When he deemed it fit to punish me for some slight misdemeanor (I remember, for instance, letting a child's marble fall from an upper landing upon his attractive, hard-looking head as he walked downstairs), he would adopt the remarkable pedagogic measure of suggesting that he and I put on boxing gloves for a bit of sparring. He would then punch me in the face with stinging accuracy. Although I preferred this to the hand-cramping *pensums* Mademoiselle would think up, such as making me copy out two hundred

times the proverb *Qui aime bien, châtie bien,* I did not miss
the good man when he left after a stormy month's stay.

Then came a Pole. He was a handsome medical student,
with liquid brown eyes and sleek hair, who looked rather
like the French actor Max Linder, a popular movie comedian.
Max lasted from 1908 to 1910 and won my admiration on a
winter day in St. Petersburg when a sudden commotion interrupted our usual morning walk. Whip-brandishing Cossacks
with fierce, imbecile faces were urging their prancing and
snorting ponies against an excited crowd. Lots of caps and
at least three galoshes lay black on the snow. For a moment
it seemed as if one of the Cossacks was heading our way, and
I saw Max half-draw from an inside pocket a small automatic
with which I forthwith fell in love—but unfortunately the
turmoil receded. Once or twice he took us to see his brother,
an emaciated Roman Catholic priest of great distinction
whose pale hands absentmindedly hovered over our little
Greek Catholic heads, while Max and he discussed political
or family matters in a stream of sibilant Polish. I visualize
my father on a summer day in the country vying with Max
in marksmanship—riddling with pistol bullets a rusty NO
HUNTING sign in our woods. He was, this pleasant Max, a
vigorous chap, and therefore I used to be taken aback when
he complained of migraine and languidly refused to join me
in kicking a football around or going for a dip in the river.
I know now that he was having an affair that summer with
a married woman whose property lay a dozen miles away. At
odd moments during the day, he would sneak off to the ken-
nels in order to feed and cajole our chained watchdogs. They
were set loose at 11 P.M. to rove around the house, and he had
to confront them in the dead of night when he slipped out
and made for the shrubbery where a bicycle with all acces-
sories—thumb bell, pump, tool case of brown leather, and

even trouser clips—had been secretly prepared for him by an ally, my father's Polish valet. Holey dirt roads and humpy forest trails would take impatient Max to the remote trysting place, which was a hunting lodge—in the grand tradition of elegant adultery. The chill mists of dawn and four Great Danes with short memories would see him cycling back, and at 8 A.M. a new day would begin. I wonder if it was not with a certain relief that, in the autumn of that year (1909), Max left the scene of his nightly exploits to accompany us on our second trip to Biarritz. Piously, penitently, he took a couple of days off to visit Lourdes in the company of the pretty and fast Irish girl who was the governess of Colette, my favorite playmate on the *plage*. Max abandoned us the next year, for a job in the X-ray department of a St. Petersburg hospital, and later on, between the two World Wars, became, I understand, something of a medical celebrity in Poland.

After the Catholic came the Protestant—a Lutheran of Jewish extraction. He will have to figure here under the name of Lenski. My brother and I went with him, late in 1910, to Germany, and after we came back in January of the following year, and began going to school in St. Petersburg, Lenski stayed on for about three years to help us with our homework. It was during his reign that Mademoiselle, who had been with us since the winter of 1905, finally gave up her struggle against intruding Muscovites and returned to Lausanne. Lenski had been born in poverty and liked to recall that between graduating from the *Gymnasium* of his native town, on the Black Sea, and being admitted to the University of St. Petersburg he had supported himself by ornamenting stones from the shingled shore with bright seascapes and selling them as paperweights. He had an oval pink face, short-lashed, curiously naked eyes behind a rimless pince-nez and a pale blue shaven head. We discovered at once three things about him: he was an excellent teacher; he lacked all sense of humor; and, in contrast to our previous tutors, he was someone we needed to defend. The security he felt as long as our parents were around might be shattered at any time in their absence by some sally on the part of our aunts. For them, my father's fierce writings against pogroms and other governmental practices were but the whims of a wayward nobleman, and I often overheard them discussing with horror Lenski's origins and my father's "insane experiments." After such an occasion, I would be dreadfully rude to them and then burst into hot tears in the seclusion of a water closet. Not that I particularly liked Lenski. There was something irritating about his dry voice, his excessive neatness, the way he had of constantly wiping his glasses with a special cloth or paring his nails with a special gadget, his pedantically correct speech and, perhaps most of all, his fantastic morning custom of marching (seemingly straight out of bed but already shod and trousered, with red braces hanging behind and a strange netlike vest enveloping his plump hairy torso) to the nearest faucet and limiting there his ablutions to a thorough sousing of his pink face, blue skull and fat neck, followed by some lusty Russian nose-blowing, after which he marched, with the same purposeful steps, but now dripping and purblind, back to his bedroom where he kept in a secret place three sacrosanct towels (incidentally he was so *brezgliv,* in the Russian untranslatable sense, that he would wash his hands after touching banknotes or banisters).

He complained to my mother that Sergey and I were little foreigners, freaks, fops, *snobï,* "pathologically indifferent," as he put it, to Goncharov, Grigorovich, Korolenko, Stanyukovich, Mamin-Sibiryak, and other stupefying bores (comparable to American "regional writers") whose works, according to him, "enthralled normal boys." To my obscure annoyance,

1910 года

My mother at thirty-four, a pastel portrait (60 cm. x 40 cm.) by Leon
Bakst, painted in 1910, in the music room of our St. Petersburg house.
The reproduction printed here was made the same year, under his super-
vision. He had had tremendous trouble with the fluctuating outline of
her lips, sometimes spending an entire sitting on one detail. The result
is an extraordinary likeness and represents an interesting stage in his
artistic development. My parents also possessed a number of watercolor
sketches made for the Scheherazade ballet. Some twenty-five years later,
in Paris, Alexandre Bénois told me that soon after the Soviet Revolution
he had had all Bakst's works, as well as some of his own, such as the
"Rainy Day in Brittany," transported from our house to the Alexander
III (now State) Museum.

My mother and her brother, Vasiliy Ivanovich Rukavishnikov (1874–1916), on the terrace of his château at Pau, Basses Pyrenees, October 1913.

he advised my parents to have their two boys—the three younger children were beyond his jurisdiction—lead a more democratic form of life, which meant, for example, switching, in Berlin, from the Adlon Hotel to a vast apartment in a gloomy pension in a lifeless lane and replacing pile-carpeted international express trains by the filthy floors and stale cigar smoke of swaying and pitching *Schnellzugs*. In foreign towns, as well as in St. Petersburg, he would freeze before shops to marvel at wares that left us completely indifferent. He was about to be married, had nothing but his salary, and was planning his future household with the utmost cunning and care. Now and then rash impulses interfered with his budget. Noticing one day a bedraggled hag who was gloating over a crimson-plumed hat on display at a milliner's, he bought it for her—and had quite a time getting rid of the woman. In his own acquisitions, he aimed at great circumspection. My brother and I patiently listened to his detailed daydreams as he analyzed every corner of the cozy yet frugal apartment he mentally prepared for his wife and himself. Sometimes his fancy would soar. Once it settled on an expensive ceiling lamp at Alexandre's, a St. Petersburg shop that featured rather painful bourgeois bric-a-brac. Not wishing the store to suspect what object he coveted, Lenski said he would take us to see it only if we swore to use self-control and not attract unnecessary attention by direct contemplation. With all kinds of precautions, he brought us under a dreadful bronze octopus and his only indication that this was the longed-for article was a purring sigh. He used the same care—tiptoeing and whispering, in order not to wake the monster of fate (which, he seemed to think, bore him a personal grudge)—when introducing us to his fiancée, a small, graceful young lady with scared-gazelle eyes, and the scent of fresh violets clinging to her black veil. We met her, I remember, near a pharmacy at

the corner of Potsdamerstrasse and Privatstrasse, a lane, full
of dead leaves, where our pension was, and he urged us to
keep his bride's presence in Berlin secret from our parents,
and a mechanical manikin in the pharmacy window was going
through the motions of shaving, and tramcars screeched by,
and it was beginning to snow.

3

We are now ready to tackle the main theme of this chapter.
Sometime during the following winter, Lenski conceived the
awful idea of showing, on alternate Sundays, Educational
Magic-Lantern Projections at our St. Petersburg home. By
their means he proposed to illustrate ("abundantly," as he
said with a smack of his thin lips) instructive readings before
a group that he fondly believed would consist of entranced
boys and girls sharing in a memorable experience. Besides
adding to our store of information, it might, he thought, help
make my brother and me into good little mixers. Using us
as a core, he accumulated around this sullen center several
layers of recruits—such coeval cousins of ours as happened to
be at hand, various youngsters we met every winter at more
or less tedious parties, some of our schoolmates (unusually
quiet they were—but, alas, registered every trifle), and the
children of the servants. Having been given a completely free
hand by my gentle and optimistic mother, he rented an elaborate apparatus and hired a dejected-looking university student to man it; as I see it now, warmhearted Lenski was,
among other things, trying to help an impecunious comrade.

Never shall I forget that first reading. Lenski had selected
a narrative poem by Lermontov dealing with the adventures
of a young monk who left his Caucasian retreat to roam
among the mountains. As usual with Lermontov, the poem

combined pedestrian statements with marvelous melting fata morgana effects. It was of goodly length, and its seven hundred and fifty rather monotonous lines were generously spread by Lenski over a mere four slides (a fifth I had clumsily broken just before the performance).

Fire-hazard considerations had led one to select for the show an obsolete nursery in a corner of which stood a columnar water heater, painted a bronzy brown, and a webfooted bath, which, for the occasion, had been chastely sheeted. The close-drawn window curtains prevented one from seeing the yard below, the stacks of birch logs, and the yellow walls of the gloomy annex containing the stables (part of which had been converted into a two-car garage). Despite the ejection of an ancient wardrobe and a couple of trunks, this depressing back room, with the magic lantern installed at one end and transverse rows of chairs, hassocks, and settees arranged for a score of spectators (including Lenski's fiancée, and three or four governesses, not counting our own Mademoiselle and Miss Greenwood), looked jammed and felt stuffy. On my left, one of my most fidgety girl cousins, a nebulous little blonde of eleven or so with long, Alice-in-Wonderland hair and a shell-pink complexion, sat so close to me that I felt the slender bone of her hip move against mine every time she shifted in her seat, fingering her locket, or passing the back of her hand between her perfumed hair and the nape of her neck, or knocking her knees together under the rustly silk of her yellow slip, which shone through the lace of her frock. On my right, I had the son of my father's Polish valet, an absolutely motionless boy in a sailor suit; he bore a striking resemblance to the Tsarevich, and by a still more striking coincidence suffered from the same tragic disease—hemophilia—so several times a year a Court carriage would bring a famous physician to our house and wait and wait in the slow, slanting snow, and if one chose the largest of those grayish flakes and kept one's eye upon it as it came down (past the oriel casement through which one peered), one could make out its rather coarse, irregular shape and also its oscillation in flight, making one feel dull and dizzy, dizzy and dull.

The lights went out. Lenski launched upon the opening lines:

> The time—not many years ago;
> The place—a point where meet and flow
> In sisterly embrace the fair
> Aragva and Kurah; right there
> A monastery stood.

The monastery, with its two rivers, dutifully appeared and stayed on, in a lurid trance (if only one swift could have swept over it!), for about two hundred lines, when it was replaced by a Georgian maiden of sorts carrying a pitcher. When the operator withdrew a slide, the picture was whisked off the screen with a peculiar flick, magnification affecting not only the scene displayed, but also the speed of its removal. Otherwise, there was little magic. We were shown conventional peaks instead of Lermontov's romantic mountains, which

> Rose in the glory of the dawn
> Like smoking altars,

and while the young monk was telling a fellow recluse of his struggle with a leopard—

> O, I was awesome to behold!
> Myself a leopard, wild and bold,
> His flaming rage, his yells were mine

—a subdued caterwauling sounded behind me; it might have come from young Rzhevuski, with whom I used to attend dancing classes, or Alec Nitte who was to win some renown a year or two later for poltergeist phenomena, or one of my cousins. Gradually, as Lenski's reedy voice went on and on, I became aware that, with a few exceptions—such as, perhaps, Samuel Rosoff, a sensitive schoolmate of mine—the audience was secretly scoffing at the performance, and that afterward I would have to cope with various insulting remarks. I felt a quiver of acute pity for Lenski—for the meek folds at the back of his shaven head, for his pluck, for the nervous move-ments of his pointer, over which, in cold, kittenish paw-play, the colors would sometimes slip, when he brought it too close to the screen. Toward the end, the monotony of the proceed-ings became quite unbearable; the flustered operator could not find the fourth slide, having got it mixed up with the used ones, and while Lenski patiently waited in the dark, some of the spectators started to project the black shadows of their raised hands upon the frightened white screen, and presently, one ribald and agile boy (could it be I after all—the Hyde of my Jekyll?) managed to silhouette his foot, which, of course, started some boisterous competition. When at last the slide was found and flashed onto the screen, I was reminded of a journey, in my early childhood, through the long, dark St. Gothard Tunnel, which our train entered during a thun-derstorm, but it was all over when we emerged, and then

> Blue, green and orange, wonderstruck
> With its own loveliness and luck,
> Across a crag a rainbow fell
> And captured there a poised gazelle.

I should add that during this and the following, still more crowded, still more awful Sunday afternoon sessions, I was haunted by the reverberations of certain family tales I had heard. In the early eighties, my maternal grandfather, Ivan

Rukavishnikov, not finding for his sons any private school to his liking, had created an academy of his own by hiring a dozen of the finest professors available and assembling a score of boys for several terms of free education in the halls of his St. Petersburg house (No. 10, Admiralty Quay). The venture was not a success. Those friends of his whose sons he wanted to consort with his own were not always compliant, and of the boys he did get, many proved disappointing. I formed a singularly displeasing image of him, exploring schools for his obstinate purpose, his sad and strange eyes, so familiar to me from photographs, seeking out the best-looking boys among the best scholars. He is said to have actually paid needy parents in order to muster companions for his two sons. Little as our tutor's naïve lantern-slide shows had to do with Rukavishnikovian extravaganzas, my mental association of the two enterprises did not help me to put up with Lenski's making a fool and a bore of himself, so I was happy when, after three more performances ("The Bronze Horseman" by Pushkin; "Don Quixote"; and "Africa—the Land of Marvels"), my mother acceded to my frantic supplications and the whole business was dropped.

Now that I come to think of it, how tawdry and tumid they looked, those jellylike pictures, projected upon the damp linen screen (moisture was supposed to make them blossom more richly), but, on the other hand, what loveliness the glass slides as such revealed when simply held between finger and thumb and raised to the light—translucent miniatures, pocket wonderlands, neat little worlds of hushed luminous hues! In later years, I rediscovered the same precise and silent beauty at the radiant bottom of a microscope's magic shaft. In the glass of the slide, meant for projection, a landscape was reduced, and this fired one's fancy; under the microscope, an insect's organ was magnified for cool study. There is, it would seem, in the dimensional scale of the world a kind of delicate meeting place between imagination and knowledge, a point, arrived at by diminishing large things and enlarging small ones, that is intrinsically artistic.

4

Considering how versatile Lenski appeared to be, how thoroughly he could explain anything related to our school studies, his constant tribulations at the university came as something of a surprise. Their cause, it transpired eventually, was his complete lack of aptitude for the financial and political problems he so stubbornly tackled. I recall the jitters he was in when he had to take one of his most important final examinations. I was as worried as he and, just before the pending event, could not resist eavesdropping at the door of the room where my father, upon Lenski's urgent request, gave him a private rehearsal by testing his knowledge of Charles Gide's *Principles of Political Economy*. Thumbing the leaves of the book, my father might inquire, for instance: "What is the cause of value?" or: "What are the differences between the banknote and paper money?" and Lenski would eagerly clear his throat—and then remain perfectly silent, as if he had expired. After a while, he ceased to produce even that brisk little cough of his, and the intervals of silence were punctuated only by my father's drumming upon the table, except that once, in a spurt of rapid and hopeful remonstration, the sufferer suddenly exclaimed: "This question is not in the book, sir!"—but it was. Finally my father sighed, closed the textbook, gently but audibly, and remarked: "*Golubchik* [my dear fellow], you cannot but fail—you simply don't know a thing." "I disagree with you there," retorted Lenski, not without dignity. Sitting as stiffly as if he were stuffed, he was driven in our car to the university, remained there till dusk, came back in a sleigh, in a heap, in a snowstorm, and in silent despair went up to his room.

Toward the end of his stay with us, he married and went away on a honeymoon to the Caucasus, to Lermontov's mountains, and then came back to us for another winter. During his absence, in the summer of 1913, a Swiss tutor, Monsieur Noyer, took over. He was a sturdily built man, with a bristly mustache, and he read us Rostand's *Cyrano de Bergerac,* mouthing every line most lusciously and changing his voice from flute to bassoon, according to the characters he mimed. At tennis, when he was server, he would firmly stand on the back line, with his thick legs, in wrinkled nankeens, wide apart, and would abruptly bend them at the knees as he gave the ball a tremendous but singularly inefficient whack.

When Lenski, in the spring of 1914, left us for good, we had a young man from a Volgan province. He was a charming fellow of gentle birth, a fair tennis player, an excellent horseman; on such accomplishments he was greatly relieved to rely, since, at that late date, neither my brother nor I needed much the educational help that an optimistic patron of his had promised my parents the wretch could give us. In the course of our very first colloquy he casually informed me that Dickens had written *Uncle Tom's Cabin,* which led to a pounce bet on my part, winning me his knuckle-duster. After that he was careful not to refer to any literary character or subject in my presence. He was very poor and a strange, dusty and etherish, not altogether unpleasant smell came from his faded university uniform. He had beautiful manners, a sweet temper, an unforgettable handwriting, all thorns and bristles (the like of which I have seen only in the letters from madmen, that, alas, I sometimes receive since the year of grace 1958), and an unlimited fund of obscene stories (which he fed me *sub rosa* in a dreamy, velvety voice, without using one gross expression) about his pals and *poules,* and also about various relations of ours, one of whom, a fashionable lady, almost twice his age, he soon married only to get rid of her—during his subsequent career in Lenin's administration—by bundling her off to a labor camp, where she perished. The more I think of that man, the more I believe that he was completely insane.

I did not quite lose track of Lenski. On a loan from his father-in-law, he started, while still with us, some fantastic business that involved the buying up and exploiting of various inventions. It would be neither kind nor fair to say that he passed them off as his own; but he adopted them and talked about them with a warmth and tenderness which hinted at something like a natural fatherhood—an emotional attitude on his part with no facts in support and no fraud in view. One day, he proudly invited all of us to try out with our car a new type of pavement he was responsible for, composed of (so far as I can make out that strange gleam through the dimness of time) a weird weave of metallic strips. The outcome was a puncture. He was consoled, however, by the purchase of another hot thing: the blueprint of what he called an "electroplane," which looked like an old Blériot but had—and here I quote him again—a "voltaic" motor. It flew only in his dreams—and mine. During the war, he launched a miracle horse food in the form of *galette*-like flat cakes (he would nibble some himself and offer bites to friends), but most horses stuck to their oats. He trafficked in a number of other patents, all of them crazy, and was deep in debt when he inherited a small fortune through his father-in-law's death. This must have been in the beginning of 1918 because, I remember, he wrote to us (we were stranded in the Yalta region) offering us money and every kind of assist-

ance. The inheritance he promptly invested in an amusement park on the East Crimean coast, and took no end of
trouble to get a good orchestra and build a roller-skating
rink of some special wood, and set up fountains and cascades
illumed by red and green bulbs. In 1919, the Bolsheviks came
and turned off the lights, and Lenski fled to France; the last
I heard of him was in the twenties, when he was said to be
earning a precarious living on the Riviera by painting pictures on seashells and stones. I do not know—and would
rather not imagine—what happened to him during the Nazi
invasion of France. Notwithstanding some of his oddities, he
was, really, a very pure, very decent human being, whose
private principles were as strict as his grammar and whose
bracing *diktantï* I recall with joy: *kolokololiteyshchiki pere-
kolotili vïkarabkavshihsya vïhuholey,* "the church-bell casters
slaughtered the desmans that had scrambled out." Many years
later, at the American Museum of Natural History in New
York, I happened to quote that tongue twister to a zoologist
who had asked me if Russian was as difficult as commonly
supposed. We met again several months later and he said:
"You know, I've been thinking a lot about those Muscovite
muskrats: *why* were they said to have scrambled out? Had
they been hibernating or hiding, or what?"

5

In thinking of my successive tutors, I am concerned less
with the queer dissonances they introduced into my young
life than with the essential stability and completeness of that
life. I witness with pleasure the supreme achievement of
memory, which is the masterly use it makes of innate harmonies when gathering to its fold the suspended and wandering tonalities of the past. I like to imagine, in consummation

and resolution of those jangling chords, something as endur-
ing, in retrospect, as the long table that on summer birthdays
and namedays used to be laid for afternoon chocolate out of
doors, in an alley of birches, limes and maples at its debouch-
ment on the smooth-sanded space of the garden proper that
separated the park and the house. I see the tablecloth and
the faces of seated people sharing in the animation of light
and shade beneath a moving, a fabulous foliage, exaggerated,
no doubt, by the same faculty of impassioned commemoration, of ceaseless return, that makes me always approach that
banquet table from the outside, from the depth of the park—
not from the house—as if the mind, in order to go back
thither, had to do so with the silent steps of a prodigal, faint
with excitement. Through a tremulous prism, I distinguish
the features of relatives and familiars, mute lips serenely
moving in forgotten speech. I see the steam of the chocolate
and the plates of blueberry tarts. I note the small helicopter
of a revolving samara that gently descends upon the tablecloth, and, lying across the table, an adolescent girl's bare
arm indolently extended as far as it will go, with its tur-
quoise-veined underside turned up to the flaky sunlight, the
palm open in lazy expectancy of something—perhaps the nutcracker. In the place where my current tutor sits, there is a
changeful image, a succession of fade-ins and fade-outs; the
pulsation of my thought mingles with that of the leaf shadows
and turns Ordo into Max and Max into Lenski and Lenski
into the schoolmaster, and the whole array of trembling trans-
formations is repeated. And then, suddenly, just when the
colors and outlines settle at last to their various duties—smiling, frivolous duties—some knob is touched and a torrent of
sounds comes to life: voices speaking all together, a walnut
cracked, the click of a nutcracker carelessly passed, thirty
human hearts drowning mine with their regular beats; the

sough and sigh of a thousand trees, the local concord of loud summer birds, and, beyond the river, behind the rhythmic trees, the confused and enthusiastic hullabaloo of bathing young villagers, like a background of wild applause.

9

1

I HAVE before me a large bedraggled scrapbook, bound in black cloth. It contains old documents, including diplomas, drafts, diaries, identity cards, penciled notes, and some printed matter, which had been in my mother's meticulous keeping in Prague until her death there, but then, between 1939 and 1961, went through various vicissitudes. With the aid of those papers and my own recollections, I have composed the following short biography of my father.

Vladimir Dmitrievich Nabokov, jurist, publicist and statesman, son of Dmitri Nikolaevich Nabokov, Minister of Justice, and Baroness Maria von Korff, was born on July 20, 1870, at Tsarskoe Selo near St. Petersburg, and was killed by an assassin's bullet on March 28, 1922, in Berlin. Till the age of thirteen he was educated at home by French and English governesses and by Russian and German tutors; from one of the latter he caught and passed on to me the *passio et morbus aureliani*. In the autumn of 1883, he started to attend the "Gymnasium" (corresponding to a combination of American "high school" and "junior college") on the then Gagarin Street (presumably renamed in the twenties by the shortsighted Soviets). His desire to excel was overwhelming. One winter night, being behind with a set task and preferring pneumonia to ridicule at the blackboard, he exposed himself to the polar frost, with the hope of a timely sickness, by sitting in nothing but his nightshirt at the open window (it gave on the Palace Square and its moon-polished pillar); on the morrow he still enjoyed perfect health, and, undeservedly, it was the dreaded teacher who happened to be laid up. At sixteen, in May 1887, he completed the Gymnasium course, with a gold medal, and studied law at the St. Petersburg University, graduating in January 1891. He continued his studies in Germany (mainly at Halle). Thirty years later, a fellow student of his, with whom he had gone for a bicycle trip in the Black Forest, sent my widowed mother the *Madame Bovary* volume which my father had had with him at the time and on the flyleaf of which he had written "The unsurpassed pearl of French literature"—a judgment that still holds.

On November 14 (a date scrupulously celebrated every subsequent year in our anniversary-conscious family), 1897, he married Elena Ivanovna Rukavishnikov, the twenty-one-year-old daughter of a country neighbor with whom he had six children (the first was a stillborn boy).

In 1895 he had been made Junior Gentleman of the Chamber. From 1896 to 1904 he lectured on criminal law at the Imperial School of Jurisprudence (*Pravovedenie*) in St. Petersburg. Gentlemen of the Chamber were supposed to ask permission of the "Court Minister" before performing a public act. This permission my father did not ask, naturally, when publishing in the review *Pravo* his celebrated article "The Blood Bath of Kishinev" in which he condemned the part played by the police in promoting the Kishinev pogrom of 1903. By imperial decree he was deprived of his court title in January 1905, after which he severed all connection with the Tsar's government and resolutely plunged into antidespotic politics, while continuing his juristic labors. From 1905 to 1915 he was president of the Russian section of the International Criminology Association and at conferences in Holland amused himself and amazed his audience by orally translating, when needed, Russian and English speeches into German and French and vice-versa. He was eloquently against capital punishment. Unswervingly he conformed to his principles in private and public matters. At an official banquet in 1904 he refused to drink the Tsar's health. He is said to have coolly advertised in the papers his court uniform for sale. From 1906 to 1917 he co-edited with I. V. Hessen and A. I. Kaminka one of the few liberal dailies in Russia, the *Rech* ("Speech") as well as the jurisprudential review *Pravo*. Politically he was a "Kadet," i.e. a member of the KD (*Konstitutsionno-demokraticheskaya partiya*), later renamed more aptly the party of the People's Freedom (*partiya Narodnoy Svobodï*). With his keen sense of humor he would have been tremendously tickled by the helpless though vicious hash Soviet lexicographers have made of his opinions and achievements in their rare biographical comments on him. In 1906 he was elected to the First Russian Parliament (*Pervaya Duma*), a humane and heroic institution, predominantly liberal (but which ignorant foreign publicists, infected by Soviet propaganda, often confuse with the ancient "boyar dumas"!). There he made several splendid speeches with nationwide repercussions. When less than a year later the Tsar dissolved the Duma, a number of members, including my father (who, as a photograph taken at the Finland Station shows, carried his railway ticket tucked under the band of his hat), repaired to Vyborg for an illegal session. In May 1908, he began a prison term of three months in somewhat belated punishment for the revolutionary mani-

festo he and his group had issued at Vyborg. "Did V. get any
'Egerias' [Speckled Woods] this summer?" he asks in one of
his secret notes from prison, which, through a bribed guard,
and a faithful friend (Kaminka), were transmitted to my
mother at Vyra. "Tell him that all I see in the prison yard
are Brimstones and Cabbage Whites." After his release he
was forbidden to participate in public elections, but (one of
the paradoxes so common under the Tsars) could freely work
in the bitterly liberal *Rech,* a task to which he devoted up
to nine hours a day. In 1913, he was fined by the government
the token sum of one hundred rubles (about as many dollars
of the present time) for his reportage from Kiev, where after
a stormy trial Beylis was found innocent of murdering a
Christian boy for "ritual" purposes: justice and public opinion could still prevail occasionally in old Russia; they had
only five years to go. He was mobilized soon after the beginning of World War One and sent to the front. Eventually
he was attached to the General Staff in St. Petersburg. Military ethics prevented him from taking an active part in the
first turmoil of the liberal revolution of March 1917. From
the very start, History seems to have been anxious of depriving him of a full opportunity to reveal his great gifts of states-
manship in a Russian republic of the Western type. In 1917,
during the initial stage of the Provisional Government—that
is, while the Kadets still took part in it—he occupied in the
Council of Ministers the responsible but inconspicuous position of Executive Secretary. In the winter of 1917–18, he was
elected to the Constituent Assembly, only to be arrested by
energetic Bolshevist sailors when it was disbanded. The
November Revolution had already entered upon its gory
course, its police was already active, but in those days the
chaos of orders and counterorders sometimes took our side:
my father followed a dim corridor, saw an open door at the

end, walked out into a side street and made his way to the Crimea with a knapsack he had ordered his valet Osip to bring him to a secluded corner and a package of caviar sandwiches which good Nikolay Andreevich, our cook, had added of his own accord. From mid-1918 to the beginning of 1919, in an interval between two occupations by the Bolshevists, and in constant friction with trigger-happy elements in Denikin's army, he was Minister of Justice ("of minimal justice" as he used to say wryly) in one of the Regional Governments, the Crimean one. In 1919, he went into voluntary exile, living first in London, then in Berlin where, in collaboration with Hessen, he edited the liberal émigré daily *Rul'* ("Rudder") until his assassination in 1922 by a sinister ruffian whom, during World War Two, Hitler made administrator of émigré Russian affairs.

He wrote prolifically, mainly on political and criminological subjects. He knew *à fond* the prose and poetry of several countries, knew by heart hundreds of verses (his favorite Russian poets were Pushkin, Tyutchev, and Fet—he published a fine essay on the latter), was an authority on Dickens, and, besides Flaubert, prized highly Stendhal, Balzac and Zola, three detestable mediocrities from *my* point of view. He used to confess that the creation of a story or poem, *any* story or poem, was to him as incomprehensible a miracle as the construction of an electric machine. On the other hand, he had no trouble at all in writing on juristic and political matters. He had a correct, albeit rather monotonous style, which today, despite all those old-world metaphors of classical education and grandiloquent clichés of Russian journalism has —at least to my jaded ear—an attractive gray dignity of its own, in extraordinary contrast (as if belonging to some older and poorer relative) to his colorful, quaint, often poetical, and sometimes ribald, everyday utterances. The preserved drafts of some of his proclamations (beginning *"Grazhdane!"*, meaning *"Citoyens!"*) and editorials are penned in a copy-book-slanted, beautifully sleek, unbelievably regular hand, almost free of corrections, a purity, a certainty, a mind-and-matter cofunction that I find amusing to compare to my own mousy hand and messy drafts, to the massacrous revisions and rewritings, and new revisions, of the very lines in which I am taking two hours now to describe a two-minute run of his flawless handwriting. His drafts were the fair copies of immediate thought. In this manner, he wrote, with phenom-enal ease and rapidity (sitting uncomfortably at a child's desk in the classroom of a mournful palace) the text of the abdica-tion of Grand Duke Mihail (next in line of succession after the Tsar had renounced his and his son's throne). No wonder he was also an admirable speaker, an "English style" cool orator, who eschewed the meat-chopping gesture and rhetor-ical bark of the demagogue, and here, too, the ridiculous cacologist I am, when not having a typed sheet before me, has inherited nothing.

Only recently have I read for the first time his important *Sbornik statey po ugolovnomu pravu* (a collection of articles on criminal law), published in 1904 in St. Petersburg, of which a very rare, possibly unique copy (formerly the prop-erty of a "Mihail Evgrafovich Hodunov," as stamped in violet ink on the flyleaf) was given me by a kind traveler, Andrew Field, who bought it in a secondhand bookshop, on his visit to Russia in 1961. It is a volume of 316 pages containing nineteen papers. In one of these ("Carnal Crimes," written in 1902), my father discusses, rather prophetically in a certain odd sense, cases (in London) "of little girls *à l'âge le plus tendre* (*v nezhneyshem vozraste*), i.e. from eight to twelve years, being sacrificed to lechers (*slastolyubtsam*)." In the same essay he reveals a very liberal and "modern" approach to various abnormal practices, incidentally coining a convenient Russian word for "homosexual": *ravnopolïy.*

It would be impossible to list the literally thousands of his articles in various periodicals, such as *Rech* or *Pravo.* In a later chapter I speak of his historically interesting book about a wartime semiofficial visit to England. Some of his memoirs pertaining to the years 1917–1919 have appeared in the *Arhiv russkoy revolyutsii,* published by Hessen in Berlin. On January 16, 1920, he delivered a lecture at King's College, London, on "Soviet Rule and Russia's Future," which was published a week later in the Supplement to *The New Commonwealth,* No. 15 (neatly pasted in my mother's album). In the spring of the same year I learned by heart most of it when preparing to speak against Bolshevism at a Union debate in Cambridge; the (victorious) apologist was a man from *The Manchester Guardian;* I forget his name, but recall drying up utterly after reciting what I had memorized, and that was my first and last political speech. A couple of months before my father's death, the émigré review *Teatr i zhizn'* ("Theater and Life") started to serialize his boyhood recollections (he and I are overlapping now—too briefly). I find therein excellently described the terrible tantrums of his pedantic master of Latin at the Third Gymnasium, as well as my father's very early, and lifelong, passion for the opera: he must have heard practically every first-rate European singer between 1880 and 1922, and although unable to play anything (except very majestically the first chords of the "Ruslan" overture) remembered every note of his favorite operas. Along this vibrant string a melodious gene that missed me glides through my father from the sixteenth-century organist Wolfgang Graun to my son.

2

I was eleven years old when my father decided that the tutoring I had had, and was still having, at home might be profitably supplemented by my attending Tenishev School. This school, one of the most remarkable in St. Petersburg, was a comparatively young institution of a much more modern and liberal type than the ordinary Gymnasium, to which general category it belonged. Its course of study, consisting of sixteen "semesters" (eight Gymnasium classes), would be roughly equivalent in America to the last six years of school plus the first two years of college. Upon my admittance, in January 1911, I found myself in the third "semester," or in the beginning of the eighth grade according to the American system.

School was taught from the fifteenth of September to the twenty-fifth of May, with a couple of interruptions: a two-week intersemestral gap—to make place, as it were, for the huge Christmas tree that touched with its star the pale-green ceiling of our prettiest drawing room—and a one-week Easter vacation, during which painted eggs enlivened the breakfast table. Since snow and frost lasted from October well into April, no wonder the mean of my school memories is definitely hiemal.

When Ivan the first (who vanished one day) or Ivan the second (who was to see the time when I would send him forth on romantic errands) came to wake me around 8 A.M., the outside world was still cowled in brown hyperborean gloom. The electric light in the bedroom had a sullen, harsh, jaundiced tinge that made my eyes smart. Leaning my singing ear on my hand and propping my elbow on the pillow, I would force myself to prepare ten pages of unfinished homework. On my bed table, next to a stocky lamp with two bronze lion heads, stood a small unconventional clock: an upright container of crystal within which black-numbered, ivory-white, pagelike lamels flipped from right to left, each stopping for a minute the way commercial stills did on the old cinema screen. I gave myself ten minutes to tintype the text in my brain (nowadays it would take me two hours!) and, say, a dozen minutes to tub, dress (with Ivan's help), scutter downstairs, and swallow a cup of tepid cocoa from the surface of which I plucked off by the center a round of wrinkled brown skin. Mornings were botched, and such things as the lessons in boxing and fencing that a wonderful rubbery Frenchman, Monsieur Loustalot, used to give me had to be discontinued.

He still came, almost daily, however, to spar or fence with my father. I would dash, with my fur coat half on, through the green drawing room (where an odor of fir, hot wax and tangerines would linger long after Christmas had gone), toward the library, from which came a medley of stamping and scraping sounds. There, I would find my father, a big, robust man, looking still bigger in his white training suit, thrusting and parrying, while his agile instructor added brisk exclamations (*"Battez!" "Rompez!"*) to the click-clink of the foils.

Panting a little, my father would remove the convex fencing mask from his perspiring pink face to kiss me good morning. The place combined pleasantly the scholarly and the athletic, the leather of books and the leather of boxing gloves. Fat armchairs stood along the book-lined walls. An elaborate "punching ball" affair purchased in England—four steel posts supporting the board from which the pear-shaped striking bag hung—gleamed at the end of the spacious room. The purpose of this apparatus, especially in connection with the machine-gunlike ra-ta-ta of its bag, was questioned and the butler's explanation of it reluctantly accepted as true, by some heavily armed street fighters who came in through the window in 1917. When the Soviet Revolution made it imperative for us to leave St. Petersburg, that library disintegrated, but queer little remnants of it kept cropping up abroad. Some twelve years later, in Berlin, I picked up from a bookstall one such waif, bearing my father's *ex libris*. Very fittingly, it turned out to be *The War of the Worlds* by Wells. And after another decade had elapsed, I discovered one day in the New York Public Library, indexed under my father's name, a copy of the neat catalogue he had had privately printed when the phantom books listed therein still stood, ruddy and sleek, on his shelves.

3

He would replace his mask and go on with his stamping and lunging while I hurried back the way I had come. After the warmth in the entrance hall, where logs were crackling in the large fireplace, the outdoor air gave an icy shock to one's lungs. I would ascertain which of our two cars, the Benz or the Wolseley, was there to take me to school. The first, a gray landaulet, manned by Volkov, a gentle, pale-faced chauffeur, was the older one. Its lines had seemed positively dynamic in comparison with those of the insipid, noseless and noiseless, electric coupé that had preceded it; but, in its turn, it acquired an old-fashioned, top-heavy look, with a sadly shrunken bonnet, as soon as the comparatively long, black English limousine came to share its garage.

To get the newer car was to start the day zestfully. Pirogov, the second chauffeur, was a very short, pudgy fellow with a russet complexion that matched well the shade of the furs he wore over his corduroy suit and the orange-brown of his leggings. When some hitch in the traffic forced him to apply the brakes (which he did by suddenly distending himself in a peculiar springy manner), or when I bothered him by trying to communicate with him through the squeaky and not very efficient speaking tube, the back of his thick neck seen through the glass partition would turn crimson. He frankly preferred to drive the hardy convertible Opel that we used in the country during three or four seasons, and would do so at sixty miles per hour (to realize how dashing that was in 1912, one should take into account the present inflation of speed): indeed, the very essence of summer freedom—schoolless untownishness—remains connected in my mind with the motor's extravagant roar that the opened muffler would release on the long, lone highway. When in the second year of World War One Pirogov was mobilized, he was replaced by dark, wild-eyed Tsiganov, a former racing ace, who had participated in various contests both in Russia and abroad and had had several ribs broken in a bad smash in Belgium. Later, sometime in 1917, soon after my father resigned from Kerenski's cabinet, Tsiganov decided—notwithstanding my father's energetic protests—to save the powerful Wolseley car from possible confiscation by dismantling it and distributing its parts over hiding places known only to him. Still later, in the gloom of a tragic autumn, with the Bolshevists gaining the upper hand, one of Kerenski's aides asked my father for a sturdy car the premier might use if forced to leave in a hurry; but our debile old Benz would not do and the Wolseley had embarrassingly vanished, and if I treasure the recollection of that request (recently denied by my eminent friend, but certainly made by his aide-de-camp), it is only from a compositional viewpoint—because of the amusing thematic echo of Christina von Korff's part in the Varennes episode of 1791.

Although heavy snowfalls were much more usual in St. Petersburg than, say, around Boston, the several automobiles that circulated among the numerous sleighs of the town before World War One somehow never seemed to get into the kind of hideous trouble that modern cars get into on a good New England white Christmas. Many strange forces had been involved in the building of the city. One is led to suppose that the arrangement of its snows—tidy drifts along the sidewalks and a smooth solid spread on the octangular wood blocks of the pavement—was arrived at by some unholy cooperation between the geometry of the streets and the physics of the snow clouds. Anyway, driving to school never took more than a quarter of an hour. Our house was No. 47 in Morskaya Street. Then came Prince Oginski's (No. 45), then the Italian Embassy (No. 43), then the German Embassy (No. 41), and then the vast Maria Square, after which the house numbers continued to dwindle. There was a small public park on the north side of the square. In one of its linden trees an ear and a finger had been found one day— remnants of a terrorist whose hand had slipped while he was arranging a lethal parcel in his room on the other side of the square. Those same trees (a pattern of silver filigree in a mother-of-pearl mist out of which the bronze dome of St. Isaac's arose in the background) had also seen children shot down at random from the branches into which they had climbed in a vain attempt to escape the mounted gendarmes who were quelling the First Revolution (1905–06). Quite a few little stories like these were attached to squares and streets in St. Petersburg.

Upon reaching Nevski Avenue, one followed it for a long stretch, during which it was a pleasure to overtake with no effort some cloaked guardsman in his light sleigh drawn by a pair of black stallions snorting and speeding along under the bright blue netting that prevented lumps of hard snow from flying into the passenger's face. A street on the left side with a lovely name—Karavannaya (the Street of Caravans)—took one past an unforgettable toyshop. Next came the Cinizelli Circus (famous for its wrestling tournaments). Finally, after crossing an ice-bound canal one drove up to the gates of Tenishev School in Mohovaya Street (the Street of Mosses).

4

Belonging, as he did by choice, to the great classless intelligentsia of Russia, my father thought it right to have me attend a school that was distinguished by its democratic principles, its policy of nondiscrimination in matters of rank, race and creed, and its up-to-date educational methods. Apart from that, Tenishev School differed in nothing from any other school in time or space. As in all schools, the boys tolerated some teachers and loathed others, and, as in all schools, there was a constant interchange of obscene quips and erotic information. Being good at games, I would not have found the whole business too dismal if only my teachers had been less intent in trying to save my soul.

They accused me of not conforming to my surroundings; of "showing off" (mainly by peppering my Russian papers with English and French terms, which came naturally to me); of refusing to touch the filthy wet towels in the washroom; of fighting with my knuckles instead of using the slaplike swing with the underside of the fist adopted by Russian scrappers. The headmaster who knew little about games, though greatly approving of their consociative virtues, was suspicious of my always keeping goal in soccer "instead of running about with the other players." Another thing that provoked resentment was my driving to and from school in an automobile and not traveling by streetcar or horsecab as the other boys, good little democrats, did. With his face all screwed up in a grimace of disgust, one teacher suggested to me that the least I could do was to have the automobile stop two or three blocks away, so that my schoolmates might be spared the sight of a liveried chauffeur doffing his cap. It was as if the school were allowing me to carry about a dead rat by the tail with the understanding that I would not dangle it under people's noses.

The worst situation, however, arose from the fact that even then I was intensely averse to joining movements or associations of any kind. I enraged the kindest and most well-meaning among my teachers by declining to participate in extracurricular group work—debating societies with the solemn election of officers and the reading of reports on historical questions, and, in the higher grades, more ambitious gatherings for the discussion of current political events. The constant pressure upon me to belong to some group or other never broke my resistance but led to a state of tension that was hardly alleviated by everybody harping upon the example set by my father.

My father was, indeed, a very active man, but as often happens with the children of famous fathers, I viewed his activities through a prism of my own, which split into many enchanting colors the rather austere light my teachers glimpsed. In connection with his varied interests—criminological, legislative, political, editorial, philanthropic—he had to attend many committee meetings, and these were often held at our house. That such a meeting was forthcoming might be always deduced from a peculiar sound in the far end of our large and resonant entrance hall. There, in a recess under the marble staircase, our *shveitsar* (doorman) would be busy sharpening pencils when I came home from school. For that purpose he used a bulky old-fashioned machine, with a whirring wheel, the handle of which he rapidly turned with one hand while holding with the other a pencil inserted into a lateral orifice. For years he had been the tritest type of "faithful retainer" imaginable, full of quaint wit and wisdom, with a dashing way of smoothing out, right and left, his mustache with two fingers, and a slight fried-fish smell always hanging about him: it originated in his mysterious basement quarters, where he had an obese wife and twins—a schoolboy of my age and a haunting, sloppy little aurora with a blue squint and coppery locks; but that pencil chore must have considerably embittered poor old Ustin—for I can readily sympathize with him, I who write my stuff only in very sharp pencil, keep bouquets of B 3's in vaselets around me, and rotate a hundred times a day the handle of the instrument (clamped to the table edge), which so speedily accumulates so much tawny-brown shag in its little drawer. It later turned out that he had long got into touch with the Tsar's secret police—tyros, of course, in comparison to Dzerzhinski's or Yagoda's men, but still fairly bothersome. As early as 1906, for instance, the police, suspecting my father of conducting clandestine meetings at Vyra, had engaged the services of Ustin who thereupon begged my father, under some pretext that I cannot recall, but with the deep purpose of spying on whatever went on, to take him to the country that summer as an extra footman (he had been pantry boy in the Rukavishnikov household); and it was he, omnipresent Ustin, who in the winter of 1917–18 heroically led representatives of the victorious Soviets up to my father's study on the second floor, and from there, through a music room and my mother's boudoir, to the southeast corner room where I was born, and to the niche in the wall, to the tiaras of colored fire, which formed an adequate recompense for the Swallowtail he had once caught for me.

Around eight in the evening, the hall would house an accumulation of greatcoats and overshoes. In a committee room, next to the library, at a long baize-covered table (where those beautifully pointed pencils had been laid out), my father and his colleagues would gather to discuss some phase of their opposition to the Tsar. Above the hubbub of voices, a tall clock in a dark corner would break into Westminster chimes; and beyond the committee room were mysterious depths—storerooms, a winding staircase, a pantry of sorts—where my cousin Yuri and I used to pause with drawn pistols on our way to Texas and where one night the police placed a fat, blear-eyed spy who went laboriously down on his knees before our librarian, Lyudmila Borisovna Grinberg, when discovered. But how on earth could I discuss all this with schoolteachers?

5

The reactionary press never ceased to attack my father's party, and I had got quite used to the more or less vulgar cartoons which appeared from time to time—my father and Milyukov handing over Saint Russia on a plate to World Jewry and that sort of thing. But one day, in the winter of 1911 I believe, the most powerful of the Rightist newspapers employed a shady journalist to concoct a scurrilous piece containing insinuations that my father could not let pass. Since the well-known rascality of the actual author of the article made him "non-duelable" (*neduelesposobnïy*, as the Russian dueling code had it), my father called out the somewhat less disreputable editor of the paper in which the article had appeared.

A Russian duel was a much more serious affair than the conventional Parisian variety. It took the editor several days to make up his mind whether or not to accept the challenge. On the last of these days, a Monday, I went, as usual, to school. In consequence of my not reading the newspapers, I was absolutely ignorant of the whole thing. Sometime during the day I became aware that a magazine opened at a certain page was passing from hand to hand and causing titters. A well-timed swoop put me in possession of what proved to be the latest copy of a cheap weekly containing a lurid account of my father's challenge, with idiotic comments on the choice of weapons he had offered his foe. Sly digs were taken at his having reverted to a feudal custom that he had criticized in his own writings. There was also a good deal about the number of his servants and the number of his suits. I found out that he had chosen for second his brother-in-law, Admiral Kolomeytsev, a hero of the Japanese war. During the battle of Tsushima, this uncle of mine, then holding the rank of captain, had managed to bring his destroyer alongside the burning flagship and save the naval commander-in-chief.

After classes, I ascertained that the magazine belonged to one of my best friends. I charged him with betrayal and mockery. In the ensuing fight, he crashed backward into a desk, catching his foot in a joint and breaking his ankle. He was laid up for a month, but gallantly concealed from his family and from our teachers my share in the matter.

The pang of seeing him carried downstairs was lost in my general misery. For some reason or other, no car came to fetch me that day, and during the cold, dreary, incredibly slow drive home in a hired sleigh I had ample time to think matters over. Now I understood why, the day before, my mother had been so little with me and had not come down to dinner. I also understood what special coaching Thernant,

a still finer *maître d'armes* than Loustalot, had of late been
giving my father. What would his adversary choose, I kept
asking myself—the blade or the bullet? Or had the choice
already been made? Carefully, I took the beloved, the familiar, the richly alive image of my father at fencing and tried to
transfer that image, minus the mask and the padding, to the
dueling ground, in some barn or riding school. I visualized
him and his adversary, both bare-chested, black-trousered, in
furious battle, their energetic movements marked by that
strange awkwardness which even the most elegant swordsmen
cannot avoid in a real encounter. The picture was so repulsive, so vividly did I feel the ripeness and nakedness of a
madly pulsating heart about to be pierced, that I found myself
hoping for what seemed momentarily a more abstract weapon.
But soon I was in even deeper distress.

As the sleigh crept along Nevski Avenue, where blurry
lights swam in the gathering dusk, I thought of the heavy
black Browning my father kept in the upper right-hand
drawer of his desk. I knew that pistol as well as I knew all
the other, more salient, things in his study; the *objets d'art*
of crystal or veined stone, fashionable in those days; the glinting family photographs; the huge, mellowly illumined Peru-
gino; the small, honey-bright Dutch oils; and, right over the
desk, the rose-and-haze pastel portrait of my mother by Bakst:
the artist had drawn her face in three-quarter view, wonderfully bringing out its delicate features—the upward sweep of
the ash-colored hair (it had grayed when she was in her
twenties), the pure curve of the forehead, the dove-blue eyes,
the graceful line of the neck.

When I urged the old, rag-doll-like driver to go faster, he
would merely lean to one side with a special half-circular
movement of his arm, so as to make his horse believe he was
about to produce the short whip he kept in the leg of his

right felt boot; and that would be sufficient for the shaggy little hack to make as vague a show of speeding up as the driver had made of getting out his *knutishko*. In the almost hallucinatory state that our snow-muffled ride engendered, I refought all the famous duels a Russian boy knew so well. I saw Pushkin, mortally wounded at the first fire, grimly sit up to discharge his pistol at d'Anthès. I saw Lermontov smile as he faced Martïnov. I saw stout Sobinov in the part of Lenski crash down and send his weapon flying into the orchestra. No Russian writer of any repute had failed to describe *une rencontre*, a hostile meeting, always of course of the classical *duel à volonté* type (not the ludicrous back-to-back-march-face-about-bang-bang performance of movie and cartoon fame). Among several prominent families, there had been tragic deaths on the dueling ground in more or less recent years. Slowly my dreamy sleigh drove up Morskaya Street, and slowly dim silhouettes of duelists advanced upon each other and leveled their pistols and fired—at the crack of dawn, in damp glades of old country estates, on bleak military training grounds, or in the driving snow between two rows of fir trees.

And behind it all there was yet a very special emotional abyss that I was desperately trying to skirt, lest I burst into a tempest of tears, and this was the tender friendship underlying my respect for my father; the charm of our perfect accord; the Wimbledon matches we followed in the London papers; the chess problems we solved; the Pushkin iambics that rolled off his tongue so triumphantly whenever I mentioned some minor poet of the day. Our relationship was marked by that habitual exchange of homespun nonsense, comically garbled words, proposed imitations of supposed intonations, and all those private jokes which are the secret code of happy families. With all that he was extremely strict

in matters of conduct and given to biting remarks when cross
with a child or a servant, but his inherent humanity was too
great to allow his rebuke to Osip for laying out the wrong
shirt to be really offensive, just as a first-hand knowledge of
a boy's pride tempered the harshness of reproval and resulted in sudden forgiveness. Thus I was more puzzled than
pleased one day when upon learning that I had deliberately
slashed my leg just above the knee with a razor (I still bear
the scar) in order to avoid a recitation in class for which
I was unprepared, he seemed unable to work up any real
wrath; and his subsequent admission of a parallel transgres-
sion in his own boyhood rewarded me for not withholding
the truth.

I remembered that summer afternoon (which already then
seemed long ago although actually only four or five years had
passed) when he had burst into my room, grabbed my net,
shot down the veranda steps—and presently was strolling back
holding between finger and thumb the rare and magnificent
female of the Russian Poplar Admirable that he had seen
basking on an aspen leaf from the balcony of his study. I remembered our long bicycle rides along the smooth Luga
highway and the efficient way in which—mighty-calved, knick-
erbockered, tweed-coated, checker-capped—he would accom-
plish the mounting of his high-saddled "Dux," which his
valet would bring up to the porch as if it were a palfrey.
Surveying the state of its polish, my father would pull on his
suede gloves and test under Osip's anxious eye whether the
tires were sufficiently tight. Then he would grip the handlebars, place his left foot on a metallic peg jutting at the rear
end of the frame, push off with his right foot on the other
side of the hind wheel and after three or four such propel-
ments (with the bicycle now set in motion), leisurely translate

his right leg into pedal position, move up his left, and settle down on the saddle.

At last I was home, and immediately upon entering the vestibule I became aware of loud, cheerful voices. With the opportuneness of dream arrangements, my uncle the Admiral was coming downstairs. From the red-carpeted landing above, where an armless Greek woman of marble presided over a malachite bowl for visiting cards, my parents were still speaking to him, and as he came down the steps, he looked up with a laugh and slapped the balustrade with the gloves he had in his hand. I knew at once that there would be no duel, that the challenge had been met by an apology, that all was right. I brushed past my uncle and reached the landing. I saw my mother's serene everyday face, but I could not look at my father. And then it happened: my heart welled in me like that wave on which the *Buynïy* rose when her captain brought her alongside the burning *Suvorov*, and I had no handkerchief, and ten years were to pass before a certain night in 1922, at a public lecture in Berlin, when my father shielded the lecturer (his old friend Milyukov) from the bullets of two Russian Fascists and, while vigorously knocking down one of the assassins, was fatally shot by the other. But no shadow was cast by that future event upon the bright stairs of our St. Petersburg house; the large, cool hand resting on my head did not quaver, and several lines of play in a difficult chess composition were not blended yet on the board.

The author in 1915, St. Petersburg.

10

THE Wild West fiction of Captain Mayne Reid (1818–1883), translated and simplified, was tremendously popular with Russian children at the beginning of this century, long after his American fame had faded. Knowing English, I could savor his *Headless Horseman* in the unabridged original. Two friends swap clothes, hats, mounts, and the wrong man gets murdered—this is the main whorl of its intricate plot. The edition I had (possibly a British one) remains in the stacks of my memory as a puffy book bound in red cloth, with a watery-gray frontispiece, the gloss of which had been gauzed over when the book was new by a leaf of tissue paper. I see this leaf as it disintegrated—at first folded improperly, then torn off—but the frontispiece itself, which no doubt depicted Louise Pointdexter's unfortunate brother (and perhaps a coyote or two, unless I am thinking of *The Death Shot,* another Mayne Reid tale), has been so long exposed to the blaze of my imagination that it is now completely bleached (but miraculously replaced by the *real* thing, as I noted when translating this chapter into Russian in the spring of 1953, and namely, by the view from a ranch you and I rented that year: a cactus-and-yucca waste whence came that morning the plaintive call of a quail—Gambel's Quail, I believe—overwhelming me with a sense of undeserved attainments and rewards).

We shall now meet my cousin Yuri, a thin, sallow-faced boy with a round cropped head and luminous gray eyes. The son of divorced parents, with no tutor to look after him, a town boy with no country home, he was in many respects different from me. He spent his winters in Warsaw, with his father, Baron Evgeniy Rausch von Traubenberg, its military governor, and his summers at Batovo or Vyra, unless taken abroad by his mother, my eccentric Aunt Nina, to dull Central European spas, where she went for long solitary walks leaving him to the care of messenger boys and chambermaids. In the country, Yuri got up late, and I did not see him before my return to lunch, after four or five hours of butterfly hunting. From his earliest boyhood, he was absolutely fearless, but was squeamish and wary of "natural history," could not make himself touch wriggly things, could not endure the amusing emprisoned tickle of a small frog groping about in one's fist like a person, or the discreet, pleasantly cool, rhythmically undulating caress of a caterpillar ascending one's bare shin. He collected little soldiers of painted lead—these meant nothing to me but he knew their uniforms as well as I did different butterflies. He did not play any ball games, was incapable of pitching a stone properly, and could not swim, but had never told me he could not, and one day, as we were trying to cross the river by walking over a jam of pine logs afloat near a sawmill, he nearly got drowned when a particularly slippery bole started to plop and revolve under his feet.

We had first become aware of each other around Christmas 1904 (I was five and a half, he seven), in Wiesbaden: I remember him coming out of a souvenir shop and running toward me with a breloque, an inch-long little pistol of silver, which he was anxious to show me—and suddenly sprawling on the sidewalk but not crying when he picked himself up, unmindful of a bleeding knee and still clutching his minuscule weapon. In the summer of 1909 or 1910, he enthusiastically initiated me into the dramatic possibilities of the Mayne Reid books. He had read them in Russian (being in everything save surname much more Russian than I) and, when looking for a playable plot, was prone to combine them with Fenimore Cooper and his own fiery inventions. I viewed our games with greater detachment and tried to keep to the script. The staging took place generally in the park of Batovo, where the trails were even more tortuous and trappy than those of Vyra. For our mutual manhunts we used spring pistols that ejected, with considerable force, pencil-long sticks (from the brass tips of which we had manfully twisted off the protective rubber suction cups). Later came airguns of various types, which shot wax pellets or small tufted darts, with nonlethal, but often quite painful consequences. In 1912, the impressive mother-of-pearl plated revolver he arrived with was calmly taken away and locked up by my tutor Lenski, but not before we had blown to pieces a shoebox lid (in prelude to the real thing, an ace), which we had been holding up by turns at a gentlemanly distance in a green avenue where a duel was rumored to have been fought many dim years ago. The following summer he was away in Switzerland with his mother—and soon after his death (in 1919), upon revisiting the same hotel and getting the same rooms they had occupied that July, she thrust her hand into the recesses of an armchair in quest of a fallen hairpin and brought up a tiny cuirassier, unhorsed but with bandy legs still compressing an invisible charger.

When he arrived for a week's visit in June 1914 (now six-

teen and a half to my fifteen, and the interval was beginning
to tell), the first thing he did, as soon as we found ourselves
alone in the garden, was to take out casually an "ambered"
cigarette from a smart silver case on the gilt inside of which
he bade me observe the formula $3 \times 4 = 12$ engraved in
memory of the three nights he had spent, at last, with Countess G. He was now in love with an old general's young wife
in Helsingfors and a captain's daughter in Gatchina. I wit-
nessed with a kind of despair every new revelation of his
man-of-the-world style. "Where can I make some rather private calls?" he asked. So I led him past the five poplars and
the old dry well (out of which we had been rope-hauled by
three frightened gardeners only a couple of years before) to
a passage in the servants' wing where the cooing of pigeons
came from an inviting windowsill and where there hung on
the sun-stamped wall the remotest and oldest of our country-
house telephones, a bulky boxlike contraption which had to
be clangorously cranked up to educe a small-voiced operator.
Yuri was now even more relaxed and sociable than the mustanger of former years. Sitting on a deal table against the
wall and dangling his long legs, he chatted with the servants
(something I was not supposed to do, and did not know
how to do)—with an aged footman with sideburns whom I
had never seen grin before or with a kitchen flirt, of whose
bare neck and bold eyes I became aware only then. After
Yuri had concluded his third long-distance conversation (I
noticed with a blend of relief and dismay how awful his
French was), we walked down to the village grocery which
otherwise I never dreamed of visiting, let alone buying there
a pound of black-and-white sunflower seeds. Throughout our
return stroll, among the late afternoon butterflies that were
preparing to roost, we munched and spat, he showing me
how to perform it conveyer-wise: split the seed open between

the right-side back teeth, ease out the kernel with the tongue, spit out the husk halves, move the smooth kernel to the left-side molars, and munch there, while the next seed which in the meantime has already been cracked on the right, is being processed in its turn. Speaking of right, he admitted he was a staunch "monarchist" (of a romantic rather than political nature) and went on to deplore my alleged (and perfectly abstract) "democratism." He recited samples of his fluent album poetry and proudly remarked that he had been complimented by Dilanov-Tomski, a fashionable poet (who favored Italian epigraphs and sectional titles, such as "Songs of Lost Love," "Nocturnal Urns," and so on), for the striking "long" rhyme *"vnemlyu múze ya"* ("I hearken to the Muse") and *"lyubvi kontúziya"* ("love's contusion"), which I countered with my best (and still unused) find: *"zápoved'"* (commandment) and *"posápïvat'"* (to sniffle). He was boiling with anger over Tolstoy's dismissal of the art of war and burning with admiration for Prince Andrey Bolkonski—for he had just discovered *War and Peace* which I had read for the first time when I was eleven (in Berlin, on a Turkish sofa, in our somberly rococo Privatstrasse flat giving on a dark, damp back garden with larches and gnomes that have remained in that book, like an old postcard, forever).

I suddenly see myself in the uniform of an officers' training school: we are strolling again villageward, in 1916, and (like Maurice Gerald and doomed Henry Pointdexter) have exchanged clothes—Yuri is wearing my white flannels and striped tie. During the short week he stayed that year we devised a singular entertainment which I have not seen described anywhere. There was a swing in the center of a small circular playground surrounded by jasmins, at the bottom of our garden. We adjusted the ropes in such a way as to have the green swingboard pass just a couple of inches above one's forehead and nose if one lay supine on the sand beneath. One of us would start the fun by standing on the board and swinging with increasing momentum; the other would lie down with the back of his head on a marked spot, and from what seemed an enormous height the swinger's board would swish swiftly above the supine one's face. And three years later, as a cavalry officer in Denikin's army, he was killed fighting the Reds in northern Crimea. I saw him dead in Yalta, the whole front of his skull pushed back by the impact of several bullets, which had hit him like the iron board of a monstrous swing, when having outstripped his detachment he was in the act of recklessly attacking alone a Red machine-gun nest. Thus was quenched his lifelong thirst for intrepid conduct in battle, for that ultimate gallant gallop with drawn pistol or unsheathed sword. Had I been competent to write his epitaph, I might have summed up matters by saying—in richer words than I can muster here—that all emotions, all thoughts, were governed in Yuri by one gift: a sense of honor equivalent, morally, to absolute pitch.

2

I have lately reread *The Headless Horseman* (in a drab edition, without pictures). It has its points. Take, for instance, that barroom in a log-walled Texan hotel, in the year of our Lord (as the captain would say) 1850, with its shirt-sleeved "saloon-clerk"—a fop in his own right, since the shirt was a ruffled one "of finest linen and lace." The colored decanters (among which a Dutch clock "quaintly ticked") were like "an iris sparkling behind his shoulders," like "an aureole surrounding his perfumed head." From glass to glass, the ice and the wine and the monongahela passed. An odor of musk, absinthe, and lemon peel filled the saloon. The glare of its camphine lamps brought out the dark asterisks produced on the white sand of its floor "by expectoration." In another year of our Lord—namely 1941—I caught some very good moths at the neon lights of a gasoline station between Dallas and Fort Worth.

Into the bar comes the villain, the "slave-whipping Mississippian," ex-captain of Volunteers, handsome, swaggering, scowling Cassius Calhoun. After toasting "America for Americans, and confusion to all foreign interlopers—especially the d—d [an evasion that puzzled me sorely when I first stumbled upon it: dead? detested?] Irish!" he intentionally collided with Maurice the Mustanger (scarlet scarf, slashed velvet trousers, hot Irish blood), a young horse trader who was really a baronet, *Sir* Maurice Gerald, as his thrilled bride was to discover at the end of the book. Wrong thrills, like this, may have been one of the reasons that the Irish-born author's fame waned so soon in his adopted country.

Immediately after the collision, Maurice performed several actions in the following order: he deposited his glass upon the counter, drew a silk handkerchief from his pocket, wiped from his embroidered shirt-bosom "the defilement of the whiskey," transferred the handkerchief from his right hand to his left, took the half-empty glass from the counter, swilled its remaining contents into Calhoun's face, quietly redeposited the glass upon the counter. This sequence I still know by heart, so often did my cousin and I enact it.

The duel took place there and then, in the emptied barroom, the men using Colt's six-shooters. Despite my interest in the fight (. . . both were wounded . . . their blood spurted all over the sanded floor . . .), I could not prevent myself from leaving the saloon in my fancy to mingle with the hushed crowd in front of the hotel, so as to make out (in the "scented dark") certain señoritas "of questionable calling."

With still more excitement did I read of Louise Pointdexter, Calhoun's fair cousin, daughter of a sugar planter,
"the highest and haughtiest of his class" (though why an old
man who planted sugar should be high and haughty was a
mystery to me). She is revealed in the throes of jealousy
(which I used to feel so keenly at miserable parties when
Mara Rzhevuski, a pale child with a white silk bow in her
black hair, suddenly and inexplicably stopped noticing me)
standing upon the edge of her *azotea,* her white hand resting
upon the copestone of the parapet which is "still wet with
the dews of night," her twin breasts sinking and swelling in
quick, spasmodic breathing, her twin breasts, let me reread,
sinking and swelling, her lorgnette directed . . .

That lorgnette I found afterward in the hands of Madame
Bovary, and later Anna Karenin had it, and then it passed
into the possession of Chekhov's Lady with the Lapdog and
was lost by her on the pier at Yalta. When Louise held it,
it was directed toward the speckled shadows under the mes-
quites, where the horseman of her choice was having an innocent conversation with the daughter of a wealthy *haciendado,*
Doña Isidora Covarubio de los Llanos (whose "head of hair
in luxuriance rivalled the tail of a wild steed").

"I had the opportunity," Maurice later explained to
Louise, as one rider to another, "of being useful to Doña
Isidora, in once rescuing her from some rude Indians." "A
slight service, you call it!" the young Creole exclaimed. "A
man who should do that much for *me—*" "What would you
do for *him?*" asked Maurice eagerly. *"Pardieu!* I should *love*
him!" "Then I would give half my life to see you in the
hands of Wild Cat and his drunken comrades—and the other
half to deliver you from the danger."

And here we find the gallant author interpolating a strange
confession: "The sweetest kiss that I ever had in my life was

when a woman—a fair creature, in the hunting field—leant over in her saddle and kissed me as I sate in mine."

The "sate," let us concede, gives duration and body to the kiss which the captain so comfortably "had," but I could not help feeling, even at the age of eleven, that centaurian love-making was not without its special limitations. Moreover, Yuri and I both knew a boy who had tried it, but the girl's horse had pushed his into a ditch. Exhausted by our adventures in the chaparral, we lay on the grass and discussed women. Our innocence seems to me now almost monstrous, in the light of various "sexual confessions" (to be found in Havelock Ellis and elsewhere), which involve tiny tots mating like mad. The slums of sex were unknown to us. Had we ever happened to hear about two normal lads idiotically masturbating in each other's presence (as described so sympathetically, with all the smells, in modern American novels), the mere notion of such an act would have seemed to us as comic and impossible as sleeping with an amelus. Our ideal was Queen Guinevere, Isolda, a not quite merciless *belle dame,* another man's wife, proud and docile, fashionable and fast, with slim ankles and narrow hands. The little girls in neat socks and pumps whom we and other little boys used to meet at dancing lessons or at Christmas Tree parties had all the enchantments, all the sweets and stars of the tree preserved in their flame-dotted iris, and they teased us, they glanced back, they delightfully participated in our vaguely festive dreams, but they belonged, those nymphets, to another class of creatures than the adolescent belles and large-hatted vamps for whom we actually yearned. After having made me sign an oath of secrecy with blood, Yuri told me about the married lady in Warsaw with whom at twelve or thirteen he was secretly in love and whom a couple of years later he made love to. By comparison it would have

sounded jejune, I feared, to tell him about my seaside playmates, but I cannot recall what substitute I invented to
match his romance. Around that time, though, a real romantic
adventure did come my way. I am now going to do something
quite difficult, a kind of double somersault with a Welsh
waggle (old acrobats will know what I mean), and I want
complete silence, please.

3

In August 1910, my brother and I were in Bad Kissingen
with our parents and tutor (Lenski); after that my father and
mother traveled to Munich and Paris, and back to St. Petersburg, and then to Berlin where we boys, with Lenski, were
spending the autumn and the beginning of the winter, having our teeth fixed. An American dentist—Lowell or Lowen,
I do not remember his name exactly—ripped some of our
teeth out and trussed up others with twine before disfiguring
us with braces. Even more hellish than the action of the rubber pear pumping hot pain into a cavity were the cotton
pads—I could not endure their dry contact and squeak—which
used to be thrust between gum and tongue for the operator's
convenience; and there would be, in the windowpane before
one's helpless eyes, a transparency, some dismal seascape or
gray grapes, shuddering with the dull reverberations of distant trams under dull skies. *"In den Zelten achtzehn A"*—
the address comes back to me dancing trochaically, immediately followed by the whispery motion of the cream-colored
electric taxi that took us there. We expected every possible
compensation in atonement for those dreadful mornings. My
brother loved the museum of wax figures in the Arcade off
the Unter den Linden—Friedrich's grenadiers, Bonaparte
communing with a mummy, young Liszt, who composed a

rhapsody in his sleep, and Marat, who died in a shoe; and for me (who did not know yet that Marat had been an ardent lepidopterist) there was, at the corner of that Arcade, Gruber's famous butterfly shop, a camphoraceous paradise at the top of a steep, narrow staircase which I climbed every other day to inquire if Chapman's new Hairstreak or Mann's recently rediscovered White had been obtained for me at last. We tried tennis on a public court; but a wintry gale kept chasing dead leaves across it, and, besides, Lenski could not really play, although insisting on joining us, without removing his overcoat, in a lopsided threesome. Subsequently, most of our afternoons were spent at a roller-skating rink in the Kurfür-stendamm. I remember Lenski rolling inexorably toward a pillar which he attempted to embrace while collapsing with a dreadful clatter; and after persevering awhile he would content himself with sitting in one of the loges that flanked the plush parapet and consuming there wedges of slightly salty mokka *torte* with whipped cream, while I kept self-suffi-ciently overtaking poor gamely stumbling Sergey, one of those galling little pictures that revolve on and on in one's mind. A military band (Germany, at the time, was the land of music), manned by an uncommonly jerky conductor, came to life every ten minutes or so but could hardly drown the ceaseless, sweeping rumble of wheels.

There existed in Russia, and still exists no doubt, a special type of school-age boy who, without necessarily being athletic in appearance or outstanding in mental scope, often having, in fact, no energy in class, a rather scrawny physique, and even, perhaps, a touch of pulmonary consumption, excels quite phenomenally at soccer *and* chess, and learns with the utmost ease and grace any kind of sport or game of skill (Borya Shik, Kostya Buketov, the famous brothers Shara-banov—where are they now, my teammates and rivals?). I was a good skater on ice and switching to rollers was for me not more difficult than for a man to replace an ordinary razor by a safety one. Very quickly I learned two or three tricky steps on the wooden floor of the rink and in no ballroom have I danced with more zest or ability (we, Shiks and Buketovs, are poor ballroom dancers, as a rule). The several instructors wore scarlet uniforms, half hussar and half hotel page. They all spoke English, of one brand or another. Among the regular visitors, I soon noticed a group of American young ladies. At first, they all merged in a common spin of bright exotic beauty. The process of differentiation began when, during one of my lone dances (and a few seconds before I came the worst cropper that I ever came on a rink), somebody said something about me as I whirled by, and a wonderful, twangy feminine voice answered, "Yes, isn't he cunning?"

I can still see her tall figure in a navy-blue tailor-made suit. Her large velvet hat was transfixed by a dazzling pin. For obvious reasons, I decided her name was Louise. At night, I would lie awake and imagine all kinds of romantic situations, and think of her willowy waist and white throat, and worry over an odd discomfort that I had associated before only with chafing shorts. One afternoon, I saw her standing in the lobby of the rink, and the most dashing of the instructors, a sleek ruffian of the Calhoun type, was holding her by the wrist and interrogating her with a crooked grin, and she was looking away and childishly turning her wrist this way and that in his grasp, and the following night he was shot, lassoed, buried alive, shot again, throttled, bitingly insulted, coolly aimed at, spared, and left to drag a life of shame.

High-principled but rather simple Lenski, who was abroad for the first time, had some trouble keeping the delights of sightseeing in harmony with his pedagogical duties. We took advantage of this and guided him toward places where our parents might not have allowed us to go. He could not resist the Wintergarten, for instance, and so, one night, we found ourselves there, drinking ice-chocolate in an orchestra box. The show developed on the usual lines: a juggler in evening clothes; then a woman, with flashes of rhinestones on her bosom, trilling a concert aria in alternating effusions of green and red light; then a comic on roller skates. Between him and a bicycle act (of which more later) there was an item on the program called "The Gala Girls," and with something of the shattering and ignominious physical shock I had experienced when coming that cropper on the rink, I recognized my American ladies in the garland of linked, shrill-voiced, shameless "girls," all rippling from left to right, and then from right to left, with a rhythmic rising of ten identical legs that shot up from ten corollas of flounces. I located my Louise's face—and knew at once that it was all over, that I had lost her, that I would never forgive her for singing so loudly, for smiling so redly, for disguising herself in that ridiculous way so unlike the charm of either "proud Creoles" or "questionable señoritas." I could not stop thinking of her altogether, of course, but the shock seems to have liberated in me a certain inductive process, for I soon noticed that *any* evocation of the feminine form would be accompanied by the puzzling discomfort already familiar to me. I asked my parents about it (they had come to Berlin to see how we were getting along) and my father ruffled the German newspaper he had just opened and replied in English (with the parody of a possible quotation—a manner of speech he often adopted in order to get going): "That, my boy, is just another of nature's absurd combinations, like shame and blushes, or grief and red eyes." "*Tolstoy vient de mourir,*" he suddenly added, in another, stunned voice, turning to my mother.

"*Da chto tï* [something like "good gracious"]!" she exclaimed in distress, clasping her hands in her lap. *"Pora domoy* [Time to go home]," she concluded, as if Tolstoy's death had been the portent of apocalyptic disasters.

4

And now comes that bicycle act—or at least my version of it. The following summer, Yuri did not visit us at Vyra, and I was left alone to cope with my romantic agitation. On rainy days, crouching at the foot of a little-used bookshelf, in a poor light that did all it could to discourage my furtive inquiry, I used to look up obscure, obscurely tantalizing and enervating terms in the Russian eighty-two-volume edition of Brockhaus' *Encyclopedia,* where, in order to save space, the title word of this or that article would be reduced, throughout a detailed discussion, to its capitalized initial, so that the columns of dense print in minion type, besides taxing one's attention, acquired the trumpery fascination of a masquerade, at which the abbreviation of a none too familiar word played hide and seek with one's avid eyes: "Moses tried to abolish P. but failed . . . In modern times, hospitable P. flourished in Austria under Maria Theresa . . . In many parts of Germany the profits from P. went to the clergy . . . In Russia, P. has been officially tolerated since 1843 . . . Seduced at the age of ten or twelve by her master, his sons or one of his menials, an orphan almost invariably ends in P."—and so forth, all of which went to enrich with mystery, rather than soberly elucidate, the allusions to meretricious love that I met with during my first immersions in Chekhov or Andreev. Butterfly hunting and various sports took care of the sunny hours, but no amount of exercise could prevent the restlessness which, every evening, launched me on vague voyages of discovery. After riding on horseback most of the afternoon, bicycling in the colored dusk was a curiously subtle, almost discarnate feeling. I had turned upside down and lowered to subsaddle level the handlebars of my Enfield bicycle, converting it into my conception of a racing model. Along the paths of the park I would skim, following yesterday's patterned imprint of Dunlop tires; neatly avoiding the ridges of tree roots; selecting a fallen twig and snapping it with my sensitive front wheel; weaving between two flat leaves and then between a small stone and the hole from which it had been dislodged the evening before; enjoying the brief smoothness of a bridge over a brook; skirting the wire fence of the tennis court; nuzzling open the little white-washed gate at the end of the park; and then, in a melancholy ecstasy of freedom, speeding along the hard-baked, pleasantly agglutinate margins of long country roads.

That summer I would always ride by a certain isba, golden in the low sun, in the doorway of which Polenka, the daughter of our head coachman Zahar, a girl of my age, would stand, leaning against the jamb, her bare arms folded on her breast in a soft, comfortable manner peculiar to rural Russia. She would watch me approach with a wonderful welcoming radiance on her face, but as I rode nearer, this would dwindle to a half smile, then to a faint light at the corners of her compressed lips, and, finally, this, too, would fade, so that when I reached her, there would be no expression at all on her round, pretty face. As soon as I had passed, however, and had turned my head for an instant to take a last look before sprinting uphill, the dimple would be back, the enigmatic light would be playing again on her dear features. I never spoke to her, but long after I had stopped riding by at that hour, our ocular relationship was renewed from time to time during two or three summers. She would appear from nowhere, always standing a little apart, always barefoot,

rubbing her left instep against her right calf or scratching
with her fourth finger the parting in her light brown hair,
and always leaning against things—against the stable door
while my horse was being saddled, against the trunk of a tree
when the whole array of country servitors would be seeing us
off to town for the winter on a crisp September morning.
Every time, her bosom seemed a little softer, her forearms a
little stronger, and once or twice I discerned, just before she
drifted out of my ken (at sixteen she married a blacksmith
in a distant village), a gleam of gentle mockery in her wide-
set hazel eyes. Strange to say, she was the first to have the
poignant power, by merely *not* letting her smile fade, of
burning a hole in my sleep and jolting me into clammy consciousness, whenever I dreamed of her, although in real life
I was even more afraid of being revolted by her dirt-caked
feet and stale-smelling clothes than of insulting her by the
triteness of quasi-seignioral advances.

5

There are two especially vivid aspects of her that I would
like to hold up simultaneously before my eyes in conclusion
of her haunting image. The first lived for a long while within
me quite separately from the Polenka I associated with door-
ways and sunsets, as if I had glimpsed a nymphean incarna-
tion of her pitiful beauty that were better left alone. One
June day, the year when she and I were both thirteen, on
the banks of the Oredezh, I was engaged in collecting some
so-called Parnassians—*Parnassius mnemosyne,* to be exact—
strange butterflies of ancient lineage, with rustling, glazed,
semitransparent wings and catkin-like flossy abdomens. My
quest had led me into a dense undergrowth of milky-white

racemosa and dark alder at the very edge of the cold, blue river, when suddenly there was an outburst of splashes and shouts, and from behind a fragrant bush, I caught sight of Polenka and three or four other naked children bathing from the ruins of an old bathhouse a few feet away. Wet, gasping, one nostril of her snub nose running, the ribs of her adolescent body arched under her pale, goose-pimpled skin, her calves flecked with black mud, a curved comb burning in her damp-darkened hair, she was scrambling away from the swish and clack of water-lily stems that a drum-bellied girl with a shaven head and a shamelessly excited stripling wearing around the loins a kind of string, locally used against the evil eye, were yanking out of the water and harrying her with; and for a second or two—before I crept away in a dismal haze of disgust and desire—I saw a strange Polenka shiver and squat on the boards of the half-broken wharf, covering her breasts against the east wind with her crossed arms, while with the tip of her tongue she taunted her pursuers.

The other picture refers to a Sunday at Christmastide in 1916. From the silent, snow-blanketed platform of the little station of Siverski on the Warsaw line (it was the nearest to our country place), I was watching a distant silvery grove as it changed to lead under the evening sky and waiting for it to emit the dull-violet smoke of the train that would take me back to St. Petersburg after a day of skiing. The smoke duly appeared and at the same moment, she and another girl walked past me, heavily kerchiefed, in huge felt boots and horrible, shapeless, long quilted jackets, with the stuffing showing at the torn spots of the coarse black cloth, and as she passed, Polenka, a bruise under her eye and a puffed-up lip (did her husband beat her on Saturdays?) remarked in wistful and melodious tones to nobody in particular: "*A barchuk-to menya ne priznal* [Look, the young master does not know me]—" and that was the only time I ever heard her speak.

6

The summer evenings of my boyhood when I used to ride by her cottage speak to me in that voice of hers now. On a road among fields, where it met the desolate highway, I would dismount and prop my bicycle against a telegraph pole. A sunset, almost formidable in its splendor, would be lingering in the fully exposed sky. Among its imperceptibly changing amassments, one could pick out brightly stained structural details of celestial organisms, or glowing slits in dark banks, or flat, ethereal beaches that looked like mirages of desert islands. I did not know then (as I know perfectly well now) what to do with such things—how to get rid of them, how to transform them into something that can be turned over to the reader in printed characters to have *him* cope with the blessed shiver—and this inability enhanced my oppression. A colossal shadow would begin to invade the fields, and the telegraph poles hummed in the stillness, and the night-feeders ascended the stems of their plants. Nibble, nibble, nibble—went a handsome striped caterpillar, not figured in Spuler, as he clung to a campanula stalk, working down with his mandibles along the edge of the nearest leaf out of which he was eating a leisurely hemicircle, then again extending his neck, and again bending it gradually, as he deepened the neat concave. Automatically, I might slip him, with a bit of his plantlet, into a matchbox to take home with me and have him produce next year a Splendid Surprise, but my thoughts were elsewhere: Zina and Colette, my seaside playmates; Louise, the prancer; all the flushed, low-sashed, silky-haired little girls at festive parties; languorous Countess G., my cousin's lady; Polenka smiling in the agony of my new dreams—all would merge to form somebody I did not know but was bound to know soon.

I recall one particular sunset. It lent an ember to my bicycle bell. Overhead, above the black music of telegraph wires, a number of long, dark-violet clouds lined with flamingo pink hung motionless in a fan-shaped arrangement; the whole thing was like some prodigious ovation in terms of color and form! It was dying, however, and everything else was darkening, too; but just above the horizon, in a lucid, turquoise space, beneath a black stratus, the eye found a vista that only a fool could mistake for the spare parts of this or any other sunset. It occupied a very small sector of the enormous sky and had the peculiar neatness of something seen through the wrong end of a telescope. There it lay in wait, a family of serene clouds in miniature, an accumulation of brilliant convolutions, anachronistic in their creaminess and extremely remote; remote but perfect in every detail; fantastically reduced but faultlessly shaped; my marvelous tomorrow ready to be delivered to me.

The author aged nineteen, with his brothers and sisters, in Yalta, November 1918. Kirill is seven; Sergey (unfortunately disfigured by flaws in the picture), wearing a rimless pince-nez and the uniform of the Yalta Gymnasium, is eighteen; Olga is fifteen; Elena (firmly clasping Box II) is twelve.

11

1

IN ORDER to reconstruct the summer of 1914, when the numb fury of verse-making first came over me, all I really need is to visualize a certain pavilion. There the lank, fifteen-year-old lad I then was, sought shelter during a thunderstorm, of which there was an inordinate number that July. I dream of my pavilion at least twice a year. As a rule, it appears in my dreams quite independently of their subject matter, which, of course, may be anything, from abduction to zoolatry. It hangs around, so to speak, with the unobtrusiveness of an artist's signature. I find it clinging to a corner of the dream canvas or cunningly worked into some ornamental part of the picture. At times, however, it seems to be suspended in the middle distance, a trifle baroque, and yet in tune with the handsome trees, dark fir and bright birch, whose sap once ran through its timber. Wine-red and bottle-green and dark-blue lozenges of stained glass lend a chapel-like touch to the latticework of its casements. It is just as it was in my boyhood, a sturdy old wooden structure above a ferny ravine in the older, riverside part of our Vyra park. Just as it was, or perhaps a little more perfect. In the real thing some of the glass was missing, crumpled leaves had been swept in by the wind. The narrow little bridge that arched across the ghyll at its deepest part, with the pavilion rising midway like a coagulated rainbow, was as slippery after a rainy spell as if it had been coated with some dark and in a sense magic ointment. Etymologically, "pavilion" and "papilio" are closely related. Inside, there was nothing in the way of furniture except a folding table hinged rustily to the wall under the east window, through the two or three glassless or pale-glassed compartments of which, among the bloated blues and drunken reds, one could catch a glimpse of the river. On a floorboard at my feet a dead horsefly lay on its back near the brown remains of a birch ament. And the patches of disintegrating whitewash on the inside of the door had been used by various trespassers for such jottings as: "Dasha, Tamara and Lena have been here" or "Down with Austria!"

The storm passed quickly. The rain, which had been a mass of violently descending water wherein the trees writhed and rolled, was reduced all at once to oblique lines of silent gold breaking into short and long dashes against a background of subsiding vegetable agitation. Gulfs of voluptuous blue were expanding between great clouds—heap upon heap of pure white and purplish gray, *lepota* (Old Russian for "stately beauty"), moving myths, gouache and guano, among the curves of which one could distinguish a mammary allusion or the death mask of a poet.

The tennis court was a region of great lakes.

Beyond the park, above steaming fields, a rainbow slipped into view; the fields ended in the notched dark border of a remote fir wood; part of the rainbow went across it, and that section of the forest edge shimmered most magically through the pale green and pink of the iridescent veil drawn before it: a tenderness and a glory that made poor relatives of the rhomboidal, colored reflections which the return of the sun had brought forth on the pavilion floor.

A moment later my first poem began. What touched it off? I think I know. Without any wind blowing, the sheer weight of a raindrop, shining in parasitic luxury on a cordate leaf, caused its tip to dip, and what looked like a globule of quicksilver performed a sudden glissando down the center vein, and then, having shed its bright load, the relieved leaf unbent. Tip, leaf, dip, relief—the instant it all took to happen seemed to me not so much a fraction of time as a fissure in it, a missed heartbeat, which was refunded at once by a patter of rhymes: I say "patter" intentionally, for when a gust of wind did come, the trees would briskly start to drip all together in as crude an imitation of the recent downpour as the stanza I was already muttering resembled the shock of wonder I had experienced when for a moment heart and leaf had been one.

2

In the avid heat of the early afternoon, benches, bridges and boles (all things, in fact, save the tennis court) were drying with incredible rapidity, and soon little remained of my initial inspiration. Although the bright fissure had closed, I doggedly went on composing. My medium happened to be Russian but could have been just as well Ukrainian, or Basic English, or Volapük. The kind of poem I produced in those days was hardly anything more than a sign I made of being alive, of passing or having passed, or hoping to pass, through certain intense human emotions. It was a phenomenon of orientation rather than of art, thus comparable to stripes of paint on a roadside rock or to a pillared heap of stones marking a mountain trail.

But then, in a sense, all poetry is positional: to try to express one's position in regard to the universe embraced by consciousness, is an immemorial urge. The arms of consciousness reach out and grope, and the longer they are the better. Tentacles, not wings, are Apollo's natural members. Vivian Bloodmark, a philosophical friend of mine, in later years, used to say that while the scientist sees everything that happens in one point of space, the poet feels everything that happens in one point of time. Lost in thought, he taps his knee with his wandlike pencil, and at the same instant a car (New York license plate) passes along the road, a child bangs the screen door of a neighboring porch, an old man yawns in a misty Turkestan orchard, a granule of cinder-gray sand is rolled by the wind on Venus, a Docteur Jacques Hirsch in Grenoble puts on his reading glasses, and trillions of other such trifles occur—all forming an instantaneous and transparent organism of events, of which the poet (sitting in a lawn chair, at Ithaca, N.Y.) is the nucleus.

That summer I was still far too young to evolve any wealth of "cosmic synchronization" (to quote my philosopher again). But I did discover, at least, that a person hoping to become a poet must have the capacity of thinking of several things at a time. In the course of the languid rambles that accompanied the making of my first poem, I ran into the village schoolmaster, an ardent Socialist, a good man, intensely devoted to my father (I welcome this image again), always with a tight posy of wild flowers, always smiling, always perspiring. While politely discussing with him my father's sudden journey to town, I registered simultaneously and with equal clarity not only his wilting flowers, his flowing tie and the blackheads on the fleshy volutes of his nostrils, but also the dull little voice of a cuckoo coming from afar, and the flash of a Queen of Spain settling on the road, and the remembered impression of the pictures (enlarged agricultural pests and bearded Russian writers) in the well-aerated classrooms of the village school which I had once or twice visited; and—to continue a tabulation that hardly does justice to the ethereal simplicity of the whole process—the throb of some utterly irrelevant recollection (a pedometer I had lost) was released from a neighboring brain cell, and the savor of the grass stalk I was chewing mingled with the cuckoo's note and the fritillary's takeoff, and all the while I was richly, serenely aware of my own manifold awareness.

He beamed and he bowed (in the effusive manner of a Russian radical), and took a couple of steps backward, and turned, and jauntily went on his way, and I picked up the thread of my poem. During the short time I had been otherwise engaged, something seemed to have happened to such words as I had already strung together: they did not look quite as lustrous as they had before the interruption. Some suspicion crossed my mind that I might be dealing in dummies. Fortunately, this cold twinkle of critical perception did not last. The fervor I had been trying to render took over again and brought its medium back to an illusory life. The ranks of words I reviewed were again so glowing, with their puffed-out little chests and trim uniforms, that I put down to mere fancy the sagging I had noticed out of the corner of my eye.

3

Apart from credulous inexperience, a young Russian versificator had to cope with a special handicap. In contrast to the rich vocabulary of satirical or narrative verse, the Russian elegy suffered from a bad case of verbal anemia. Only in very expert hands could it be made to transcend its humble origin —the pallid poetry of eighteenth-century France. True, in my day a new school was in the act of ripping up the old rhythms, but it was still to the latter that the conservative beginner turned in search of a neutral instrument—possibly because he did not wish to be diverted from the simple expression of simple emotions by adventures in hazardous form. Form, however, got its revenge. The rather monotonous designs into which early nineteenth-century Russian poets had twisted the pliant elegy resulted in certain words, or types of words (such as the Russian equivalents of *fol amour* or *langoureux et rêvant*) being coupled again and again, and this later lyricists could not shake off for a whole century.

In an especially obsessive arrangement, peculiar to the iambic of four to six feet, a long, wriggly adjective would occupy the first four or five syllables of the last three feet of the line. A good tetrametric example would be *ter-pi bes-chis-len-ni-e mu-ki* (en-dure in-cal-cu-la-ble tor-ments). The young Russian poet was liable to slide with fatal ease into this alluring abyss of syllables, for the illustration of which I have chosen *beschislennïe* only because it translates well; the real favorites were such typical elegiac components as *zadumchivïe* (pensive), *utrachennïe* (lost), *muchitel'nïe* (anguished), and so forth, all accented on the second syllable. Despite its great length, a word of that kind had but a single accent of its own, and, consequently, the penultimate metrical stress of the line encountered a normally unstressed syllable (*ni* in the Russian example, "la" in the English one). This produced a pleasant scud, which, however, was much too familiar an effect to redeem banality of meaning.

An innocent beginner, I fell into all the traps laid by the singing epithet. Not that I did not struggle. In fact, I was working at my elegy very hard, taking endless trouble over every line, choosing and rejecting, rolling the words on my tongue with the glazed-eyed solemnity of a tea-taster, and still it would come, that atrocious betrayal. The frame impelled the picture, the husk shaped the pulp. The hackneyed order of words (short verb or pronoun—long adjective—short noun) engendered the hackneyed disorder of thought, and some such line as *poeta gorestnïe gryozï*, translatable and accented as "the poet's melancholy daydreams," led fatally to a rhyming line ending in *rozï* (roses) or *beryozï* (birches) or *grozï* (thunderstorms), so that certain emotions were connected with certain surroundings not by a free act of one's will but by the faded ribbon of tradition. Nonetheless, the nearer my poem got to its completion, the more certain I became that whatever I saw before me would be seen by others. As I focused my eyes upon a kidney-shaped flower bed (and noted one pink petal lying on the loam and a small ant investigating its decayed edge) or considered the tanned midriff of a birch trunk where some hoodlum had stripped it of its papery, pepper-and-salt bark, I really believed that all this would be perceived by the reader through the magic veil of my words such as *utrachennïe rozï* or *zadumchivoy beryozï*. It did not occur to me then that far from being a veil, those poor words were so opaque that, in fact, they formed a wall in which all one could distinguish were the well-worn bits of the major and minor poets I imitated. Years later, in the squalid suburb of a foreign town, I remember seeing a paling, the boards of which had been brought from some other place where they had been used, apparently, as the inclosure of an itinerant circus. Animals had been painted on it by a versatile barker; but whoever had removed the boards, and then knocked them together again, must have been blind or insane, for now the fence showed only disjointed parts of animals (some of them, moreover, upside down)—a tawny haunch, a zebra's head, the leg of an elephant.

4

On the physical plane, my intense labors were marked by a number of dim actions or postures, such as walking, sitting, lying. Each of these broke again into fragments of no spatial importance: at the walking stage, for instance, I might be wandering one moment in the depths of the park and the next pacing the rooms of the house. Or, to take the sitting stage, I would suddenly become aware that a plate of something I could not even remember having sampled was being removed and that my mother, her left cheek twitching as it did whenever she worried, was narrowly observing from her place at the top of the long table my moodiness and lack of appetite. I would lift my head to explain—but the table had gone, and I was sitting alone on a roadside stump, the stick of my butterfly net, in metronomic motion, drawing arc after arc on the brownish sand; earthen rainbows, with variations in depth of stroke rendering the different colors.

When I was irrevocably committed to finish my poem or die, there came the most trancelike state of all. With hardly a twinge of surprise, I found myself, of all places, on a leathern couch in the cold, musty, little-used room that had been my grandfather's study. On that couch I lay prone, in a kind of reptilian freeze, one arm dangling, so that my knuckles loosely touched the floral figures of the carpet. When next I came out of that trance, the greenish flora was still there, my arm was still dangling, but now I was prostrate on the edge of a rickety wharf, and the water lilies I touched were real, and the undulating plump shadows of alder foliage on the water—apotheosized inkblots, oversized amoebas—were rhythmically palpitating, extending and drawing in dark pseudopods, which, when contracted, would break at their rounded margins into elusive and fluid macules, and these would come together again to reshape the groping terminals. I relapsed into my private mist, and when I emerged again, the support of my extended body had become a low bench in the park, and the live shadows, among which my hand dipped, now moved on the ground, among violet tints instead of aqueous black and green. So little did ordinary measures of existence mean in that state that I would not have been surprised to come out of its tunnel right into the park of Versailles, or the Tiergarten, or Sequoia National Forest; and, inversely, when the old trance occurs nowadays, I am quite prepared to find myself, when I awaken from it, high up in a certain tree, above the dappled bench of my boyhood, my belly pressed against a thick, comfortable branch and one arm hanging down among the leaves upon which the shadows of other leaves move.

Various sounds reached me in my various situations. It might be the dinner gong, or something less usual, such as the foul music of a barrel organ. Somewhere near the stables the old tramp would grind, and on the strength of more direct impressions imbibed in earlier years, I would see him mentally from my perch. Painted on the front of his instrument were Balkan peasants of sorts dancing among palmoid willows. Every now and then he shifted the crank from one hand to the other. I saw the jersey and skirt of his little bald female monkey, her collar, the raw sore on her neck, the chain which she kept plucking at every time the man pulled it, hurting her badly, and the several servants standing around, gaping, grinning—simple folks terribly tickled by a monkey's "antics." Only the other day, near the place where I am recording these matters, I came across a farmer and his son (the kind of keen healthy kid you see in breakfast food ads), who were similarly diverted by the sight of a young cat torturing a baby chipmunk—letting him run a few inches and then pouncing upon him again. Most of his tail was gone, the stump was bleeding. As he could not escape by running, the game little fellow tried one last measure: he stopped and lay down on his side in order to merge with a bit of light and shade on the ground, but the too violent heaving of his flank gave him away.

The family phonograph, which the advent of the evening set in action, was another musical machine I could hear through my verse. On the veranda where our relatives and friends assembled, it emitted from its brass mouthpiece the so-called *tsïganskie romansï* beloved of my generation. These were more or less anonymous imitations of gypsy songs—or imitations of such imitations. What constituted their gypsiness was a deep monotonous moan broken by a kind of hiccup, the audible cracking of a lovesick heart. At their best, they were responsible for the raucous note vibrating here and there in the works of true poets (I am thinking especially of Alexander Blok). At their worst, they could be likened to the apache stuff composed by mild men of letters and delivered by thickset ladies in Parisian night clubs. Their natural environment was characterized by nightingales in tears, lilacs in bloom and the alleys of whispering trees that graced the parks of the landed gentry. Those nightingales trilled, and in a pine grove the setting sun banded the trunks at different levels with fiery red. A tambourine, still throbbing, seemed to lie on the darkening moss. For a spell, the last notes of the husky contralto pursued me through the dusk. When silence returned, my first poem was ready.

5

It was indeed a miserable concoction, containing many borrowings besides its pseudo-Pushkinian modulations. An echo of Tyutchev's thunder and a refracted sunbeam from Fet were alone excusable. For the rest, I vaguely remember the mention of "memory's sting"—*vospominan'ya zhalo* (which I had really visualized as the ovipositor of an ichneumon fly straddling a cabbage caterpillar, but had not dared say so)—and something about the old-world charm of a distant barrel organ. Worst of all were the shameful gleanings from Apuhtin's and Grand Duke Konstantin's lyrics of the *tsiganski* type. They used to be persistently pressed upon me by a youngish and rather attractive aunt, who could also spout Louis Bouilhet's famous piece (*À Une Femme*), in which a metaphorical violin bow is incongruously used to play on a metaphorical guitar, and lots of stuff by Ella Wheeler Wilcox —a tremendous hit with the empress and her ladies-in-waiting. It seems hardly worthwhile to add that, as themes go, my elegy dealt with the loss of a beloved mistress—Delia, Tamara or Lenore—whom I had never lost, never loved, never met but was all set to meet, love, lose.

In my foolish innocence, I believed that what I had written was a beautiful and wonderful thing. As I carried it homeward, still unwritten, but so complete that even its punctuation marks were impressed on my brain like a pillow crease on a sleeper's flesh, I did not doubt that my mother would greet my achievement with glad tears of pride. The possibility of her being much too engrossed, that particular night, in other events to listen to verse did not enter my mind at all. Never in my life had I craved more for her praise. Never had I been more vulnerable. My nerves were on edge because of the darkness of the earth, which I had not noticed muffling itself up, and the nakedness of the firmament, the disrobing of which I had not noticed either. Overhead, between the formless trees bordering my dissolving path, the night sky was pale with stars. In those years, that marvelous mess of

constellations, nebulae, interstellar gaps and all the rest of
the awesome show provoked in me an indescribable sense of
nausea, of utter panic, as if I were hanging from earth upside
down on the brink of infinite space, with terrestrial gravity
still holding me by the heels but about to release me any
moment.

Except for two corner windows in the upper story (my
mother's sitting room), the house was already dark. The night
watchman let me in, and slowly, carefully, so as not to disturb
the arrangement of words in my aching head, I mounted the
stairs. My mother reclined on the sofa with the St. Petersburg
Rech in her hands and an unopened London *Times* in her
lap. A white telephone gleamed on the glass-topped table
near her. Late as it was, she still kept expecting my father
to call from St. Petersburg where he was being detained by
the tension of approaching war. An armchair stood by the
sofa, but I always avoided it because of its golden satin, the
mere sight of which caused a laciniate shiver to branch from
my spine like nocturnal lightning. With a little cough, I sat
down on a footstool and started my recitation. While thus
engaged, I kept staring at the farther wall upon which I see
so clearly in retrospect some small daguerreotypes and silhouettes in oval frames, a Somov aquarelle (young birch trees,
the half of a rainbow—everything very melting and moist),
a splendid Versailles autumn by Alexandre Benois, and a
crayon drawing my mother's mother had made in her girlhood—that park pavilion again with its pretty windows partly
screened by linked branches. The Somov and the Benois are
now in some Soviet Museum but that pavilion will never be
nationalized.

As my memory hesitated for a moment on the threshold of
the last stanza, where so many opening words had been tried
that the finally selected one was now somewhat camouflaged

by an array of false entrances, I heard my mother sniff. Presently I finished reciting and looked up at her. She was smiling ecstatically through the tears that streamed down her face. "How wonderful, how beautiful," she said, and with the tenderness in her smile still growing, she passed me a hand mirror so that I might see the smear of blood on my cheekbone where at some indeterminable time I had crushed a gorged mosquito by the unconscious act of propping my cheek on my fist. But I saw more than that. Looking into my own eyes, I had the shocking sensation of finding the mere dregs of my usual self, odds and ends of an evaporated identity which it took my reason quite an effort to gather again in the glass.

The author in Cambridge, Spring 1920. It was not unnatural for a Russian, when gradually discovering the pleasures of the Cam, to prefer, at first, a rowboat to the more proper canoe or punt.

12

WHEN I first met Tamara—to give her a name concolorous with her real one—she was fifteen, and I was a year older. The place was the rugged but comely country (black fir, white birch, peatbogs, hayfields, and barrens) just south of St. Petersburg. A distant war was dragging on. Two years later, that trite *deus ex machina*, the Russian Revolution, came, causing my removal from the unforgettable scenery. In fact, already then, in July 1915, dim omens and backstage rumblings, the hot breath of fabulous upheavals, were affecting the so-called "Symbolist" school of Russian poetry—especially the verse of Alexander Blok.

During the beginning of that summer and all through the previous one, Tamara's name had kept cropping up (with the feigned naïveté so typical of Fate, when meaning business) here and there on our estate (Entry Forbidden) and on my uncle's land (Entry Strictly Forbidden) on the opposite bank of the Oredezh. I would find it written with a stick on the reddish sand of a park avenue, or penciled on a whitewashed wicket, or freshly carved (but not completed) in the wood of some ancient bench, as if Mother Nature were giving me mysterious advance notices of Tamara's existence. That hushed July afternoon, when I discovered her standing quite still (only her eyes were moving) in a birch grove, she seemed to have been spontaneously generated there, among those watchful trees, with the silent completeness of a mythological manifestation.

She slapped dead the horsefly that she had been waiting for to light and proceeded to catch up with two other, less pretty girls who were calling to her. Presently, from a vantage point above the river, I saw them walking over the bridge, clicking along on brisk high heels, all three with their hands tucked into the pockets of their navy-blue jackets and, because of the flies, every now and then tossing their beribboned and beflowered heads. Very soon I traced Tamara to the modest *dachka* (summer cottage) that her family rented in the village. I would ride my horse or my bicycle in the vicinity, and with the sudden sensation of a dazzling explosion (after which my heart would take quite a time to get back from where it had landed) I used to come across Tamara at this or that bland bend of the road. Mother Nature eliminated first one of her girl companions, then the other, but not until August—August 9, 1915, to be Petrarchally exact, at half-past four of that season's fairest afternoon in the rainbow-windowed pavilion that I had noticed my trespasser enter—not until then, did I muster sufficient courage to speak to her.

Seen through the carefully wiped lenses of time, the beauty of her face is as near and as glowing as ever. She was short and a trifle on the plump side but very graceful, with her slim ankles and supple waist. A drop of Tatar or Circassian blood might have accounted for the slight slant of her merry dark eye and the duskiness of her blooming cheek. A light down, akin to that found on fruit of the almond group, lined her profile with a fine rim of radiance. She accused her rich-

brown hair of being unruly and oppressive and threatened
to have it bobbed, and did have it bobbed a year later, but
I always recall it as it looked first, fiercely braided into a thick
plait that was looped up at the back of her head and tied
there with a big bow of black silk. Her lovely neck was always
bare, even in winter in St. Petersburg, for she had managed
to obtain permission to eschew the stifling collar of a Russian
schoolgirl's uniform. Whenever she made a funny remark or
produced a jingle from her vast store of minor poetry, she had
a most winning way of dilating her nostrils with a little snort
of amusement. Still, I was never quite sure when she was
serious and when she was not. The rippling of her ready
laughter, her rapid speech, the roll of her very uvular *r*, the
tender, moist gleam on her lower eyelid—indeed, all her features were ecstatically fascinating to me, but somehow or
other, instead of divulging her person, they tended to form
a brilliant veil in which I got entangled every time I tried to
learn more about her. When I used to tell her we would
marry in the last days of 1917, as soon as I had finished school,
she would quietly call me a fool. I visualized her home but
vaguely. Her mother's first name and patronymic (which
were all I knew of the woman) had merchant-class or clerical
connotations. Her father, who, I gathered, took hardly any
interest in his family, was the steward of a large estate somewhere in the south.

Autumn came early that year. Layers of fallen leaves piled
up ankle-deep by the end of August. Velvet-black Camberwell Beauties with creamy borders sailed through the glades.
The tutor to whose erratic care my brother and I were en-
trusted that season used to hide in the bushes in order to spy
upon Tamara and me with the aid of an old telescope he had
found in the attic; but in his turn, one day, the peeper was
observed by my uncle's purple-nosed old gardener Apostolski

(incidentally, a great tumbler of weeding-girls) who very kindly reported it to my mother. She could not tolerate snooping, and besides (though I never spoke to her about Tamara) she knew all she cared to know of my romance from my poems which I recited to her in a spirit of praise-worthy objectivity, and which she lovingly copied out in a special album. My father was away with his regiment; he did feel it his duty, after acquainting himself with the stuff, to ask me some rather awkward questions when he returned from the front a month later; but my mother's purity of heart had carried her, and was to carry her, over worse diffi-culties. She contented herself with shaking her head dubi-ously though not untenderly, and telling the butler to leave every night some fruit for me on the lighted veranda.

I took my adorable girl to all those secret spots in the woods, where I had daydreamed so ardently of meeting her, of creating her. In one particular pine grove everything fell into place, I parted the fabric of fancy, I tasted reality. As my uncle was absent that year, we could also stray freely in his huge, dense, two-century-old park with its classical crip-ples of green-stained stone in the main avenue and labyrin-thine paths radiating from a central fountain. We walked "swinging hands," country-fashion. I picked dahlias for her on the borders along the gravel drive, under the distant benevolent eye of old Priapostolski. We felt less safe when I used to see her home, or near-home, or at least to the village bridge. I remember the coarse graffiti linking our first names, in strange diminutives, on a certain white gate and, a little apart from that village-idiot scrawl, the adage "Prudence is the friend of Passion," in a bristly hand well-known to me. Once, at sunset, near the orange and black river, a young *dachnik* (vacationist) with a riding crop in his hand bowed to her in passing; whereupon she blushed like a girl in a novel but only said, with a spirited sneer, that he had never ridden a horse in his life. And another time, as we emerged onto a turn of the highway, my two little sisters in their wild curiosity almost fell out of the red family "torpedo" swerving toward the bridge.

On dark rainy evenings I would load the lamp of my bicycle with magical lumps of calcium carbide, shield a match from the gusty wind and, having imprisoned a white flame in the glass, ride cautiously into the darkness. The circle of light cast by my lamp would pick out the damp, smooth shoulder of the road, between its central system of puddles and the long bordering grasses. Like a tottering ghost, the pale ray would weave across a clay bank at the turn as I began the downhill ride toward the river. Beyond the bridge the road sloped up again to meet the Rozhestveno–Luga highway, and just above that junction a footpath among dripping jasmin bushes ascended a steep escarpment. I had to dismount and push my bicycle. As I reached the top, my livid light flitted across the six-pillared white portico at the back of my uncle's mute, shuttered manor—as mute and shuttered as it may be today, half a century later. There, in a corner of that arched shelter, from where she had been following the zigzags of my ascending light, Tamara would be waiting, perched on the broad parapet with her back to a pillar. I would put out my lamp and grope my way toward her. One is moved to speak more eloquently about these things, about many other things that one always hopes might survive captivity in the zoo of words—but the ancient limes crowding close to the house drown Mnemosyne's monologue with their creaking and heaving in the restless night. Their sigh would subside. The rain pipe at one side of the porch, a small busybody of water, could be heard steadily bubbling. At times, some additional rustle, troubling the rhythm of the rain in the leaves, would cause Tamara to turn her head in the direction of an imagined footfall, and then, by a faint luminosity—now rising above the horizon of my memory despite all that rain—I could distinguish the outline of her face; but there was nothing and nobody to fear, and presently she would gently exhale the breath she had held for a moment and her eyes would close again.

2

With the coming of winter our reckless romance was transplanted to grim St. Petersburg. We found ourselves horribly deprived of the sylvan security we had grown accustomed to. Hotels disreputable enough to admit us stood beyond the limits of our daring, and the great era of parked amours was still remote. The secrecy that had been so pleasurable in the country now became a burden, yet neither of us could face the notion of chaperoned meetings at her home or mine. Consequently, we were forced to wander a good deal about the town (she, in her little gray-furred coat, I, white-spatted and karakul-collared, with a knuckle-duster in my velvet-lined pocket), and this permanent quest for some kind of refuge produced an odd sense of hopelessness, which, in its turn, foreshadowed other, much later and lonelier, roamings.

We skipped school: I forget what Tamara's procedure was; mine consisted of talking either of the two chauffeurs into dropping me at this or that corner on the way to school (both were good sports and actually refused to accept my gold—handy five-rouble pieces coming from the bank in appetizing, weighty sausages of ten or twenty shining pieces, in the aesthetic recollection of which I can freely indulge now that my proud émigré destitution is also a thing of the past). Nor had I any trouble with our wonderful, eminently bribable Ustin, who took the calls on our ground-floor telephone, the number of which was 24-43, *dvadtsat' chetïre sorok tri;* he briskly replied I had a sore throat. I wonder, by the way, what would happen if I put in a long-distance call from my desk right now? No answer? No such number? No such country? Or the voice of Ustin saying *"moyo pochtenietse!"* (the ingratiating diminutive of "my respects")? There exist, after all, well-publicized Slavs and Kurds who are well over one hundred and fifty. My father's telephone in his study (584-51) was not listed, and my form master in his attempts to learn the truth about my failing health never got anywhere, though sometimes I missed three days in a row.

We walked under the white lacery of berimed avenues in public parks. We huddled together on cold benches—after having removed first their tidy cover of snow, then our snow-incrusted mittens. We haunted museums. They were drowsy and deserted on weekday mornings, and very warm, in contrast to the glacial haze and its red sun that, like a flushed moon, hung in the eastern windows. There we would seek the quiet back rooms, the stopgap mythologies nobody looked at, the etchings, the medals, the paleographic items, the Story of Printing—poor things like that. Our best find, I think, was a small room where brooms and ladders were kept; but a batch of empty frames that suddenly started to slide and topple in the dark attracted an inquisitive art lover, and we fled. The Hermitage, St. Petersburg's Louvre, offered nice nooks, especially in a certain hall on the ground floor, among cabinets with scarabs, behind the sarcophagus of Nana, high priest of Ptah. In the Russian Museum of Emperor Alexander III, two halls (Nos. 30 and 31, in its northeastern corner), harboring repellently academic paintings by Shishkin ("Clearing in a Pine Forest") and by Harlamov ("Head of a Young Gypsy"), offered a bit of privacy because of some tall stands with drawings—until a foul-mouthed veteran of the Turkish campaign threatened to call the police. So from these great museums we graduated to smaller ones, such as the Suvorov, for instance, where I recall a most silent room full of old armor and tapestries, and torn silk banners, with several bewigged, heavily booted dummies in green uniforms standing guard over us. But wherever we went, invariably, after a few visits, this or that hoary, blear-eyed, felt-soled attendant would grow suspicious and we would have to transfer our furtive frenzy elsewhere—to the Pedagogical Museum, to the Museum of Court Carriages, or to a tiny museum of old maps, which guidebooks do not even list—and then out again into the cold, into some lane of great gates and green lions with rings in their jaws, into the stylized snowscape of the "Art World," *Mir Iskusstva*—Dobuzhinski, Alexandre Benois—so dear to me in those days.

On late afternoons, we got into the last row of seats in one of the two movie theatres (the Parisiana and the Piccadilly) on Nevski Avenue. The art was progressing. Sea waves were tinted a sickly blue and as they rode in and burst into foam against a black, remembered rock (Rocher de la Vierge, Biarritz—funny, I thought, to see again the beach of my cosmopolitan childhood), there was a special machine that imitated the sound of the surf, making a kind of washy swish that never quite managed to stop short with the scene but for three or four seconds accompanied the next feature—a brisk funeral, say, or shabby prisoners of war with their dapper captors. As often as not, the title of the main picture was a quotation from some popular poem or song and might be quite long-winded, such as *The Chrysanthemums Blossom No More in the Garden* or *Her Heart Was a Toy in His Hands and Like a Toy It Got Broken.* Female stars had low foreheads, magnificent eyebrows, lavishly shaded eyes. The favorite actor of the day was Mozzhuhin. One famous director had acquired in the Moscow countryside a white-pillared mansion (not unlike that of my uncle), and it appeared in all the pictures he made. Mozzhuhin would drive up to it in a smart sleigh and fix a steely eye on a light in one window while a celebrated little muscle twitched under the tight skin of his jaw.

When museums and movie houses failed us and the night was young, we were reduced to exploring the wilderness of the world's most gaunt and enigmatic city. Solitary street lamps were metamorphosed into sea creatures with prismatic spines by the icy moisture on our eyelashes. As we crossed the vast squares, various architectural phantoms arose with silent suddenness right before us. We felt a cold thrill, generally associated not with height but with depth—with an abyss opening at one's feet—when great, monolithic pillars of polished granite (polished by slaves, repolished by the moon, and rotating smoothly in the polished vacuum of the night) zoomed above us to support the mysterious rotundities of St. Isaac's cathedral. We stopped on the brink, as it were, of these perilous massifs of stone and metal, and with linked hands, in Lilliputian awe, craned our heads to watch new colossal visions rise in our way—the ten glossy-gray atlantes of a palace portico, or a giant vase of porphyry near the iron gate of a garden, or that enormous column with a black angel on its summit that obsessed, rather than adorned, the moon-flooded Palace Square, and went up and up, trying in vain to reach the subbase of Pushkin's *"Exegi monumentum."*

She contended afterward, in her rare moments of moodiness, that our love had not withstood the strain of that winter; a flaw had appeared, she said. Through all those months, I had kept writing verse to her, for her, about her, two or three poems per week; in the spring of 1916 I published a collection of them—and was horrified when she drew my attention to something I had not noticed at all when concocting the book. There it was, the same ominous flaw, the banal hollow note, and glib suggestion that our love was doomed since it could never recapture the miracle of its initial moments, the rustle and rush of those limes in the rain, the compassion of the wild countryside. Moreover—but this neither of us saw at the time—my poems were juvenile stuff, quite devoid of merit and ought never to have been put on sale. The book (a copy of which still exists, alas, in the "closed stacks" of the Lenin Library, Moscow) deserved what it got at the tearing claws of the few critics who noticed it in obscure periodicals. My Russian literature teacher at school, Vladimir Hippius, a first-rate though somewhat esoteric poet whom I greatly admired (he surpassed in talent, I think, his much better known cousin, Zinaïda Hippius, woman poet and critic) brought a copy with him to class and provoked the delirious hilarity of the majority of my classmates by applying his fiery sarcasm (he was a fierce man with red hair) to my most romantic lines. His famous cousin at a session of the Literary Fund asked my father, its president, to tell me, please, that I would never, never be a writer. A well-meaning, needy and talentless journalist, who had reasons to be grateful to my father, wrote an impossibly enthusiastic piece about me, some five hundred lines dripping with fulsome praise; it was intercepted in time by my father, and I remember him and me, while we read it in manuscript, grinding our teeth and groaning—the ritual adopted by our family when faced by something in awful taste or by somebody's *gaffe*. The whole business cured me permanently of all interest in literary fame and was probably the cause of that almost pathological and not always justified indifference to reviews which in later years deprived me of the emotions most authors are said to experience.

That spring of 1916 is the one I see as the very type of a St. Petersburg spring, when I recall such specific images as Tamara, wearing an unfamiliar white hat, among the spectators of a hard-fought interscholastic soccer game, in which, that Sunday, the most sparkling luck helped me to make save after save in goal; and a Camberwell Beauty, exactly as old as our romance, sunning its bruised black wings, their borders now bleached by hibernation, on the back of a bench in Alexandrovski Garden; and the booming of cathedral bells in the keen air, above the corrugated dark blue of the Neva, voluptuously free of ice; and the fair in the confetti-studded slush of the Horse Guard Boulevard during Catkin Week, with its squeaking and popping din, its wooden toys, its loud hawking of Turkish delight and Cartesian devils called *amerikanskie zhiteli* ("American inhabitants")—minute goblins of glass riding up and down in glass tubes filled with pink- or lilac-tinted alcohol as real Americans do (though all the epithet meant was "outlandish") in the shafts of transparent skyscrapers as the office lights go out in the greenish sky. The excitement in the streets made one drunk with desire for the woods and the fields. Tamara and I were especially eager to return to our old haunts, but all through April her mother kept wavering between renting the same cottage again and economically staying in town. Finally, under a certain condition (accepted by Tamara with the fortitude of Hans Andersen's little mermaid), the cottage was rented, and a glorious summer immediately enveloped us, and there she was, my happy Tamara, on the points of her toes, trying to pull down a racemosa branch in order to pick its puckered fruit, with all the world and its trees wheeling in the orb of her laughing eye, and a dark patch from her exertions in the sun forming under her raised arm on the raw shantung of her yellow frock. We lost ourselves in mossy woods and bathed in a fairy-tale cove and swore eternal love by the crowns of flowers that, like all little Russian mermaids, she was so fond of weaving, and early in the fall she moved to town in search of a job (this was the condition set by her mother), and in the course of the following months I did not see her at all, engrossed as I was in the kind of varied experience which I thought an elegant *littérateur* should seek. I had already entered an extravagant phase of sentiment and sensuality, that was to last about ten years. In looking at it from my present tower I see myself as a hundred different young men at once, all pursuing one changeful girl in a series of simultaneous or overlapping love affairs, some delightful, some sordid, that ranged from one-night adventures to protracted involvements and dissimulations, with very meager artistic results. Not only is the experience in question, and the shadows of all those charming ladies useless to me now in recomposing my past, but it creates a bothersome defocalization, and no matter how I worry the screws of memory, I cannot recall the way Tamara and I parted. There is possibly another reason, too, for this blurring: we had parted too many times before. During that last summer in the country, we used to part forever after each secret meeting when, in the fluid blackness of the night, on that old wooden bridge between masked moon and misty river, I would kiss her warm, wet eyelids and rain-chilled face, and immediately after go back to her for yet another farewell—and then the long, dark, wobbly uphill ride, my slow, laboriously pedaling feet trying to press down the monstrously strong and resilient darkness that refused to stay under.

I do remember, however, with heartbreaking vividness, a

certain evening in the summer of 1917 when, after a winter of incomprehensible separation, I chanced to meet Tamara on a suburban train. For a few minutes between two stops, in the vestibule of a rocking and rasping car, we stood next to each other, I in a state of intense embarrassment, of crushing regret, she consuming a bar of chocolate, methodically breaking off small, hard bits of the stuff, and talking of the office where she worked. On one side of the tracks, above bluish bogs, the dark smoke of burning peat was mingling with the smoldering wreck of a huge, amber sunset. It can be proved, I think, by published records that Alexander Blok was even then noting in his diary the very peat smoke I saw, and the wrecked sky. There was later a period in my life when I might have found this relevant to my last glimpse of Tamara as she turned on the steps to look back at me before descending into the jasmin-scented, cricket-mad dusk of a small station; but today no alien marginalia can dim the purity of the pain.

3

When, at the end of the year, Lenin took over, the Bolsheviks immediately subordinated everything to the retention of power, and a regime of bloodshed, concentration camps, and hostages entered upon its stupendous career. At the time many believed one could fight Lenin's gang and save the achievements of the March Revolution. My father, who had been elected to the Constituent Assembly which, in its preliminary phase, strove to prevent the entrenchment of the Soviets, decided to remain as long as possible in St. Petersburg but to send his large family to the Crimea, a region that was still free (this freedom was to last for only a few weeks longer). We traveled in two parties, my brother and I going separately from my mother and the three younger children. The Soviet era was a dull week old; liberal newspapers still came out; and while seeing us off at the Nikolaevski station and waiting with us, my imperturbable father settled down at a corner table in the buffet to write, in his flowing, "celestial" hand (as the typesetters said, marveling at the absence of corrections), a leading article for the moribund *Rech* (or perhaps some emergency publication) on those special long strips of ruled paper, which corresponded proportionally to columns of print. As far as I remember, the main reason for sending my brother and me off so promptly was the probability of our being inducted into the new "Red" army if we stayed in town. I was annoyed at going to a fascinating region in mid-November, long after the collecting season was over, having never been very good at digging for pupae (though, eventually, I did turn up a few beneath a big oak in our Crimean garden). Annoyance changed to distress, when after making a precise little cross over the face of each of us, my father rather casually added that very possibly, *ves'ma vozmozhno,* he would never see us again; whereupon, in trench coat and khaki cap, with his briefcase under his arm, he strode away into the steamy fog.

The long journey southward started tolerably well, with the heat still humming and the lamps still intact in the Petrograd–Simferopol first-class sleeper, and a passably famous singer in dramatic makeup, with a bouquet of chrysanthemums in brown paper pressed to her breast, stood in the corridor, tapping upon the pane, along which somebody walked and waved as the train started to glide, without one jolt to indicate we were leaving that gray city forever. But soon after Moscow, all comfort came to an end. At several points of our slow dreary progression, the train, including our sleeping car, was invaded by more or less Bolshevized

soldiers who were returning to their homes from the front
(one called them either "deserters" or "Red Heroes," depend-
ing upon one's political views). My brother and I thought it
rather fun to lock ourselves up in our compartment and
thwart every attempt to disturb us. Several soldiers traveling
on the roof of the car added to the sport by trying to use, not
unsuccessfully, the ventilator of our room as a toilet. My
brother, who was a first-rate actor, managed to simulate all
the symptoms of a bad case of typhus, and this helped us
out when the door finally gave way. Early on the third morning, at a vague stop, I took advantage of a lull in those merry
proceedings to get a breath of fresh air. I moved gingerly
along the crowded corridor, stepping over the bodies of snoring men, and got off. A milky mist hung over the platform
of an anonymous station—we were somewhere not far from
Kharkov. I wore spats and a derby. The cane I carried, a
collector's item that had belonged to my uncle Ruka, was of
a light-colored, beautifully freckled wood, and the knob was
a smooth pink globe of coral cupped in a gold coronet. Had
I been one of the tragic bums who lurked in the mist of that
station platform where a brittle young fop was pacing back
and forth, I would not have withstood the temptation to
destroy him. As I was about to board the train, it gave a jerk
and started to move; my foot slipped and my cane was sent
flying under the wheels. I had no special affection for the
thing (in fact, I carelessly lost it a few years later), but I was
being watched, and the fire of adolescent *amour propre*
prompted me to do what I cannot imagine my present self
ever doing. I waited for one, two, three, four cars to pass
(Russian trains were notoriously slow in gaining momentum) and when, at last, the rails were revealed, I picked up
my cane from between them and raced after the nightmar-
ishly receding bumpers. A sturdy proletarian arm conformed

to the rules of sentimental fiction (rather than to those of Marxism) by helping me to swarm up. Had I been left behind, those rules might still have held good, since I would have been brought near Tamara, who by that time had also moved south and was living in a Ukrainian hamlet less than a hundred miles from the scene of that ridiculous occurrence.

4

Of her whereabouts I learned unexpectedly a month or so after my arrival in southern Crimea. My family settled in the vicinity of Yalta, at Gaspra, near the village of Koreiz. The whole place seemed completely foreign; the smells were not Russian, the sounds were not Russian, the donkey braying every evening just as the muezzin started to chant from the village minaret (a slim blue tower silhouetted against a peach-colored sky) was positively Baghdadian. And there was I standing on a chalky bridle path near a chalky stream bed where separate, serpentlike bands of water thinly glided over oval stones—there was I, holding a letter from Tamara. I looked at the abrupt Yayla Mountains, covered up to their rocky brows with the karakul of the dark Tauric pine; at the maquis-like stretch of evergreen vegetation between mountain and sea; at the translucent pink sky, where a self-conscious crescent shone, with a single humid star near it; and the whole artificial scene struck me as something in a prettily illustrated, albeit sadly abridged, edition of *The Arabian Nights*. Suddenly I felt all the pangs of exile. There had been the case of Pushkin, of course—Pushkin who had wandered in banishment here, among those naturalized cypresses and laurels—but though some prompting might have come from his elegies, I do not think my exaltation was a pose. Thenceforth for several years, until the writing of a novel relieved

me of that fertile emotion, the loss of my country was equated
for me with the loss of my love.

Meanwhile, the life of my family had completely changed.
Except for a few jewels astutely buried in the normal filling
of a talcum powder container, we were absolutely ruined.
But this was a very minor matter. The local Tatar government had been swept away by a brand-new Soviet, and we
were subjected to the preposterous and humiliating sense of
utter insecurity. During the winter of 1917–18 and well into
the windy and bright Crimean spring, idiotic death toddled
by our side. Every other day, on the white Yalta pier (where,
as you remember, the lady of Chekhov's "Lady with the Lapdog" lost her lorgnette among the vacational crowd), various
harmless people had, in advance, weights attached to their
feet and then were shot by tough Bolshevik sailors imported
from Sebastopol for the purpose. My father, who was not
harmless, had joined us by this time, after some dangerous
adventures, and, in that region of lung specialists, had adopted
the mimetic disguise of a doctor without changing his name
("simple and elegant," as a chess annotator would have said
of a corresponding move on the board). We dwelt in an
inconspicuous villa that a kind friend, Countess Sofia Panin,
had placed at our disposal. On certain nights, when rumors
of nearing assassins were especially strong, the men of our
family took turns patrolling the house. The slender shadows
of oleander leaves would cautiously move in the sea breeze
along a pale wall, as if pointing at something, with a great
show of stealth. We had a shotgun and a Belgian automatic,
and did our best to pooh-pooh the decree which said that
anyone unlawfully possessing firearms would be executed on
the spot.

Chance treated us kindly; nothing happened beyond the
shock we got in the middle of a January night, when a

brigand-like figure, all swathed in leather and fur, crept into our midst—but it turned out to be only our former chauffeur, Tsiganov, who had thought nothing of riding all the way from St. Petersburg, on buffers and in freight cars, through the immense, frosty and savage expanse of Russia, for the mere purpose of bringing us a very welcome sum of money unexpectedly sent us by some good friends of ours. He also brought the mail received at our St. Petersburg address; among it was that letter from Tamara. After a month's stay, Tsiganov declared the Crimean scenery bored him and departed—to go all the way back north, with a big bag over his shoulder, containing various articles which we would have gladly given him had we thought he coveted them (such as a trouser press, tennis shoes, nightshirts, an alarm clock, a flat-iron, several other ridiculous things I have forgotten) and the absence of which only gradually came to light if not pointed out, with vindictive zeal, by an anemic servant girl whose pale charms he had also rifled. Curiously enough, he had prevailed upon us to transfer my mother's precious stones from the talcum powder container (that he had at once detected) to a hole dug in the garden under a versatile oak— and there they all were after his departure.

Then, one spring day in 1918, when the pink puffs of blossoming almond trees enlivened the dark mountainside, the Bolsheviks vanished and a singularly silent army of Germans replaced them. Patriotic Russians were torn between the animal relief of escaping native executioners and the necessity of owing their reprieve to a foreign invader—especially to the Germans. The latter, however, were losing their war in the west and came to Yalta on tiptoe, with diffident smiles, an army of gray apparitions easy for a patriot to ignore, and ignored it was, save for some rather ungrateful snickers at the halfhearted KEEP OFF THE GRASS signs that appeared on park lawns. A couple of months later, having nicely repaired the plumbing in various villas vacated by commissars, the Germans faded out in their turn; the Whites trickled in from the east and soon began fighting the Red Army, which was attacking the Crimea from the north. My father became Minister of Justice in the Regional Government located in Simferopol, and his family was lodged near Yalta on the Livadia grounds, the Tsar's former domain. A brash, hectic gaiety associated with White-held towns brought back, in a vulgarized version, the amenities of peaceful years. Cafés did a wonderful business. All kinds of theatres thrived. One morning, on a mountain trail, I suddenly met a strange cavalier, clad in a Circassian costume, with a tense, perspiring face painted a fantastic yellow. He kept furiously tugging at his horse, which, without heeding him, proceeded down the steep path at a curiously purposeful walk, like that of an offended person leaving a party. I had seen runaway horses, but I had never seen a walkaway one before, and my astonishment was given a still more pleasurable edge when I recognized the unfortunate rider as Mozzhuhin, whom Tamara and I had so often admired on the screen. The film *Haji Murad* (after Tolstoy's tale of that gallant, rough-riding mountain chief) was being rehearsed on the mountain pastures of the range. "Stop that brute [*Derzhite proklyatoe zhivotnoe*]," he said through his teeth as he saw me, but at the same moment, with a mighty sound of crunching and crashing stones, two authentic Tatars came running down to the rescue, and I trudged on, with my butterfly net, toward the upper crags where the Euxine race of the Hippolyte Grayling was expecting me.

In that summer of 1918, a poor little oasis of miraged youth, my brother and I used to frequent the amiable and eccentric family who owned the coastal estate Oleiz. A banter-

ing friendship soon developed between my coeval Lidia T. and
me. Many young people were always around, brown-limbed
braceleted young beauties, a well-known painter called Sorin,
actors, a male ballet dancer, merry White Army officers, some
of whom were to die quite soon, and what with beach parties,
blanket parties, bonfires, a moon-spangled sea and a fair
supply of Crimean Muscat Lunel, a lot of amorous fun went
on; and all the while, against this frivolous, decadent and
somehow unreal background (which I was pleased to believe
conjured up the atmosphere of Pushkin's visit to the Crimea
a century earlier), Lidia and I played a little oasal game of
our own invention. The idea consisted of parodizing a bio-
graphic approach projected, as it were, into the future and
thus transforming the very specious present into a kind of
paralyzed past as perceived by a doddering memoirist who recalls, through a helpless haze, his acquaintance with a great
writer when both were young. For instance, either Lidia or
I (it was a matter of chance inspiration) might say, on the
terrace after supper: "The writer liked to go out on the terrace after supper," or "I shall always remember the remark
V. V. made one warm night: 'It is,' he remarked, 'a warm
night' "; or, still sillier: "He was in the habit of lighting his
cigarette, before smoking it"—all this delivered with much
pensive, reminiscent fervor which seemed hilarious and
harmless to us at the time; but now—now I catch myself
wondering if we did not disturb unwittingly some perverse
and spiteful demon.

Through all those months, every time a bag of mail managed to get from the Ukraine to Yalta, there would be a
letter for me from my Cynara. Nothing is more occult than
the way letters, under the auspices of unimaginable car-
riers, circulate through the weird mess of civil wars; but
whenever, owing to that mess, there was some break in our

correspondence, Tamara would act as if she ranked deliveries with ordinary natural phenomena such as the weather or tides, which human affairs could not affect, and she would accuse me of not answering her, when in fact I did nothing but write to her and think of her during those months— despite my many betrayals.

5

Happy is the novelist who manages to preserve an actual love letter that he received when he was young within a work of fiction, embedded in it like a clean bullet in flabby flesh and quite secure there, among spurious lives. I wish I had kept the whole of our correspondence that way. Tamara's letters were a sustained conjuration of the rural landscape we knew so well. They were, in a sense, a distant but wonderfully clear antiphonal response to the much less expressive lyrics I had once dedicated to her. By means of unpampered words, whose secret I fail to discover, her high-school-girlish prose could evoke with plangent strength every whiff of damp leaf, every autumn-rusted frond of fern in the St. Petersburg countryside. "Why did we feel so cheerful when it rained?" she asked in one of her last letters, reverting as it were to the pure source of rhetorics. *"Bozhe moy"* (*mon Dieu*—rather than "My God"), where has it gone, all that distant, bright, endearing (*Vsyo eto dalyokoe, svetloe, miloe*—in Russian no subject is needed here, since these are neuter adjectives that play the part of abstract nouns, on a bare stage, in a subdued light).

Tamara, Russia, the wildwood grading into old gardens, my northern birches and firs, the sight of my mother getting down on her hands and knees to kiss the earth every time we came back to the country from town for the summer,

et la montagne et le grand chêne—these are things that fate
one day bundled up pell-mell and tossed into the sea,
completely severing me from my boyhood. I wonder, however, whether there is really much to be said for more
anesthetic destinies, for, let us say, a smooth, safe, small-town
continuity of time, with its primitive absence of perspective,
when, at fifty, one is still dwelling in the clapboard house
of one's childhood, so that every time one cleans the attic
one comes across the same pile of old brown schoolbooks,
still together among later accumulations of dead objects, and
where, on summery Sunday mornings, one's wife stops on
the sidewalk to endure for a minute or two that terrible,
garrulous, dyed, church-bound McGee woman, who, way
back in 1915, used to be pretty, naughty Margaret Ann of
the mint-flavored mouth and nimble fingers.

The break in my own destiny affords me in retrospect a
syncopal kick that I would not have missed for worlds. Ever
since that exchange of letters with Tamara, homesickness
has been with me a sensuous and particular matter. Nowadays, the mental image of matted grass on the Yayla, of
a canyon in the Urals or of salt flats in the Aral Region, affects
me nostalgically and patriotically as little, or as much, as,
say, Utah; but give me anything on any continent resembling
the St. Petersburg countryside and my heart melts. What
it would be actually to see again my former surroundings,
I can hardly imagine. Sometimes I fancy myself revisiting
them with a false passport, under an assumed name. It could
be done.

But I do not think I shall ever do it. I have been dream-
ing of it too idly and too long. Similarly, during the latter
half of my sixteen-month stay in the Crimea, I planned for
so long a time to join Denikin's army, with the intention
not so much of clattering astride a chamfrained charger into

the cobbled outskirts of St. Petersburg (my poor Yuri's dream) as of reaching Tamara in her Ukrainian hamlet, that the army ceased to exist by the time I had made up my mind. In March of 1919, the Reds broke through in northern Crimea, and from various ports a tumultuous evacuation of anti-Bolshevik groups began. Over a glassy sea in the bay of Sebastopol, under wild machine-gun fire from the shore (the Bolshevik troops had just taken the port), my family and I set out for Constantinople and Piraeus on a small and shoddy Greek ship *Nadezhda* (Hope) carrying a cargo of dried fruit. I remember trying to concentrate, as we were zigzagging out of the bay, on a game of chess with my father —one of the knights had lost its head, and a poker chip replaced a missing rook—and the sense of leaving Russia was totally eclipsed by the agonizing thought that Reds or no Reds, letters from Tamara would be still coming, miraculously and needlessly, to southern Crimea, and would search there for a fugitive addressee, and weakly flap about like bewildered butterflies set loose in an alien zone, at the wrong altitude, among an unfamiliar flora.

13

1

IN 1919, by way of the Crimea and Greece, a flock of
Nabokovs—three families in fact—fled from Russia to
western Europe. It was arranged that my brother and I would
go up to Cambridge, on a scholarship awarded more in
atonement for political tribulations than in acknowledge-
ment of intellectual merit. The rest of my family expected
to stay for a while in London. Living expenses were to be
paid by the handful of jewels which Natasha, a farsighted
old chambermaid, just before my mother's departure from
St. Petersburg in November 1917, had swept off a dresser
into a *nécessaire* and which for a brief spell had undergone
interment or perhaps some kind of mysterious maturation
in a Crimean garden. We had left our northern home for
what we thought would be a brief wait, a prudent perching
pause on the southern ledge of Russia; but the fury of the
new regime had refused to blow over. In Greece, during
two spring months, braving the constant resentment of in-
tolerant shepherd dogs, I searched in vain for Gruner's
Orange-tip, Heldreich's Sulphur, Krueper's White: I was in
the wrong part of the country. On the Cunard liner *Pan-
nonia* which left Greece on May 18, 1919 (twenty-one years

too soon as far as I was concerned) for New York, but let us off at Marseilles, I learned to foxtrot. France rattled by in the coal-black night. The pale Channel was still oscillating inside us, when the Dover–London train quietly came to a stop. Repetitive pictures of gray pears on the grimy walls of Victoria Station advertised the bath soap English governesses had used upon me in my childhood. A week later I was already shuffling cheek-to-cheek at a charity ball with my first English sweetheart, a wayward willowy girl five years my senior.

My father had visited London before—the last time in February 1916, when, with five other prominent representatives of the Russian press, he had been invited by the British Government to take a look at England's war effort (which, it was hinted, did not meet with sufficient appreciation on the part of Russia's public opinion). On the way there, being challenged by my father and Korney Chukovski to rhyme on *Afrika*, the poet and novelist Aleksey Tolstoy (no relation to Count Lyov Nikolaevich) had supplied, though seasick, the charming couplet

> *Vizhu pal'mu i Kafrika.*
> *Eto—Afrika.*
> (I see a palm and a little Kaffir. That's Afrika.)

In England the visitors had been shown the Fleet. Dinners and speeches had followed in noble succession. The timely capture of Erzerum by the Russians and the pending introduction of conscription in England ("Will you march too or wait till March 2?" as the punning posters put it) had provided the speakers with easy topics. There had been an official banquet presided over by Sir Edward Grey, and a funny interview with George V whom Chukovski, the *enfant terrible* of the group, insisted on asking if he liked the works of Oscar Wilde—"dze ooarks of OOald." The king, who was baffled by his interrogator's accent and who, anyway, had never been a voracious reader, neatly countered by inquiring how his guests liked the London fog (later Chukovski used to cite this triumphantly as an example of British cant—tabooing a writer because of his morals).

A recent visit to the Public Library in New York has revealed that the above incident does not appear in my father's book *Iz Voyuyushchey Anglii,* Petrograd, 1916 (*A Report on England at War*)—and indeed there are not many samples therein of his habitual humor beyond, perhaps, a description of a game of badminton (or was it fives?) that he had with H. G. Wells, and an amusing account of a visit to some first-line trenches in Flanders, where hospitality went so far as to allow the explosion of a German grenade within a few feet of the visitors. Before publication in book form, this report appeared serially in a Russian daily. There, with a certain old-world naïveté, my father had mentioned making a present of his Swan fountain pen to Admiral Jellicoe, who at table had borrowed it to autograph a menu card and had praised its fluent and suave nib. This unfortunate disclosure of the pen's make was promptly echoed in the London papers by a Mabie, Todd and Co., Ltd., advertisement, which quoted a translation of the passage and depicted my father handing the firm's product to the Commander-in-Chief of the Grand Fleet, under the chaotic sky of a sea battle.

But now there were no banquets, no speeches, and even no fives with Wells whom it proved impossible to convince that Bolshevism was but an especially brutal and thorough form of barbaric oppression—in itself as old as the desert sands—and not at all the attractively new revolutionary experiment that so many foreign observers took it to be. After several expensive months in a rented house in Elm Park Gardens, my parents and the three younger children left London for Berlin (where, until his death in March, 1922, my father joined Iosif Hessen, a fellow member of the People's Freedom Party, in editing a Russian émigré newspaper), while my brother and I went to Cambridge—he to Christ College, I to Trinity.

2

I had two brothers, Sergey and Kirill. Kirill, the youngest child (1911–1964), was also my godson as happened in Russian families. At a certain stage of the baptismal ceremony, in our Vyra drawing room, I held him gingerly before handing him to his godmother, Ekaterina Dmitrievna Danzas (my father's first cousin and a grandniece of Colonel K. K. Danzas, Pushkin's second in his fatal duel). In his childhood Kirill belonged, with my two sisters, to the remote nurseries which were so distinctly separated from his elder brothers' apartments in town house and manor. I saw very little of him during my two decades of European expatriation, 1919–1940, and nothing at all after that, until my next visit to Europe, in 1960, when a brief period of very friendly and joyful meetings ensued.

Kirill went to school in London, Berlin and Prague, and to college at Louvain. He married Gilberte Barbanson, a Belgian girl, ran (humorously but not unsuccessfully) a travel agency in Brussels, and died of a heart attack in Munich.

He loved seaside resorts and rich food. He loathed, as much as I do, bullfighting. He spoke five languages. He was a dedicated practical joker. His one great reality in life was literature, especially Russian poetry. His own verse reflects the influence of Gumilyov and Hodasevich. He pub-

My wife took, unnoticed, this picture, unposed, of me in the act of writing a novel in our hotel room. The hotel is the Établissement Thermal at Le Boulou, in the East Pyrenees. The date (discernible on the captured calendar) is February 27, 1929. The novel, *Zashchita Luzhina (The Defense)*, deals with the defense invented by an insane chess player. Note the pat pattern of the tablecloth. A half-empty package of Gauloises cigarettes can be made out between the ink bottle and an overful ashtray. Family photos are propped against the four volumes of Dahl's Russian dictionary. The end of my robust, dark-brown penholder (a beloved tool of young oak that I used during all my twenty years of literary labors in Europe and may rediscover yet in one of the trunks stored at Dean's, Ithaca, N. Y.) is already well chewed. My writing hand partly conceals a stack of setting boards. Spring moths would float in through the open window on overcast nights and settle upon the lighted wall on my left. In that way we collected a number of rare Pugs in perfect condition and spread them at once (they are now in an American museum). Seldom does a casual snapshot compendiate a life so precisely.

Many years ago, in St. Petersburg, I remember being amused by the Collected Poems of a tram conductor, and especially by his picture, in uniform, sturdily booted, with a pair of new rubbers on the floor beside him and his father's war medals on the photographer's console near which the author stood at attention. Wise conductor, farseeing photographer!

A snapshot taken by my wife of our three-year-old son Dmitri (born May 10, 1934) standing with me in front of our boardinghouse, Les Hesperides, in Mentone, at the beginning of December 1937. We looked it up twenty-two years later. Nothing had changed, except the management and the porch furniture. There is always, of course, the natural thrill of retrieved time; beyond that, however, I get no special kick out of revisiting old émigré haunts in those incidental countries. The winter mosquitoes, I remember, were terrible. Hardly had I extinguished the light in my room than it would come, that ominous whine whose unhurried, doleful, and wary rhythm contrasted so oddly with the actual mad speed of the satanic insect's gyrations. One waited for the touch in the dark, one freed a cautious arm from under the bedclothes—and mightily slapped one's own ear, whose sudden hum mingled with that of the receding mosquito. But then, next morning, how eagerly one reached for a butterfly net upon locating one's replete tormentor—a thick dark little bar on the white of the ceiling!

lished sparsely and was always as reticent about his writing as he was about his persiflage-misted inner existence.

For various reasons I find it inordinately hard to speak about my other brother. That twisted quest for Sebastian Knight (1940), with its gloriettes and self-mate combinations, is really nothing in comparison to the task I balked in the first version of this memoir and am faced with now. Except for the two or three poor little adventures I have sketched in earlier chapters, his boyhood and mine seldom mingled. He is a mere shadow in the background of my richest and most detailed recollections. I was the coddled one; he, the witness of coddling. Born, caesareanally, ten and a half months after me, on March 12, 1900, he matured earlier than I and physically looked older. We seldom played together, he was indifferent to most of the things I was fond of —toy trains, toy pistols, Red Indians, Red Admirables. At six or seven he developed a passionate adulation, condoned by Mademoiselle, for Napoleon and took a little bronze bust of him to bed. As a child, I was rowdy, adventurous and something of a bully. He was quiet and listless, and spent much more time with our mentors than I. At ten, began his interest in music, and thenceforth he took innumerable lessons, went to concerts with our father, and spent hours on end playing snatches of operas, on an upstairs piano well within earshot. I would creep up behind and prod him in the ribs—a miserable memory.

We attended different schools; he went to my father's former *gimnasiya* and wore the regulation black uniform to which, at fifteen, he added an illegal touch: mouse-gray spats. About that time, a page from his diary that I found on his desk and read, and in stupid wonder showed to my tutor, who promptly showed it to my father, abruptly pro-

vided a retroactive clarification of certain oddities of behavior on his part.

The only game we both liked was tennis. We played a
lot of it together, especially in England, on an erratic grass
court in Kensington, on a good clay court in Cambridge.
He was left-handed. He had a bad stammer that hampered
discussions of doubtful points. Despite a weak service and
an absence of any real backhand, he was not easy to beat,
being the kind of player who never double-faults, and returns everything with the consistency of a banging wall. In
Cambridge, we saw more of each other than anywhere before
and had, for once, a few friends in common. We both
graduated in the same subjects, with the same honors, after
which he moved to Paris where, during the following years,
he gave lessons of English and Russian, just as I did in Berlin.

We again met in the nineteen-thirties, and were on quite
amiable terms in 1938–1940, in Paris. He often dropped in
for a chat, rue Boileau where I lodged in two shabby rooms
with you and our child, but it so happened (he had been
away for a while) that he learned of our departure to America only after we had left. My bleakest recollections are
associated with Paris, and the relief of leaving it was overwhelming, but I am sorry he had to stutter his astonishment
to an indifferent concierge. I know little of his life during
the war. At one time he was employed as translator at an
office in Berlin. A frank and fearless man, he criticized the
regime in front of colleagues, who denounced him. He was
arrested, accused of being a "British spy" and sent to a Ham-
burg concentration camp where he died of inanition, on
January 10, 1945. It is one of those lives that hopelessly
claim a belated something—compassion, undestanding, no
matter what—which the mere recognition of such a want can
neither replace nor redeem.

3

The beginning of my first term in Cambridge was inauspicious. Late in the afternoon of a dull and damp October day, with the sense of indulging in some weird theatricals, I put on my newly acquired, dark-bluish academic gown and black square cap for my first formal visit to E. Harrison, my college tutor. I went up a flight of stairs and knocked on a massive door that stood slightly ajar. "Come in," said a distant voice with hollow abruptness. I crossed a waiting room of sorts and entered my tutor's study. The brown dusk had forestalled me. There was no light in the study save for the glow of a large fireplace near which a dim figure sat in a dimmer chair. I advanced saying: "My name is—" and stepped into the tea things that stood on the rug beside Mr. Harrison's low wicker armchair. With a grunt, he bent sideways from his seat to right the pot, and then scooped up and dumped back into it the wet black mess of tea leaves it had disgorged. Thus the college period of my life began on a note of embarrassment, a note that was to recur rather persistently during my three years of residence.

Mr. Harrison thought it a fine idea to have one "White Russian" lodge with another, and so, at first, I shared an apartment in Trinity Lane with a puzzled compatriot. After a few months he left college, and I remained sole occupant of those lodgings. They seemed intolerably squalid in comparison with my remote and by now nonexistent home. Well do I remember the ornaments on the mantelpiece (a glass ashtray, with the Trinity crest, left by some former lodger; a seashell in which I found the imprisoned hum of one of my own seaside summers), and my landlady's old mechanical piano, a pathetic contraption, full of ruptured, crushed, knotted music, which one sampled once and no more. Narrow Trinity Lane was a staid and rather sad little street, with almost no traffic, but with a long, lurid past beginning in the sixteenth century, when it used to be Findsilver Lane, although commonly called at the time by a coarser name because of the then abominable state of its gutters. I suffered a good deal from the cold, but it is quite untrue, as some have it, that the polar temperature in Cambridge bedrooms caused the water to freeze solid in one's washstand jug. As a matter of fact, there would be hardly more than a thin layer of ice on the surface, and this was easily broken by means of one's toothbrush into tinkling bits, a sound which, in retrospect, has even a certain festive appeal to my Americanized ear. Otherwise, getting up was no fun at all. I still feel in my bones the bleakness of the morning walk up Trinity Lane to the Baths, as one shuffled along, exuding pallid puffs of breath, in a thin dressing gown over one's pajamas and with a cold, fat sponge-bag under one's arm. Nothing in the world could induce me to wear next to my skin the "woolies" that kept Englishmen secretly warm. Overcoats were considered sissy. The usual attire of the average Cambridge undergraduate, whether athlete or leftist poet, struck a sturdy and dingy note: his shoes had thick rubber soles, his flannel trousers were dark gray, and the buttoned sweater, called a "jumper," under his Norfolk jacket was a conservative brown. What I suppose might be termed the gay set wore old pumps, very light gray flannel trousers, a bright-yellow "jumper," and the coat part of a good suit. By that time my youthful preoccupation with clothes was on the wane, but it did seem rather a lark, after the formal fashions in Russia, to go about in slippers, eschew garters, and wear one's collar sewn onto one's shirt—a daring innovation in those days.

The mild masquerade in which I indolently joined has

left such trifling impressions upon my mind that it would be tedious to continue in this strain. The story of my college years in England is really the story of my trying to become a Russian writer. I had the feeling that Cambridge and all its famed features—venerable elms, blazoned windows, loquacious tower clocks—were of no consequence in themselves but existed merely to frame and support my rich nostalgia. Emotionally, I was in the position of a man who, having just lost a fond kinswoman, realized—too late—that through some laziness of the routine-drugged human soul, he had neither troubled to know her as fully as she deserved, nor had shown her in full the marks of his not quite conscious then, but now unrelieved, affection. As with smarting eyes I meditated by the fire in my Cambridge room, all the potent banality of embers, solitude and distant chimes pressed against me, contorting the very folds of my face as an airman's face is disfigured by the fantastic speed of his flight. And I thought of all I had missed in my country, of the things I would not have omitted to note and treasure, had I suspected before that my life was to veer in such a violent way.

To some of the several fellow émigrés I met in Cambridge the general trend of my feelings was so obvious and familiar a thing that it would have fallen flat and seemed almost improper if put into words. With the whiter of those White Russians I soon found out that patriotism and politics boiled down to a snarling resentment which was directed more against Kerenski than against Lenin and which proceeded solely from material discomforts and losses. Then, too, I ran into some quite unexpected difficulties with such of my English acquaintances as were considered to be cultured and subtle, and humane, but who, for all their decency and refinement, would lapse into the most astonishing drivel when Russia was being discussed. I want to single out here a young

Socialist I knew, a lanky giant whose slow and multiple ma-
nipulations of a pipe were horribly aggravating when you
did not agree with him and delightfully soothing when you
did. With him, I had many political wrangles, the bitterness
of which invariably dissolved when we turned to the poets
we both cherished. Today he is not unknown among his
peers, which is, I readily admit, a pretty meaningless phrase,
but then, I am doing my best to obscure his identity; let me
refer to him by the name of "Nesbit" as I dubbed him (or
affirm now having dubbed him), not only because of his
alleged resemblance to early portraits of Maxim Gorki, a
regional mediocrity of that era, one of whose first stories
("My Fellow Traveler"—another apt note) had been translated by a certain R. Nesbit Bain, but also because "Nesbit"
has the advantage of entering into a voluptuous palindromic
association with "Ibsen," a name I shall have to evoke presently.

It is probably true, as some have argued, that sympathy
for Leninism on the part of English and American liberal
opinion in the twenties was swung by consideration of home
politics. But it was also due to simple misinformation. My
friend knew little of Russia's past and this little had come
to him through polluted Communist channels. When challenged to justify the bestial terror that had been sanctioned
by Lenin—the torture-house, the blood-bespattered wall—
Nesbit would tap the ashes out of his pipe against the fender
knob, recross sinistrally his huge, heavily shod, dextrally
crossed legs, and murmur something about the "Allied
Blockade." He lumped together as "Czarist elements" Russian émigrés of all hues, from peasant Socialist to White
general—much as today Soviet writers wield the term "Fas-
cist." He never realized that had he and other foreign
idealists been Russians in Russia, he and they would have

been destroyed by Lenin's regime as naturally as rabbits are by ferrets and farmers. He maintained that the reason for what he demurely called "less variety of opinion" under the Bolsheviks than in the darkest Tsarist days was "the want of any tradition of free speech in Russia," a statement he got, I believe, from the sort of fatuous "Dawn in Russia" stuff that eloquent English and American Leninists wrote in those years. But the thing that irritated me perhaps most was Nesbit's attitude toward Lenin himself. All cultured and discriminating Russians knew that this astute politician had about as much taste and interest in aesthetic matters as an ordinary Russian bourgeois of the Flaubertian *épicier* sort (the type that admired Pushkin on the strength of Chaykovski's vile librettos, wept at the Italian opera, and was allured by any painting that told a story); but Nesbit and his highbrow friends saw in him a kind of sensitive, poetic-minded patron and promoter of the newest trends in art and would smile a superior smile when I tried to explain that the connection between advanced politics and advanced art was a purely verbal one (gleefully exploited by Soviet propaganda), and that the more radical a Russian was in politics, the more conservative he was on the artistic side.

I had at my disposal a number of such truths that I liked to air, but that Nesbit, firmly entrenched in his ignorance, regarded as mere fancies. The history of Russia (I might, for example, declare) could be considered from two points of views (both of which, for some reason, equally annoyed Nesbit): first, as the evolution of the police (a curiously impersonal and detached force, sometimes working in a kind of void, sometimes helpless, and at other times outdoing the government in brutal persecution); and second, as the development of a marvelous culture. Under the Tsars (I might go on), despite the fundamentally inept and ferocious character of their rule, a freedom-loving Russian had had incomparably more means of expressing himself, and used to run incomparably less risk in doing so, than under Lenin. Since the reforms of the eighteen-sixties, the country had possessed (though not always adhered to) a legislation of which any Western democracy might have been proud, a vigorous public opinion that held despots at bay, widely read periodicals of all shades of liberal political thought, and what was especially striking, fearless and independent judges ("Oh come . . ." Nesbit would interpose). When revolutionaries did get caught, banishment to Tomsk or Omsk (now Bombsk) was a restful vacation in comparison to the concentration camps that Lenin introduced. Political exiles escaped from Siberia with farcical ease, witness the famous flight of Trotsky—Santa Leo, Santa Claws Trotsky—merrily riding back in a Yuletide sleigh drawn by reindeer: On, Rocket, on, Stupid, on, Butcher and Blitzen!

I soon became aware that if my views, the not unusual views of Russian democrats abroad, were received with pained surprise or polite sneers by English democrats *in situ,* another group, the English ultraconservatives, rallied eagerly to my side but did so from such crude reactionary motivation that I was only embarrassed by their despicable support. Indeed, I pride myself with having discerned even then the symptoms of what is so clear today, when a kind of family circle has gradually been formed, linking representatives of all nations, jolly empire-builders in their jungle clearings, French policemen, the unmentionable German product, the good old churchgoing Russian or Polish *pogromshchik,* the lean American lyncher, the man with the bad teeth who squirts antiminority stories in the bar or the lavatory, and, at another point of the same subhuman circle, those ruthless, paste-faced automatons in opulent John Held

trousers and high-shouldered jackets, those *Sitzriesen* loom-
ing at all our conference tables, whom—or shall I say which?
—the Soviet State began to export around 1945 after more
than two decades of selective breeding and tailoring, during
which men's fashions abroad had had time to change, so
that the symbol of infinitely available cloth could only provoke cruel derision (as occurred in postwar England when
a famous Soviet team of professional soccer players happened
to parade in mufti).

4

Very soon I turned away from politics and concentrated
on literature. I invited to my Cambridge rooms the vermilion
shields and blue lightning of the Song of *Igor's Campaign*
(that incomparable and mysterious epic of the late twelfth
or late eighteenth century), the poetry of Pushkin and
Tyutchev, the prose of Gogol and Tolstoy, and also the
wonderful works of the great Russian naturalists who had
explored and described the wilds of Central Asia. At a bookstall in the Market Place, I unexpectedly came upon a Russian work, a secondhand copy of Dahl's *Interpretative Dictionary of the Living Russian Language* in four volumes. I
bought it and resolved to read at least ten pages per day,
jotting down such words and expressions as might especially
please me, and I kept this up for a considerable time. My
fear of losing or corrupting, through alien influence, the only
thing I had salvaged from Russia—her language—became
positively morbid and considerably more harassing than the
fear I was to experience two decades later of my never being
able to bring my English prose anywhere close to the level
of my Russian. I used to sit up far into the night, surrounded
by an almost Quixotic accumulation of unwieldy volumes,

and make polished and rather sterile Russian poems not so
much out of the live cells of some compelling emotion as
around a vivid term or a verbal image that I wanted to use
for its own sake. It would have horrified me at the time
to discover what I see so clearly now, the direct influence
upon my Russian structures of various contemporaneous
("Georgian") English verse patterns that were running about
my room and all over me like tame mice. And to think of
the labor I expended! Suddenly, in the small hours of a
November morning, I would become conscious of the silence
and chill (my second winter in Cambridge seems to have
been the coldest, and most prolific one). The red and blue
flames wherein I had been seeing a fabled battle had sunk to
the lugubrious glow of an arctic sunset among hoary firs. Still
I could not force myself to go to bed, dreading not so much
insomnia as the inevitable double systole, abetted by the cold
of the sheets, and also the curious affection called *anxietas
tibiarum,* a painful condition of unrest, an excruciating increase of muscular sense, which leads to a continual change
in the position of one's limbs. So I would heap on more coals
and help revive the flames by spreading a sheet of the London
Times over the smoking black jaws of the fireplace, thus
screening completely its open recess. A humming noise
would start behind the taut paper, which would acquire the
smoothness of drumskin and the beauty of luminous parch-
ment. Presently, as the hum turned into a roar, an orange-
colored spot would appear in the middle of the sheet, and
whatever patch of print happened to be there (for example,
"The League does not command a guinea or a gun," or
"... the revenges that Nemesis has had upon Allied hesitation and indecision in Eastern and Central Europe...")
stood out with ominous clarity—until suddenly the orange
spot burst. Then the flaming sheet, with the whirr of a lib-

erated phoenix, would fly up the chimney to join the stars.
It cost one a fine of twelve shillings if that firebird was
observed.

The literary set, Nesbit and his friends, while commending
my nocturnal labors, frowned upon various other things I
went in for, such as entomology, practical jokes, girls, and,
especially, athletics. Of the games I played at Cambridge,
soccer has remained a wind-swept clearing in the middle of
a rather muddled period. I was crazy about goal keeping. In
Russia and the Latin countries, that gallant art had been
always surrounded with a halo of singular glamour. Aloof,
solitary, impassive, the crack goalie is followed in the streets
by entranced small boys. He vies with the matador and the
flying ace as an object of thrilled adulation. His sweater, his
peaked cap, his kneeguards, the gloves protruding from the
hip pocket of his shorts, set him apart from the rest of the
team. He is the lone eagle, the man of mystery, the last
defender. Photographers, reverently bending one knee, snap
him in the act of making a spectacular dive across the goal
mouth to deflect with his fingertips a low, lightning-like shot,
and the stadium roars in approval as he remains for a moment or two lying full length where he fell, his goal still
intact.

But in England, at least in the England of my youth, the
national dread of showing off and a too grim preoccupation
with solid teamwork were not conducive to the development
of the goalie's eccentric art. This at least was the explanation
I dug up for not being oversuccessful on the playing fields
of Cambridge. Oh, to be sure, I had my bright, bracing days
—the good smell of turf, that famous inter-Varsity forward,
dribbling closer and closer to me with the new tawny ball
at his twinkling toe, then the stinging shot, the lucky save,
its protracted tingle.... But there were other, more memor-

able, more esoteric days, under dismal skies, with the goal
area a mass of black mud, the ball as greasy as a plum pud-
ding, and my head racked with neuralgia after a sleepless
night of verse-making. I would fumble badly—and retrieve
the ball from the net. Mercifully the game would swing to
the opposite end of the sodden field. A weak, weary drizzle
would start, hesitate, and go on again. With an almost cooing
tenderness in their subdued croaking, dilapidated rooks
would be flapping about a leafless elm. Mists would gather.
Now the game would be a vague bobbing of heads near the
remote goal of St. John's or Christ, or whatever college we
were playing. The far, blurred sounds, a cry, a whistle, the
thud of a kick, all that was perfectly unimportant and had
no connection with me. I was less the keeper of a soccer goal
than the keeper of a secret. As with folded arms I leant my
back against the left goalpost, I enjoyed the luxury of closing
my eyes, and thus I would listen to my heart knocking and
feel the blind drizzle on my face and hear, in the distance,
the broken sounds of the game, and think of myself as of a
fabulous exotic being in an English footballer's disguise,
composing verse in a tongue nobody understood about a
remote country nobody knew. Small wonder I was not very
popular with my teammates.

Not once in my three years of Cambridge—repeat: not once
—did I visit the University Library, or even bother to locate
it (I know its new place now), or find out if there existed a
college library where books might be borrowed for reading
in one's digs. I skipped lectures. I sneaked to London and
elsewhere. I conducted several love affairs simultaneously. I
had dreadful interviews with Mr. Harrison. I translated into
Russian a score of poems by Rupert Brooke, *Alice in Wonderland,* and Romain Rolland's *Colas Breugnon.* Scholastically,
I might as well have gone up to the Inst. M. M. of Tirana.

Such things as the hot muffins and crumpets one had with one's tea after games or the newsboys' cockneyish cries of "Piper, piper!" mingling with the bicycle bells in the darkening streets, seemed to me at the time more characteristic of Cambridge than they do now. I cannot help realizing that, aside from striking but more or less transient customs, and deeper than ritual or rule, there did exist the residual something about Cambridge that many a solemn alumnus has tried to define. I see this basic property as the constant awareness one had of an untrammeled extension of time. I do not know if anyone will ever go to Cambridge in search of the imprints which the teat-cleats on my soccer boots have left in the black mud before a gaping goal or follow the shadow of my cap across the quadrangle to my tutor's stairs; but I know that I thought of Milton, and Marvell, and Marlowe, with more than a tourist's thrill as I passed beside the reverend walls. Nothing one looked at was shut off in terms of time, everything was a natural opening into it, so that one's mind grew accustomed to work in a particularly pure and ample environment, and because, in terms of space, the narrow lane, the cloistered lawn, the dark archway hampered one physically, that yielding diaphanous texture of time was, by contrast, especially welcome to the mind, just as a sea view from a window exhilarates one hugely, even though one does not care for sailing. I had no interest whatever in the history of the place, and was quite sure that Cambridge was in no way affecting my soul, although actually it was Cambridge that supplied not only the casual frame, but also the very colors and inner rhythms for my very special Russian thoughts. Environment, I suppose, does act upon a creature if there is, in that creature, already a certain responsive particle or strain (the English I had imbibed in my childhood). Of this I had my first inkling just before leaving

Cambridge, during my last and saddest spring there, when I suddenly felt that something in me was as naturally in contact with my immediate surroundings as it was with my Russian past, and that this state of harmony had been reached at the very moment that the careful reconstruction of my artificial but beautifully exact Russian world had been at last completed. I think one of the very few "practical" actions I have ever been guilty of was to use part of that crystalline material to obtain an Honours degree.

5

I remember the dreamy flow of punts and canoes on the Cam, the Hawaiian whine of phonographs slowly passing through sunshine and shade and a girl's hand gently twirling this way and that the handle of her peacock-bright parasol as she reclined on the cushions of the punt which I dreamily navigated. The pink-coned chestnuts were in full fan; they made overlapping masses along the banks, they crowded the sky out of the river, and their special pattern of flowers and leaves produced a kind of *en escalier* effect, the angular figuration of some splendid green and old-rose tapestry. The air was as warm as in the Crimea, with the same sweet, fluffy smell of a certain flowering bush that I never could quite identify (I later caught whiffs of it in the gardens of the southern States). The three arches of an Italianate bridge, spanning the narrow stream, combined to form, with the help of their almost perfect, almost unrippled replicas in the water, three lovely ovals. In its turn, the water cast a patch of lacy light on the stone of the intrados under which one's gliding craft passed. Now and then, shed by a blossoming tree, a petal would come down, down, down, and with the odd feeling of seeing something neither worshiper nor casual spectator ought to see, one would manage to glimpse its reflection which swiftly—more swiftly than the petal fell—rose to meet it; and, for the fraction of a second, one feared that the trick would not work, that the blessed oil would not catch fire, that the reflection might miss and the petal float away alone, but every time the delicate union did take place, with the magic precision of a poet's word meeting halfway his, or a reader's, recollection.

When, after an absence of almost seventeen years I revisited England, I made the dreadful mistake of going to see Cambridge again not at the glorious end of the Easter term but on a raw February day that reminded me only of my own confused old nostalgia. I was hopelessly trying to find an academic job in England (the ease with which I obtained that type of employment in the U.S.A. is to me, in backthought, a constant source of grateful wonder). In every way the visit was not a success. I had lunch with Nesbit at a little place, which ought to have been full of memories but which, owing to various changes, was not. He had given up smoking. Time had softened his features and he no longer resembled Gorki or Gorki's translator, but looked a little like Ibsen, minus the simian vegetation. An accidental worry (the cousin or maiden sister who kept house for him had just been removed to Binet's clinic or something) seemed to prevent him from concentrating on the very personal and urgent matter I wanted to speak to him about. Bound volumes of *Punch* were heaped on a table in a kind of small vestibule where a bowl of goldfish had formerly stood—and it all looked so different. Different too were the garish uniforms worn by the waitresses, of whom none was as pretty as the particular one I remembered so clearly. Rather desperately, as if struggling against boredom, Ibsen launched into politics. I knew well what to expect—denunciation of Sta-

linism. In the early twenties Nesbit had mistaken his own
ebullient idealism for a romantic and humane something in
Lenin's ghastly rule. Ibsen, in the days of the no less ghastly
Stalin, was mistaking a quantitative increase in his own
knowledge for a qualitative change in the Soviet regime.
The thunderclap of purges that had affected "old Bolsheviks," the heroes of his youth, had given him a salutary shock,
something that in Lenin's day all the groans coming from
the Solovki forced labor camp or the Lubyanka dungeon
had not been able to do. With horror he pronounced the
names of Ezhov and Yagoda—but quite forgot their predecessors, Uritski and Dzerzhinski. While time had improved
his judgment regarding contemporaneous Soviet affairs, he
did not bother to reconsider the preconceived notions of his
youth, and still saw in Lenin's short reign a kind of glamorous *quinquennium Neronis.*

He looked at his watch, and I looked at mine, and we
parted, and I wandered around the town in the rain, and
then visited the Backs, and for some time peered at the rooks
in the black network of the bare elms and at the first crocuses
in the mist-beaded turf. As I strolled under those sung trees,
I tried to put myself into the same ecstatically reminiscent
mood in regard to my student years as during those years I
had experienced in regard to my boyhood, but all I could
evoke were fragmentary little pictures: M. K., a Russian,
dyspeptically cursing the aftereffects of a College Hall dinner; N. R., another Russian, romping about like a child; P.
M. storming into my room with a copy of *Ulysses* freshly
smuggled from Paris; J. C. quietly dropping in to say that
he, too, had just lost his father; R. C. charmingly inviting
me to join him on a trip to the Swiss Alps; Christopher
something or other, wriggling out of a proposed tennis
double upon learning that his partner was to be a Hindu;

T., a very old and fragile waiter, spilling the soup in Hall on Professor A. E. Housman, who then abruptly stood up as one shooting out of a trance; S. S., who was in no way connected with Cambridge, but who, having dozed off in his chair at a literary party (in Berlin) and being nudged by a neighbor, also stood up suddenly—in the middle of a story someone was reading; Lewis Carroll's Dormouse, unexpectedly starting to tell a tale; E. Harrison unexpectedly making me a present of *The Shropshire Lad,* a little volume of verse about young males and death.

The dull day had dwindled to a pale yellow streak in the gray west when, acting upon an impulse, I decided to visit my old tutor. Like a sleepwalker, I mounted the familiar steps and automatically knocked on the half-open door bearing his name. In a voice that was a jot less abrupt, and a trifle more hollow, he bade me come in. "I wonder if you remember me . . ." I started to say, as I crossed the dim room to where he sat near a comfortable fire. "Let me see," he said, slowly turning around in his low chair, "I do not quite seem . . ." There was a dismal crunch, a fatal clatter: I had stepped into the tea things that stood at the foot of his wicker chair. "Oh, yes, of course," he said, "I know who you are."

The small butterfly, light blue above, grayish beneath, of which the two type specimens (male holotype on the left, both sides, one hindwing slightly damaged; and male paratype on the right, both sides), preserved in the American Museum of Natural History and figured now for the first time from photographs made by that institution, is *Plebejus (Lysandra) cormion* Nabokov. The first name is that of the genus, the second that of the subgenus, the third that of the species, and the fourth that of the author of the original description which I published in September 1941 (*Journal of the New York Entomological Society*, Vol. 49, p. 265), later figuring the genitalia of the paratype (October 26, 1945, *Psyche*, Vol. 52, Pl. 1). Possibly, as I pointed out, my butterfly owed its origin to hybridization between *Plebejus (Lysandra) coridon* Poda (in the large sense) and *Plebejus (Meleageria) daphnis* Schiffermüller. Live organisms are less conscious of specific or subgeneric differences than the taxonomist is. I took the two males figured, and saw at least two more (but no females) on July 20 (paratype) and 22 (holotype), 1938, at about 4,000 ft. near the village of Moulinet, Alpes Maritimes. It may not rank high enough to deserve a name, but whatever it be—a new species in the making, a striking sport, or a chance cross—it remains a great and delightful rarity.

14

THE spiral is a spiritualized circle. In the spiral form, the circle, uncoiled, unwound, has ceased to be vicious; it has been set free. I thought this up when I was a schoolboy, and I also discovered that Hegel's triadic series (so popular in old Russia) expressed merely the essential spirality of all things in their relation to time. Twirl follows twirl, and every synthesis is the thesis of the next series. If we consider the simplest spiral, three stages may be distinguished in it, corresponding to those of the triad: We can call "thetic" the small curve or arc that initiates the convolution centrally; "antithetic" the larger arc that faces the first in the process of continuing it; and "synthetic" the still ampler arc that continues the second while following the first along the outer side. And so on.

A colored spiral in a small ball of glass, this is how I see my own life. The twenty years I spent in my native Russia (1899–1919) take care of the thetic arc. Twenty-one years of voluntary exile in England, Germany and France (1919–1940) supply the obvious antithesis. The period spent in my adopted country (1940–1960) forms a synthesis—and a new thesis. For the moment I am concerned with my antithetic stage, and more particularly with my life in Continental Europe after I had graduated from Cambridge in 1922.

As I look back at those years of exile, I see myself, and thousands of other Russians, leading an odd but by no means unpleasant existence, in material indigence and intellectual luxury, among perfectly unimportant strangers, spectral Germans and Frenchmen in whose more or less illusory cities we, émigrés, happened to dwell. These aborigines were to the mind's eye as flat and transparent as figures cut out of cellophane, and although we used their gadgets, applauded their clowns, picked their roadside plums and apples, no real communication, of the rich human sort so widespread in our own midst, existed between us and them. It seemed at times that we ignored them the way an arrogant or very stupid invader ignores a formless and faceless mass of natives; but occasionally, quite often in fact, the spectral world through which we serenely paraded our sores and our arts would produce a kind of awful convulsion and show us who was the discarnate captive and who the true lord. Our utter physical dependence on this or that nation, which had coldly granted us political refuge, became painfully evident when some trashy "visa," some diabolical "identity card" had to be obtained or prolonged, for then an avid bureaucratic hell would attempt to close upon the petitioner and he might wilt while his dossier waxed fatter and fatter in the desks of rat-whiskered consuls and policemen. *Dokumentï,* it has been said, is a Russian's placenta. The League of Nations equipped émigrés who had lost their Russian citizenship with a so-called "Nansen" passport, a very inferior document of a sickly green hue. Its holder was little better than a criminal on parole and had to go through most hideous ordeals every time he wished to travel from one country to another, and the smaller the countries the worse the fuss they made. Somewhere at the back of their glands, the authorities secreted the notion that no matter how bad a state—say, Soviet Russia—might be, any fugitive from it was intrinsically despicable since he existed outside a national administration; and therefore he was viewed with the preposterous disapproval with which certain religious groups regard a child born out of wedlock. Not all of us consented to be bastards and ghosts. Sweet are the recollections some Russian émigrés treasure of how they insulted or fooled high officials at various ministries, *Préfectures* and *Polizeipraesidiums*.

In Berlin and Paris, the two capitals of exile, Russians formed compact colonies, with a coefficient of culture that greatly surpassed the cultural mean of the necessarily more diluted foreign communities among which they were placed. Within those colonies they kept to themselves. I have in view, of course, Russian intellectuals, mostly belonging to democratic groups, and not the flashier kind of person who "was, you know, adviser to the Tsar or something" that American clubwomen immediately think of whenever "White Russians" are mentioned. Life in those settlements was so full and intense that these Russian *"intelligenti"* (a word that had more socially idealistic and less highbrow connotations than "intellectuals" as used in America) had neither time nor reason to seek ties beyond their own circle. Today, in a new and beloved world, where I have learned to feel at home as easily as I have ceased barring my sevens, extroverts and cosmopolitans to whom I happen to mention these past matters think I am jesting, or accuse me of snobbery in reverse, when I maintain that in the course of almost one-fifth of a century spent in Western Europe I have not had, among the sprinkling of Germans and Frenchmen I knew (mostly landladies and literary people), more than two good friends all told.

, during my secluded years in Germany, I never
those gentle musicians of yore who, in Turgenev's
d their rhapsodies far into the summer night;
or those happy old hunters with their captures pinned to the
crown of their hats, of whom the Age of Reason made such
fun: La Bruyère's gentleman who sheds tears over a para-
sitized caterpillar, Gay's "philosophers more grave than wise"
who, if you please, "hunt science down in butterflies," and,
less insultingly, Pope's "curious Germans," who "hold so
rare" those "insects fair"; or simply the so-called wholesome
and kindly folks that during the last war homesick soldiers
from the Middle West seem to have preferred so much to the
cagey French farmer and to brisk Madelon II. On the contrary, the most vivid figure I find when sorting out in memory the meager stack of my non-Russian and non-Jewish
acquaintances in the years between the two wars is the image
of a young German university student, well-bred, quiet,
bespectacled, whose hobby was capital punishment. At our
second meeting he showed me a collection of photographs
among which was a purchased series (*"Ein bischen retou-
chiert,"* he said wrinkling his freckled nose) that depicted
the successive stages of a routine execution in China; he com-
mented, very expertly, on the splendor of the lethal sword
and on the spirit of perfect cooperation between headsman
and victim, which culminated in a veritable geyser of mist-
gray blood spouting from the very clearly photographed neck
of the decapitated party. Being pretty well off, this young
collector could afford to travel, and travel he did, in between
the humanities he studied for his Ph.D. He complained, however, of continuous ill luck and added that if he did not see
something really good soon, he might not stand the strain.
He had attended a few passable hangings in the Balkans and
a well-advertised, although rather bleak and mechanical *guil-*

lotinade (he liked to use what he thought was colloquial French) on the Boulevard Arago in Paris; but somehow he never was sufficiently close to observe everything in detail, and the highly expensive teeny-weeny camera in the sleeve of his raincoat did not work as well as he had hoped. Despite a bad cold, he had journeyed to Regensburg where beheading was violently performed with an axe; he had expected great things from that spectacle but, to his intense disappointment, the subject had apparently been drugged and had hardly reacted at all, beyond feebly flopping about on the ground while the masked executioner and his clumsy mate fell all over him. Dietrich (my acquaintance's first name) hoped some day to go to the States so as to witness a couple of electrocutions; from this word, in his innocence, he derived the adjective "cute," which he had learned from a cousin of his who had been to America, and with a little frown of wistful worry Dietrich wondered if it were really true that, during the performance, sensational puffs of smoke issued from the natural orifices of the body. At our third and last encounter (there still remained bits of him I wanted to file for possible use) he related to me, more in sorrow than in anger, that he had once spent a whole night patiently watching a good friend of his who had decided to shoot himself and had agreed to do so, in the roof of the mouth, facing the hobbyist in a good light, but having no ambition or sense of honor, had got hopelessly tight instead. Although I have lost track of Dietrich long ago, I can well imagine the look of calm satisfaction in his fish-blue eyes as he shows, nowadays (perhaps at the very minute I am writing this), a never-expected profusion of treasures to his thigh-clapping, guffawing co-veterans—the absolutely *wunderbar* pictures he took during Hitler's reign.

2

I have sufficiently spoken of the gloom and the glory of
exile in my Russian novels, and especially in the best of them,
Dar (recently published in English as *The Gift*); but a quick
recapitulation here may be convenient. With a very few exceptions, all liberal-minded creative forces—poets, novelists,
critics, historians, philosophers and so on—had left Lenin's
and Stalin's Russia. Those who had not were either wither-
ing away there or adulterating their gifts by complying with
the political demands of the state. What the Tsars had never
been able to achieve, namely the complete curbing of minds
to the government's will, was achieved by the Bolsheviks in
no time after the main contingent of the intellectuals had
escaped abroad or had been destroyed. The lucky group of
expatriates could now follow their pursuits with such utter
impunity that, in fact, they sometimes asked themselves if the
sense of enjoying absolute mental freedom was not due to
their working in an absolute void. True, there was among
émigrés a sufficient number of good readers to warrant the
publication, in Berlin, Paris, and other towns, of Russian
books and periodicals on a comparatively large scale; but
since none of those writings could circulate within the Soviet
Union, the whole thing acquired a certain air of fragile un-
reality. The number of titles was more impressive than the
number of copies any given work sold, and the names of the
publishing houses—Orion, Cosmos, Logos, and so forth—had
the hectic, unstable and slightly illegal appearance that firms
issuing astrological or facts-of-life literature have. In serene
retrospect, however, and judged by artistic and scholarly
standards alone, the books produced *in vacuo* by émigré
writers seem today, whatever their individual faults, more
permanent and more suitable for human consumption than

the slavish, singularly provincial and conventional streams of political consciousness that came during those same years from the pens of young Soviet authors whom a fatherly state provided with ink, pipes and pullovers.

The editor of the daily *Rul'* (and the publisher of my first books), Iosif Vladimirovich Hessen, allowed me with great leniency to fill his poetry section with my unripe rhymes. Blue evenings in Berlin, the corner chestnut in flower, light-headedness, poverty, love, the tangerine tinge of premature shoplights, and an animal aching yearn for the still fresh reek of Russia—all this was put into meter, copied out in long-hand and carted off to the editor's office, where myopic I. V. would bring the new poem close to his face and after this brief, more or less tactual, act of cognition put it down on his desk. By 1928, my novels were beginning to bring a little money in German translations, and in the spring of 1929, you and I went butterfly hunting in the Pyrenees. But only at the end of the nineteen-thirties did we leave Berlin for good, although long before that I used to take trips to Paris for public readings of my stuff.

Quite a feature of émigré life, in keeping with its itinerant and dramatic character, was the abnormal frequency of those literary readings in private houses or hired halls. The various types of performers stand out very distinctly in the puppet show going on in my mind. There was the faded actress, with eyes like precious stones, who having pressed for a moment a clenched handkerchief to a feverish mouth, proceeded to evoke nostalgic echoes of the Moscow Art Theatre by subjecting some famous piece of verse to the action, half dissection and half caress, of her slow limpid voice. There was the hopelessly second-rate author whose voice trudged through a fog of rhythmic prose, and one could watch the nervous trembling of his poor, clumsy but careful fingers every time he tucked the page he had finished under those to come, so that his manuscript retained throughout the reading its appalling and pitiful thickness. There was the young poet in whom his envious brethren could not help seeing a disturbing streak of genius as striking as the stripe of a skunk; erect on the stage, pale and glazed-eyed, with nothing in his hands to anchor him to this world, he would throw back his head and deliver his poem in a highly irritating, rolling chant and stop abruptly at the end, slamming the door of the last line and waiting for applause to fill the hush. And there was the old *cher maître* dropping pearl by pearl an admirable tale he had read innumerable times, and always in the same manner, wearing the expression of fastidious distaste that his nobly furrowed face had in the frontispiece of his collected works.

I suppose it would be easy for a detached observer to poke fun at all those hardly palpable people who imitated in foreign cities a dead civilization, the remote, almost legendary, almost Sumerian mirages of St. Petersburg and Moscow, 1900–1916 (which, even then, in the twenties and thirties, sounded like 1916–1900 B.C.). But at least they were rebels as most major Russian writers had been ever since Russian literature had existed, and true to this insurgent condition which their sense of justice and liberty craved for as strongly as it had done under the oppression of the Tsars, émigrés regarded as monstrously un-Russian and subhuman the behavior of pampered authors in the Soviet Union, the servile response on the part of those authors to every shade of every governmental decree; for the art of prostration was growing there in exact ratio to the increasing efficiency of first Lenin's, then Stalin's political police, and the successful Soviet writer was the one whose fine ear caught the soft whisper of an official suggestion long before it had become a blare.

Owing to the limited circulation of their works abroad, even the older generation of émigré writers, whose fame had been solidly established in pre-Revolution Russia, could not hope that their books would make a living for them. Writing a weekly column for an émigré paper was never quite sufficient to keep body and pen together. Now and then translations into other languages brought in an unexpected scoop; but, otherwise, grants from various émigré organizations, earnings from public readings and lavish private charity were responsible for prolonging elderly authors' lives. Younger, less known but more adaptable writers supplemented chance subsidies by engaging in various jobs. I remember teaching English and tennis. Patiently I thwarted the persistent knack Berlin businessmen had of pronouncing "business" so as to rhyme with "dizziness"; and like a slick automaton, under the slow-moving clouds of a long summer day, on dusty courts, I ladled ball after ball over the net to their tanned, bob-haired daughters. I got five dollars (quite a sum during the inflation in Germany) for my Russian *Alice in Wonderland.* I helped compile a Russian grammar for foreigners in which the first exercise began with the words *Madam, ya doktor, vot banan* (Madam, I am the doctor, here is a banana). Best of all, I used to compose for a daily émigré paper, the Berlin *Rul',* the first Russian crossword puzzles, which I baptized *krestoslovitsï.* I find it strange to recall that freak existence. Deeply beloved of blurbists is the list of more or less earthy professions that a young author (writing about Life and Ideas —which are so much more important, of course, than mere "art") has followed: newspaper boy, soda jerk, monk, wrestler, foreman in a steel mill, bus driver and so on. Alas, none of these callings has been mine.

My passion for good writing put me in close contact with various Russian authors abroad. I was young in those days and much more keenly interested in literature than I am now. Current prose and poetry, brilliant planets and pale galaxies, flowed by the casement of my garret night after night. There were independent authors of diverse age and talent, and there were groupings and cliques within which a number of young or youngish writers, some of them very gifted, clustered around a philosophizing critic. The most important of these mystagogues combined intellectual talent and moral mediocrity, an uncanny sureness of taste in modern Russian poetry and a patchy knowledge of Russian classics. His group believed that neither a mere negation of Bolshevism nor the routine ideals of Western democracies were sufficient to build a philosophy upon which émigré literature could lean. They thirsted for a creed as a jailed drug addict thirsts for his pet heaven. Rather pathetically, they envied Parisian Catholic groups for the seasoned subtleties that Russian mysticism so obviously lacked. Dostoevskian drisk could not compete with neo-Thomist thought; but were there not other ways? The longing for a system of faith, a constant teetering on the brink of some accepted religion was found to provide a special satisfaction of its own. Only much later, in the forties, did some of those writers finally discover a definite slope down which to slide in a more or less genuflectory attitude. This slope was the enthusiastic nationalism that could call a state (Stalin's Russia, in this case) good and lovable for no other reason than because its army had won a war. In the early thirties, however, the nationalistic precipice was only faintly perceived and the mystagogues were still enjoying the thrills of slippery suspension. In their attitude toward literature they were curiously conservative; with them soul-saving came first, logrolling next, and art last. A retrospective glance nowadays notes the surprising fact of these free belles-lettrists abroad aping fettered thought at home by decreeing that to be a representative of a group or an epoch was more important than to be an individual writer.

Vladislav Hodasevich used to complain, in the twenties and thirties, that young émigré poets had borrowed their art form from him while following the leading cliques in modish *angoisse* and soul-reshaping. I developed a great liking for this bitter man, wrought of irony and metallic-like genius, whose poetry was as complex a marvel as that of Tyutchev or Blok. He was, physically, of a sickly aspect, with contemptuous nostrils and beetling brows, and when I conjure him up in my mind he never rises from the hard chair on which he sits, his thin legs crossed, his eyes glittering with malevolence and wit, his long fingers screwing into a holder the half of a *Caporal Vert* cigarette. There are few things in modern world poetry comparable to the poems of his *Heavy Lyre*, but unfortunately for his fame the perfect frankness he indulged in when voicing his dislikes made him some terrible enemies among the most powerful critical coteries. Not all the mystagogues were Dostoevskian Alyoshas; there were also a few Smerdyakovs in the group, and Hodasevich's poetry was played down with the thoroughness of a revengeful racket.

Another independent writer was Ivan Bunin. I had always preferred his little-known verse to his celebrated prose (their interrelation, within the frame of his work, recalls Hardy's case). At the time I found him tremendously perturbed by the personal problem of aging. The first thing he said to me was to remark with satisfaction that his posture was better than mine, despite his being some thirty years older than I. He was basking in the Nobel prize he had just received and invited me to some kind of expensive and fashionable eating place in Paris for a heart-to-heart talk. Unfortunately

I happen to have a morbid dislike for restaurants and cafés, especially Parisian ones—I detest crowds, harried waiters, Bohemians, vermouth concoctions, coffee, *zakuski*, floor shows and so forth. I like to eat and drink in a recumbent position (preferably on a couch) and in silence. Heart-to-heart talks, confessions in the Dostoevskian manner, are also not in my line. Bunin, a spry old gentleman, with a rich and unchaste vocabulary, was puzzled by my irresponsiveness to the hazel grouse of which I had had enough in my childhood and exasperated by my refusal to discuss eschatological matters. Toward the end of the meal we were utterly bored with each other. "You will die in dreadful pain and complete isolation," remarked Bunin bitterly as we went toward the cloakroom. An attractive, frail-looking girl took the check for our heavy overcoats and presently fell with them in her embrace upon the low counter. I wanted to help Bunin into his raglan but he stopped me with a proud gesture of his open hand. Still struggling perfunctorily—*he* was now trying to help *me* —we emerged into the pallid bleakness of a Paris winter day. My companion was about to button his collar when a look of surprise and distress twisted his handsome features. Gingerly opening his overcoat, he began tugging at something under his armpit. I came to his assistance and together we finally dragged out of his sleeve my long woolen scarf which the girl had stuffed into the wrong coat. The thing came out inch by inch; it was like unwrapping a mummy and we kept slowly revolving around each other in the process, to the ribald amusement of three sidewalk whores. Then, when the operation was over, we walked on without a word to a street corner where we shook hands and separated. Subsequently we used to meet quite often, but always in the midst of other people, generally in the house of I. I. Fondaminski (a saintly and heroic soul who did more for Russian émigré literature than

any other man and who died in a German prison). Somehow
Bunin and I adopted a bantering and rather depressing mode
of conversation, a Russian variety of American "kidding,"
and this precluded any real commerce between us.

I met many other émigré Russian authors. I did not meet
Poplavski who died young, a far violin among near balalaikas.

Go to sleep, O Morella, how awful are aquiline lives

His plangent tonalities I shall never forget, nor shall I ever
forgive myself the ill-tempered review in which I attacked
him for trivial faults in his unfledged verse. I met wise, prim,
charming Aldanov; decrepit Kuprin, carefully carrying a
bottle of *vin ordinaire* through rainy streets; Ayhenvald—a
Russian version of Walter Pater—later killed by a trolleycar;
Marina Tsvetaev, wife of a double agent, and poet of genius,
who, in the late thirties, returned to Russia and perished
there. But the author that interested me most was naturally
Sirin. He belonged to my generation. Among the young
writers produced in exile he was the loneliest and most arrogant one. Beginning with the appearance of his first novel
in 1925 and throughout the next fifteen years, until he vanished as strangely as he had come, his work kept provoking
an acute and rather morbid interest on the part of critics.
Just as Marxist publicists of the eighties in old Russia would
have denounced his lack of concern with the economic structure of society, so the mystagogues of émigré letters deplored
his lack of religious insight and of moral preoccupation.
Everything about him was bound to offend Russian conven-
tions and especially that Russian sense of decorum which, for
example, an American offends so dangerously today, when in
the presence of Soviet military men of distinction he happens
to lounge with both hands in his trouser pockets. Conversely,
Sirin's admirers made much, perhaps too much, of his un-

usual style, brilliant precision, functional imagery and that sort of thing. Russian readers who had been raised on the sturdy straightforwardness of Russian realism and had called the bluff of decadent cheats, were impressed by the mirror-like angles of his clear but weirdly misleading sentences and by the fact that the real life of his books flowed in his figures of speech, which one critic has compared to "windows giving upon a contiguous world . . . a rolling corollary, the shadow of a train of thought." Across the dark sky of exile, Sirin passed, to use a simile of a more conservative nature, like a meteor, and disappeared, leaving nothing much else behind him than a vague sense of uneasiness.

3

In the course of my twenty years of exile I devoted a prodigious amount of time to the composing of chess problems. A certain position is elaborated on the board, and the problem to be solved is how to mate Black in a given number of moves, generally two or three. It is a beautiful, complex and sterile art related to the ordinary form of the game only insofar as, say, the properties of a sphere are made use of both by a juggler in weaving a new act and by a tennis player in winning a tournament. Most chess players, in fact, amateurs and masters alike, are only mildly interested in these highly specialized, fanciful, stylish riddles, and though appreciative of a catchy problem would be utterly baffled if asked to compose one.

Inspiration of a quasi-musical, quasi-poetical, or to be quite exact, poetico-mathematical type, attends the process of thinking up a chess composition of that sort. Frequently, in the friendly middle of the day, on the fringe of some trivial occupation, in the idle wake of a passing thought, I would experience, without warning, a twinge of mental pleasure as the bud of a chess problem burst open in my brain, promising me a night of labor and felicity. It might be a new way of blending an unusual strategic device with an unusual line of defense; it might be a glimpse of the actual configuration of men that would render at last, with humor and grace, a difficult theme that I had despaired of expressing before; or it might be a mere gesture made in the mist of my mind by the various units of force represented by chessmen—a kind of swift dumb show, suggesting new harmonies and new conflicts; whatever it was, it belonged to an especially exhilarating order of sensation, and my only quarrel with it today is that the maniacal manipulation of carved figures, or of their mental counterparts, during my most ebullient and prolific years engulfed so much of the time I could have devoted to verbal adventure.

Experts distinguish several schools of the chess-problem art: the Anglo-American one that combines accurate construction with dazzling thematic patterns, and refuses to be bound by any conventional rules; the rugged splendor of the Teutonic school; the highly finished but unpleasantly slick and insipid products of the Czech style with its strict adherence to certain artificial conditions; the old Russian end-game studies, which attain the sparkling summits of the art, and the mechanical Soviet problem of the so-called "task" type, which replaces artistic strategy by the ponderous working of themes to their utmost capacity. Themes in chess, it may be explained, are such devices as forelaying, withdrawing, pinning, unpinning and so forth; but it is only when they are combined in a certain way that a problem is satisfying. Deceit, to the point of diabolism, and originality, verging upon the grotesque, were my notions of strategy; and although in matters of construction I tried to conform, whenever possible, to classical rules, such as economy of force, unity, weeding out of loose ends, I was always ready to sacrifice purity of form to the exigencies of fantastic content, causing form to bulge and burst like a sponge-bag containing a small furious devil.

It is one thing to conceive the main play of a composition and another to construct it. The strain on the mind is formidable; the element of time drops out of one's consciousness altogether: the building hand gropes for a pawn in the box, holds it, while the mind still ponders the need for a foil or a stopgap, and when the fist opens, a whole hour, perhaps, has gone by, has burned to ashes in the incandescent cerebration of the schemer. The chessboard before him is a magnetic field, a system of stresses and abysses, a starry firmament. The bishops move over it like searchlights. This or that knight is a lever adjusted and tried, and readjusted and tried again, till the problem is tuned up to the necessary level of beauty and surprise. How often I have struggled to bind the terrible force of White's queen so as to avoid a dual solution! It should be understood that competition in chess problems is not really between White and Black but between the composer and the hypothetical solver (just as in a first-rate work of fiction the real clash is not between the characters but between the author and the world), so that a great part of a problem's value is due to the number of "tries"—delusive opening moves, false scents, specious lines of play, astutely and lovingly prepared to lead the would-be solver astray. But whatever I can say about this matter of problem composing, I do not seem to convey sufficiently the ecstatic core of the process and its points of connection with various other, more overt and fruitful, operations of the creative mind, from the charting of dangerous seas to the writing of one of those incredible novels where the author, in a fit of lucid madness, has set himself certain unique rules that he observes, certain nightmare obstacles that he surmounts, with the zest of a deity building a live world from the most unlikely ingredients—rocks, and carbon, and blind throbbings. In the case of problem composition, the event is accompanied by a mellow physical satisfaction, especially when the chessmen are beginning to enact adequately, in a penultimate rehearsal, the composer's dream. There is a feeling of snugness (which goes back to one's childhood, to play-planning in bed, with parts of toys fitting into corners of one's brain); there is the nice way one piece is ambushed behind another, within the comfort and warmth of an out-of-the-way square; and there is the smooth motion of a well-oiled and polished machine that runs sweetly at the touch of two forked fingers lightly lifting and lightly lowering a piece.

I remember one particular problem I had been trying to compose for months. There came a night when I managed at last to express that particular theme. It was meant for the delectation of the very expert solver. The unsophisticated might miss the point of the problem entirely, and discover its fairly simple, "thetic" solution without having passed through the pleasurable torments prepared for the sophisticated one. The latter would start by falling for an illusory pattern of play based on a fashionable avant-garde theme (exposing White's King to checks), which the composer had taken the greatest pains to "plant" (with only one obscure little move by an inconspicuous pawn to upset it). Having passed through this "antithetic" inferno the by now ultrasophisticated solver would reach the simple key move (bishop to c2) as somebody on a wild goose chase might go from Albany to New York by way of Vancouver, Eurasia and the Azores. The pleasant experience of the roundabout route (strange landscapes, gongs, tigers, exotic customs, the thrice-repeated circuit of a newly married couple around the sacred fire of an earthen brazier) would amply reward him for the misery of the deceit, and after that, his arrival at the simple key move would provide him with a synthesis of poignant artistic delight.

I remember slowly emerging from a swoon of concentrated chess thought, and there, on a great English board of cream and cardinal leather, the flawless position was at last balanced like a constellation. It worked. It lived. My Staunton chessmen (a twenty-year-old set given to me by my father's Englished brother, Konstantin), splendidly massive pieces, of tawny or black wood, up to four and a quarter inches tall, displayed their shiny contours as if conscious of the part they played. Alas, if examined closely, some of the men were seen to be chipped (after traveling in their box through the fifty or sixty lodgings I had changed during those years); but the top of the king's rook and the brow of the king's knight still showed a small crimson crown painted upon them, recalling the round mark on a happy Hindu's forehead.

A brooklet of time in comparison to its frozen lake on the chessboard, my watch showed half-past three. The season was May—mid-May, 1940. The day before, after months of soliciting and cursing, the emetic of a bribe had been administered to the right rat at the right office and had resulted finally in a *visa de sortie* which, in its turn, conditioned the permission to cross the Atlantic. All of a sudden, I felt that with the completion of my chess problem a whole period of my life had come to a satisfactory close. Everything around was very quiet; faintly dimpled, as it were, by the quality of my relief. Sleeping in the next room were you and our child. The lamp on my table was bonneted with blue sugarloaf paper (an amusing military precaution) and the resulting light lent a lunar tinge to the voluted air heavy with tobacco smoke. Opaque curtains separated me from blacked-out Paris. The headline of a newspaper drooping from the seat of a chair spoke of Hitler's striking at the Low Countries.

I have before me the sheet of paper upon which, that night in Paris, I drew the diagram of the problem's position. White: King on a7 (meaning first file, seventh rank), Queen on b6, Rooks on f4 and h5, Bishops on e4 and h8, Knights on d8 and e6, Pawns on b7 and g3; Black: King on e5, Rook on g7, Bishop on h6, Knights on e2 and g5, Pawns on c3, c6 and d7. White begins and mates in two moves. The false scent, the irresistible "try" is: Pawn to b8, becoming a knight, with three beautiful mates following in answer to disclosed checks by Black; but Black can defeat the whole brilliant affair by *not* checking White and making instead a modest dilatory move elsewhere on the board. In one corner of the sheet with the diagram, I notice a certain stamped mark that also adorns other papers and books I took out of France to America in May 1940. It is a circular imprint, in the ultimate tint of the spectrum—*violet de bureau*. In its center there are two capital letters of pica size, *R.F.*, meaning of course *République Française*. Other letters in lesser type, running peripherally, spell *Contrôle des Informations*. However, it is only now, many years later, that the information concealed in my chess symbols, which that control permitted to pass, may be, and in fact is, divulged.

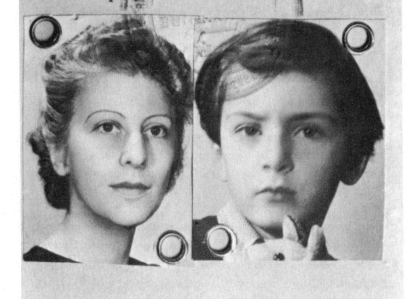

Photographie du titulaire et, le cas échéant, photographies des enfants qui l'accompagnent.

Signature du titulaire.

Véra Nabokoff

A Nansen passport picture taken in Paris in April 1940, of the author's wife, Véra, and son Dmitri, aged five. A few weeks later, in May, the last chapter of our European period was to end as it ends in this book.

15

1

THEY are passing, posthaste, posthaste, the gliding years—
to use a soul-rending Horatian inflection. The years are
passing, my dear, and presently nobody will know what you
and I know. Our child is growing; the roses of Paestum, of
misty Paestum, are gone; mechanically minded idiots are
tinkering and tampering with forces of nature that mild
mathematicians, to their own secret surprise, appear to have
foreshadowed; so perhaps it is time we examined ancient
snapshots, cave drawings of trains and planes, strata of toys
in the lumbered closet.

We shall go still further back, to a morning in May 1934,
and plot with respect to this fixed point the graph of a section of Berlin. There I was walking home, at 5 A.M., from the
maternity hospital near Bayerischer Platz, to which I had
taken you a couple of hours earlier. Spring flowers adorned
the portraits of Hindenburg and Hitler in the window of a
shop that sold frames and colored photographs. Leftist groups
of sparrows were holding loud morning sessions in lilacs and
limes. A limpid dawn had completely unsheathed one side of
the empty street. On the other side, the houses still looked
blue with cold, and various long shadows were gradually

being telescoped, in the matter-of-fact manner young day has when taking over from night in a well-groomed, well-watered city, where the tang of tarred pavements underlies the sappy smells of shade trees; but to me the optical part of the business seemed quite new, like some unusual way of laying the table, because I had never seen that particular street at daybreak before, although, on the other hand, I had often passed there, childless, on sunny evenings.

In the purity and vacuity of the less familiar hour, the shadows were on the wrong side of the street, investing it with a sense of not inelegant inversion, as when one sees reflected in the mirror of a barbershop the window toward which the melancholy barber, while stropping his razor, turns his gaze (as they all do at such times), and, framed in that reflected window, a stretch of sidewalk shunting a procession of unconcerned pedestrians in the wrong direction, into an abstract world that all at once stops being droll and loosens a torrent of terror.

Whenever I start thinking of my love for a person, I am in the habit of immediately drawing radii from my love—from my heart, from the tender nucleus of a personal matter—to monstrously remote points of the universe. Something impels me to measure the consciousness of my love against such unimaginable and incalculable things as the behavior of nebulae (whose very remoteness seems a form of insanity), the dreadful pitfalls of eternity, the unknowledgeable beyond the unknown, the helplessness, the cold, the sickening involutions and interpenetrations of space and time. It is a pernicious habit, but I can do nothing about it. It can be compared to the uncontrollable flick of an insomniac's tongue checking a jagged tooth in the night of his mouth and bruising itself in doing so but still persevering. I have known people who, upon accidentally touching something—a doorpost, a wall—

had to go through a certain very rapid and systematic sequence of manual contacts with various surfaces in the room
before returning to a balanced existence. It cannot be helped;
I must know where I stand, where you and my son stand.
When that slow-motion, silent explosion of love takes place
in me, unfolding its melting fringes and overwhelming me
with the sense of something much vaster, much more endur-
ing and powerful than the accumulation of matter or energy
in any imaginable cosmos, then my mind cannot but pinch
itself to see if it is really awake. I have to make a rapid inven-
tory of the universe, just as a man in a dream tries to con-
done the absurdity of his position by making sure he is dream-
ing. I have to have all space and all time participate in my
emotion, in my mortal love, so that the edge of its mortality
is taken off, thus helping me to fight the utter degradation,
ridicule, and horror of having developed an infinity of sensation and thought within a finite existence.

Since, in my metaphysics, I am a confirmed non-unionist
and have no use for organized tours through anthropomor-
phic paradises, I am left to my own, not negligible devices
when I think of the best things in life; when, as now, I look
back upon my almost couvade-like concern with our baby.
You remember the discoveries we made (supposedly made by
all parents): the perfect shape of the miniature fingernails of
the hand you silently showed me as it lay, stranded starfish-
wise, on your palm; the epidermic texture of limb and cheek,
to which attention was drawn in dimmed, faraway tones, as
if the softness of touch could be rendered only by the softness
of distance; that swimming, sloping, elusive something about
the dark-bluish tint of the iris which seemed still to retain
the shadows it had absorbed of ancient, fabulous forests where
there were more birds than tigers and more fruit than thorns,
and where, in some dappled depth, man's mind had been

born; and, above all, an infant's first journey into the next
dimension, the newly established nexus between eye and
reachable object, which the career boys in biometrics or in
the rat-maze racket think they can explain. It occurs to me
that the closest reproduction of the mind's birth obtainable
is the stab of wonder that accompanies the precise moment
when, gazing at a tangle of twigs and leaves, one suddenly
realizes that what had seemed a natural component of that
tangle is a marvelously disguised insect or bird.

There is also keen pleasure (and, after all, what else should
the pursuit of science produce?) in meeting the riddle of the
initial blossoming of man's mind by postulating a voluptuous
pause in the growth of the rest of nature, a lolling and loaf-
ing which allowed first of all the formation of *Homo poe-
ticus*—without which *sapiens* could not have been evolved.
"Struggle for life" indeed! The curse of battle and toil leads
man back to the boar, to the grunting beast's crazy obsession
with the search for food. You and I have frequently remarked
upon that maniacal glint in a housewife's scheming eye as
it roves over food in a grocery or about the morgue of a
butcher's shop. Toilers of the world, disband! Old books are
wrong. The world was made on a Sunday.

2

Throughout the years of our boy's infancy, in Hitler's Germany and Maginot's France, we were more or less constantly
hard up, but wonderful friends saw to his having the best
things available. Although powerless to do much about it,
you and I jointly kept a jealous eye on any possible rift between his childhood and our own incunabula in the opulent
past, and this is where those friendly fates came in, doctoring
the rift every time it threatened to open. Then, too, the sci-

ence of building up babies had made the same kind of phe-
nomenal, streamlined progress that flying or tilling had—*I,*
when nine months old, did not get a pound of strained
spinach at one feeding or the juice of a dozen oranges per
day; and the pediatric hygiene you adopted was incomparably more artistic and scrupulous than anything old nurses
could have dreamed up when we were babes.

I think bourgeois fathers—wing-collar workers in pencil-
striped pants, dignified, office-tied fathers, so different from
young American veterans of today or from a happy, jobless
Russian-born expatriate of fifteen years ago—will not understand my attitude toward our child. Whenever you held him
up, replete with his warm formula and grave as an idol, and
waited for the postlactic all-clear signal before making a horizontal baby of the vertical one, I used to take part both in
your wait and in the tightness of his surfeit, which I exaggerated, therefore rather resenting your cheerful faith in the
speedy dissipation of what I felt to be a painful oppression;
and when, at last, the blunt little bubble did rise and burst
in his solemn mouth, I used to experience a lovely relief
while you, with a congratulatory murmur, bent low to de-
posit him in the white-rimmed twilight of his crib.

You know, I still feel in my wrists certain echoes of the
pram-pusher's knack, such as, for example, the glib downward pressure one applied to the handle in order to have the
carriage tip up and climb the curb. First came an elaborate
mouse-gray vehicle of Belgian make, with fat autoid tires and
luxurious springs, so large that it could not enter our puny
elevator. It rolled on sidewalks in slow stately mystery, with
the trapped baby inside lying supine, well covered with
down, silk and fur; only his eyes moved, warily, and sometimes they turned upward with one swift sweep of their
showy lashes to follow the receding of branch-patterned blue-

ness that flowed away from the edge of the half-cocked hood
of the carriage, and presently he would dart a suspicious
glance at my face to see if the teasing trees and sky did not
belong, perhaps, to the same order of things as did rattles
and parental humor. There followed a lighter carriage, and
in this, as he spun along, he would tend to rise, straining at
his straps; clutching at the edges; standing there less like the
groggy passenger of a pleasure boat than like an entranced
scientist in a spaceship; surveying the speckled skeins of a
live, warm world; eyeing with philosophic interest the pillow
he had managed to throw overboard; falling out himself
when a strap burst one day. Still later he rode in one of those
small contraptions called strollers; from initial springy and
secure heights the child came lower and lower, until, when
he was about one and a half, he touched ground in front of
the moving stroller by slipping forward out of his seat and
beating the sidewalk with his heels in anticipation of being
set loose in some public garden. A new wave of evolution
started to swell, gradually lifting him again from the ground,
when, for his second birthday, he received a four-foot-long,
silver-painted Mercedes racing car operated by inside pedals,
like an organ, and in this he used to drive with a pumping,
clanking noise up and down the sidewalk of the Kurfürs-
tendamm while from open windows came the multiplied roar
of a dictator still pounding his chest in the Neander valley
we had left far behind.

It might be rewarding to go into the phylogenetic aspects
of the passion male children have for things on wheels,
particularly railway trains. Of course, we know what the
Viennese Quack thought of the matter. We will leave him
and his fellow travelers to jog on, in their third-class carriage
of thought, through the police state of sexual myth (incidentally, what a great mistake on the part of dictators to

ignore psychoanalysis—a whole generation might be so easily corrupted that way!). Rapid growth, quantum-quick thought, the roller coaster of the circulatory system—all forms of vitality are forms of velocity, and no wonder a growing child desires to out-Nature Nature by filling a minimum stretch of time with a maximum of spatial enjoyment. Innermost in man is the spiritual pleasure derivable from the possibilities of outtugging and outrunning gravity, of overcoming or re-enacting the earth's pull. The miraculous paradox of smooth round objects conquering space by simply tumbling over and over, instead of laboriously lifting heavy limbs in order to progress, must have given young mankind a most salutary shock. The bonfire into which the dreamy little savage peered as he squatted on naked haunches, or the unswerving advance of a forest fire—these have also affected, I suppose, a chromosome or two behind Lamarck's back, in the mysterious way which Western geneticists are as disinclined to elucidate as are professional physicists to discuss the outside of the inside, the whereabouts of the curvature; for every dimension presupposes a medium within which it can act, and if, in the spiral unwinding of things, space warps into something akin to time, and time, in its turn, warps into something akin to thought, then, surely, another dimension follows—a special Space maybe, not the old one, we trust, unless spirals become vicious circles again.

But whatever the truth may be, we shall never forget, you and I, we shall forever defend, on this or some other battleground, the bridges on which we spent hours waiting with our little son (aged anything from two to six) for a train to pass below. I have seen older and less happy children stop for a moment in order to lean over the railing and spit into the asthmatic stack of the engine that happened to pass under, but neither you nor I is ready to admit that the more

normal of two children is the one who resolves pragmatically
the aimless exaltation of an obscure trance. You did nothing
to curtail or rationalize those hour-long stops on windy
bridges when, with an optimism and a patience that knew
no bounds, our child would hope for a semaphore to click
and for a growing locomotive to take shape at a point where
all the many tracks converged, in the distance, between the
blank backs of houses. On cold days he wore a lambskin coat,
with a similar cap, both a brownish color mottled with rime-
like gray, and these, and mittens, and the fervency of his
faith kept him glowing, and kept *you* warm too, since all you
had to do to prevent your delicate fingers from freezing was
to hold one of his hands alternately in your right and left,
switching every minute or so, and marveling at the incredible amount of heat generated by a big baby's body.

3

Besides dreams of velocity, or in connection with them,
there is in every child the essentially human urge to reshape
the earth, to act upon a friable environment (unless he is a
born Marxist or a corpse and meekly waits for the environment to fashion *him*). This explains a child's delight in
digging, in making roads and tunnels for his favorite toys.
Our son had a tiny model of Sir Malcolm Campbell's Blue-
bird, of painted steel and with detachable tires, and this he
would play with endlessly on the ground, and the sun would
make a kind of nimbus of his longish fair hair and turn to
a toffee tint his bare back crisscrossed by the shoulder straps
of his knitted navy-blue shorts (under which, when undressed, he was seen to be bottomed and haltered with natural white). Never in my life have I sat on so many benches
and park chairs, stone slabs and stone steps, terrace parapets

and brims of fountain basins as I did in those days. The popular pine barrens around the lake in Berlin's Grunewald we visited but seldom. You questioned the right of a place to call itself a forest when it was so full of refuse, so much more littered with rubbish than the glossy, self-conscious streets of the adjoining town. Curious things turned up in this Grunewald. The sight of an iron bedstead exhibiting the anatomy of its springs in the middle of a glade or the presence of a dressmaker's black dummy lying under a hawthorn bush in bloom made one wonder who, exactly, had troubled to carry these and other widely scattered articles to such remote points of a pathless forest. Once I came across a badly disfigured but still alert mirror, full of sylvan reflections—drunk, as it were, on a mixture of beer and chartreuse —leaning, with surrealistic jauntiness, against a tree trunk. Perhaps such intrusions on these burgherish pleasure grounds were a fragmentary vision of the mess to come, a prophetic bad dream of destructive explosions, something like the heap of dead heads the seer Cagliostro glimpsed in the ha-ha of a royal garden. And nearer to the lake, in summer, especially on Sundays, the place was infested with human bodies in various stages of nudity and solarization. Only the squirrels and certain caterpillars kept their coats on. Gray-footed goodwives sat on greasy gray sand in their slips; repulsive, seal-voiced males, in muddy swimming trunks, gamboled around; remarkably comely but poorly groomed girls, destined to bear a few years later—early in 1946, to be exact—a sudden crop of infants with Turkic or Mongol blood in their innocent veins, were chased and slapped on the rear (whereupon they would cry out, "Ow-wow!"); and the exhalations coming from these unfortunate frolickers, and their shed clothes (neatly spread out here and there on the ground) mingled with the stench of stagnant water to form an inferno

of odors that, somehow, I have never found duplicated anywhere else. People in Berlin's public gardens and city parks
were not permitted to undress; but shirts might be unbut-
toned, and rows of young men, of a pronounced Nordic type,
sat with closed eyes on benches and exposed their frontal and
pectoral pimples to the nationally approved action of the sun.
The squeamish and possibly exaggerated shudder that ob-
tains in these notes may be attributed, I suppose, to the constant fear we lived in of some contamination affecting our
child. You always considered abominably trite, and not
devoid of a peculiar Philistine flavor, the notion that small
boys, in order to be delightful, should hate to wash and love
to kill.

I would like to remember every small park we visited; I
would like to have the ability Professor Jack, of Harvard and
the Arnold Arboretum, told his students he had of identifying twigs with his eyes shut, merely from the sound of their
swish through the air ("Hornbeam, honeysuckle, Lombardy
poplar. Ah—a folded *Transcript*"). Quite often, of course,
I can determine the geographic position of this or that park
by some particular trait or combination of traits: dwarf-box
edgings along narrow gravel walks, all of which meet like
people in plays; a low blue bench against a cuboid hedge of
yew; a square bed of roses framed in a border of heliotrope
—these features are obviously associated with small park
areas at street intersections in suburban Berlin. Just as
clearly, a chair of thin iron, with its spidery shadow lying
beneath it a little to one side of center, or a pleasantly supercilious, although plainly psychopathic, rotatory sprinkler,
with a private rainbow hanging in its spray above gemmed
grass, spells a Parisian park; but, as you will well understand,
the eye of memory is so firmly focused upon a small figure
squatting on the ground (loading a toy truck with pebbles

or contemplating the bright, wet rubber of a gardener's hose to which some of the gravel over which the hose has just slithered adheres) that the various loci—Berlin, Prague, Franzensbad, Paris, the Riviera, Paris again, Cap d'Antibes and so forth—lose all sovereignty, pool their petrified generals and fallen leaves, cement the friendship of their interlocked paths, and unite in a federation of light and shade through which bare-kneed, graceful children drift on whirring roller skates.

Now and then a recognized patch of historical background aids local identification—and substitutes other bonds for those a personal vision suggests. Our child must have been almost three on that breezy day in Berlin (where, of course, no one could escape familiarity with the ubiquitous picture of the Führer) when we stood, he and I, before a bed of pallid pansies, each of their upturned faces showing a dark mustache-like smudge, and had great fun, at my rather silly prompting, commenting on their resemblance to a crowd of bobbing little Hitlers. Likewise, I can name a blooming garden in Paris as the place where I noticed, in 1938 or 1939, a quiet girl of ten or so, with a deadpan white face, looking, in her dark, shabby, unseasonable clothes, as if she had escaped from an orphanage (congruously, I was granted a later glimpse of her being swept away by two flowing nuns), who had deftly tied a live butterfly to a thread and was promenading the pretty, weakly fluttering, slightly crippled insect on that elfish leash (the by-product, perhaps, of a good deal of dainty needlework in that orphanage). You have often accused me of unnecessary callousness in my matter-of-fact entomological investigations on our trips to the Pyrenees or the Alps; so, if I diverted our child's attention from that would-be Titania, it was not because I pitied her Red Admirable (Admiral, in vulgar parlance) but because there was some vaguely repulsive symbolism about her sullen sport. I may have been reminded, in fact, of the simple, old-fashioned trick a French policeman had—and no doubt still has—when leading a florid-nosed workman, a Sunday rowdy, away to jail, of turning him into a singularly docile and even alacritous satellite by catching a kind of small fishhook in the man's uncared-for but sensitive and responsive flesh. You and I did our best to encompass with vigilant tenderness the trustful tenderness of our child but were inevitably confronted by the fact that the filth left by hoodlums in a sandbox on a playground was the least serious of possible offenses, and that the horrors which former generations had mentally dismissed as anachronisms or things occurring only in remote khanates and mandarinates, were all around us.

As time went on and the shadow of fool-made history vitiated even the exactitude of sundials, we moved more restlessly over Europe, and it seemed as if not we but those gardens and parks traveled along. Le Nôtre's radiating avenues and complicated parterres were left behind, like side-tracked trains. In Prague, to which we journeyed to show our child to my mother in the spring of 1937, there was Stromovka Park, with its atmosphere of free undulating remoteness beyond man-trained arbors. You will also recall those rock gardens of Alpine plants—sedums and saxifrages —that escorted us, so to speak, into the Savoy Alps, joining us on a vacation (paid for by something my translators had sold), and then followed us back into the towns of the plains. Cuffed hands of wood nailed to boles in the old parks of curative resorts pointed in the direction whence came a subdued thumping of bandstand music. An intelligent walk accompanied the main driveway; not everywhere paralleling it but freely recognizing its guidance, and from duck pond or lily pool gamboling back to join the procession of plane

trees at this or that point where the park had developed a
city-father fixation and dreamed up a monument. Roots,
roots of remembered greenery, roots of memory and pungent
plants, roots, in a word, are enabled to traverse long distances
by surmounting some obstacles, penetrating others and in-
sinuating themselves into narrow cracks. So those gardens
and parks traversed Central Europe with us. Graveled walks
gathered and stopped at a *rond-point* to watch you or me
bend and wince as we looked for a ball under a privet hedge
where, on the dark, damp earth, nothing but a perforated
mauve trolley ticket or a bit of soiled gauze and cotton wool
could be detected. A circular seat would go around a thick
oak trunk to see who was sitting on the other side and find
there a dejected old man reading a foreign-language newspaper and picking his nose. Glossy-leaved evergreens enclos-
ing a lawn where our child discovered his first live frog broke
into a trimmed maze of topiary work, and you said you
thought it was going to rain. At some farther stage, under less
leaden skies, there was a great show of rose dells and pleached
alleys, and trellises swinging their creepers, ready to turn
into the vines of columned pergolas if given a chance, or, if
not, to disclose the quaintest of quaint public toilets, a
miserable chalet-like affair of doubtful cleanliness, with a
woman attendant in black, black-knitting on its porch.

Down a slope, a flagged path stepped cautiously, putting
the same foot first every time, through an iris garden; under
beeches; and then was transformed into a fast-moving earthy
trail patterned with rough imprints of horse hooves. The
gardens and parks seemed to move ever faster as our child's
legs grew longer, and when he was about four, the trees and
flowering shrubs turned resolutely toward the sea. Like a
bored stationmaster seen standing alone on the speed-clipped
platform of some small station at which one's train does not

stop, this or that gray park watchman receded as the park
streamed on and on, carrying us south toward the orange
trees and the arbutus and the chick-fluff of mimosas and the
pâte tendre of an impeccable sky.

Graded gardens on hillsides, a succession of terraces whose
every stone step ejected a gaudy grasshopper, dropped from
ledge to ledge seaward, with the olives and the oleanders
fairly toppling over each other in their haste to obtain a view
of the beach. There our child kneeled motionless to be photographed in a quivering haze of sun against the scintillation
of the sea, which is a milky blur in the snapshots we have
preserved but was, in life, silvery blue, with great patches
of purple-blue farther out, caused by warm currents in collaboration with and corroboration of (hear the pebbles rolled
by the withdrawing wave?) eloquent old poets and their
smiling similes. And among the candy-like blobs of sea-licked
glass—lemon, cherry, peppermint—and the banded pebbles,
and the little fluted shells with lustered insides, sometimes
small bits of pottery, still beautiful in glaze and color, turned
up. They were brought to you or me for inspection, and if
they had indigo chevrons, or bands of leaf ornament, or any
kind of gay emblemata, and were judged precious, down
they went with a click into the toy pail, and, if not, a plop
and a flash marked their return to the sea. I do not doubt
that among those slightly convex chips of majolica ware
found by our child there was one whose border of scroll-
work fitted exactly, and continued, the pattern of a fragment
I had found in 1903 on the same shore, and that the two
tallied with a third my mother had found on that Mentone
beach in 1882, and with a fourth piece of the same pottery
that had been found by *her* mother a hundred years ago—
and so on, until this assortment of parts, if all had been preserved, might have been put together to make the complete,

the absolutely complete, bowl, broken by some Italian child, God knows where and when, and now mended by *these* rivets of bronze.

In the fall of 1939, we returned to Paris, and around May 20 of the following year we were again near the sea, this time on the western coast of France, at St. Nazaire. There, one last little garden surrounded us, as you and I, and our child, by now six, between us, walked through it on our way to the docks, where, behind the buildings facing us, the liner *Champlain* was waiting to take us to New York. That garden was what the French call, phonetically, *skwarr* and the Russians *skver*, perhaps because it is the kind of thing usually found in or near public squares in England. Laid out on the last limit of the past and on the verge of the present, it remains in my memory merely as a geometrical design which no doubt I could easily fill in with the colors of plausible flowers, if I were careless enough to break the hush of pure memory that (except, perhaps, for some chance tinnitus due to the pressure of my own tired blood) I have left undisturbed, and humbly listened to, from the beginning. What I really remember about this neutrally blooming design, is its clever thematic connection with transatlantic gardens and parks; for suddenly, as we came to the end of its path, you and I saw something that we did not immediately point out to our child, so as to enjoy in full the blissful shock, the enchantment and glee he would experience on discovering ahead the ungenuinely gigantic, the unrealistically real prototype of the various toy vessels he had doddled about in his bath. There, in front of us, where a broken row of houses stood between us and the harbor, and where the eye encountered all sorts of stratagems, such as pale-blue and pink underwear cakewalking on a clothesline, or a lady's bicycle and a striped cat oddly sharing a rudimentary balcony of cast iron, it was most satisfying to make out among the jumbled angles of roofs and walls, a splendid ship's funnel, showing from behind the clothesline as something in a scrambled picture—Find What the Sailor Has Hidden—that the finder cannot unsee once it has been seen.

Index

ABOUT THE AUTHOR

Vladimir Nabokov was born in St. Petersburg on April 23, 1899. His family fled to the Crimea in 1917, during the Bolshevik Revolution, then went into exile in Europe. Nabokov studied at Trinity College, Cambridge, earning a degree in French and Russian literature in 1922, and lived in Berlin and Paris for the next two decades, writing prolifically, mainly in Russian, under the pseudonym Sirin. In 1940 he moved to the United States, where he pursued a brilliant literary career (as a poet, novelist, memoirist, critic, and translator) while teaching Russian, creative writing, and literature at Stanford, Wellesley, Cornell, and Harvard. The monumental success of his novel *Lolita* (1955) enabled him to give up teaching and devote himself fully to his writing. In 1961 he moved to Montreux, Switzerland, where he died in 1977. Recognized as one of the master prose stylists of the century in both Russian and English, he translated a number of his original English works—including *Lolita*—into Russian, and collaborated on English translations of his original Russian works.

ALSO BY VLADIMIR NABOKOV

ADA, OR ARDOR

Ada, or Ardor tells a love story troubled by incest. But more: it is also at once a fairy tale, an epic, and a philosophical treatise on the nature of time; a parody of the history of the novel; and an erotic catalogue.

Fiction/Literature/978-0-679-72522-0

BEND SINISTER

Bend Sinister is a haunting and compelling narrative about a civilized man caught in the tyranny of a police state. Professor Adam Krug, the country's foremost philosopher, offers the only hope of resistance to Paduk, dictator and leader of the Party of the Average Man.

Fiction/Literature/978-0-679-72727-9

THE DEFENSE

As a young boy, Luzhin was unattractive, distracted, withdrawn, an enigma to his parents, and an object of ridicule to his classmates. Taking up chess, he rises to the rank of grandmaster, but in his obsessive mind, the game of chess gradually supplants reality.

Fiction/Literature/978-0-679-72722-4

THE ENCHANTER

The Enchanter is the Ur-*Lolita*, the precursor to Nabokov's classic novel. It tells the story of an outwardly respectable man and his fatal obsession with certain pubescent girls, whose coltish grace and subconscious coquetry reveal, to his mind, a bud on the verge of bloom.

Fiction/Literature/978-0-679-72886-3

THE EYE

The Eye is as much a farcical detective story as it is a profoundly refractive tale about the vicissitudes of identities and appearances. Smurov is a lovelorn, excruciatingly self-conscious Russian émigré living in prewar Berlin who commits suicide after being humiliated by a jealous husband, only to suffer even greater indignities in the afterlife.

Fiction/Literature/978-0-679-72723-1

THE GIFT

The Gift is an ode to Russian literature, evoking the works of Pushkin, Gogol, and others in the course of its narrative: the story of Fyodor Godunov-Cherdyntsev, an impoverished émigré poet living in Berlin, who dreams of the book he will someday write.

Fiction/Literature/978-0-679-72725-5

GLORY

Glory is the wryly ironic story of Martin Edelweiss, a young Russian émigré of no account, who is in love with a girl who refuses to marry him. Hoping to impress his love, he embarks on a "perilous, daredevil project"—to illegally reenter the Soviet Union.

Fiction/Literature/978-0-679-72724-8

INVITATION TO A BEHEADING

In a dream country, the young man Cincinnatus C. is condemned to death by beheading for "gnostical turpitude," an imaginary crime that defies definition. Cincinnatus spends his last days in an absurd jail, where he is visited by chimerical jailers, an executioner who masquerades as a fellow prisoner, and by his in-laws.

Fiction/Literature/978-0-679-72531-2

KING, QUEEN, KNAVE

Dreyer, a wealthy and boisterous proprietor of a men's clothing store is ruddy, self-satisfied, and masculine, but he is repugnant to his exquisite but cold middle-class wife, Martha. Attracted to his money but repelled by his oblivious passion, she longs for their nephew instead.

Fiction/Literature/978-0-679-72340-0

LAUGHTER IN THE DARK

Albinus, a respectable, middle-aged man and aspiring filmmaker, abandons his wife for a lover half his age: Margot, who wants to become a movie star herself. When Albinus introduces her to Rex, an American movie producer, disaster ensues.

Fiction/Literature/978-0-679-72450-6

PNIN

A professor of Russian at an American college, Pnin takes the wrong train to deliver a lecture in a language he cannot master. Although he is the focal point of subtle academic conspiracies he cannot begin to comprehend, he stages the faculty party to end all faculty parties.

Fiction/Literature/978-0-679-72341-7

TRANSPARENT THINGS

"*Transparent Things* revolves around the four visits of the hero—sullen, gawky Hugh Person—to Switzerland. . . . As a young publisher, Hugh is sent to interview R., falls in love with Armande on the way, wrests her, after multiple humiliations, from a grinning Scandinavian and returns to NY with his bride. . . . Eight years later—following a murder, a period of madness and a brief imprisonment—Hugh makes a lone sentimental journey to wheedle out his past" (Martin Amis).

Fiction/Literature/978-0-679-72541-1

ALSO AVAILABLE:

VINTAGE INTERNATIONAL
Available from your local bookstore, or visit
www.randomhouse.com

A PUBLISHING EVENT

The final, unfinished novel from

Vladimir Nabokov

The Original of Laura

After years of controversy surrounding the
fate of Nabokov's final manuscript, Knopf will
publish the last work by one of the 20th
century's acknowledged masters of literature.
An essential part of Nabokov's oeuvre,
The Original of Laura blurs the line between
the author's life and fiction. This edition,
uniquely designed by Chip Kidd, includes
facsimiles of the 138 note cards on which it
was written.

Available November 2009 in hardcover from Knopf

$35.00 • 304 pages • 978-0-307-27189-1

Please visit www.aaknopf.com